The Spanish *quinqui* film

Manchester University Press

The Spanish *quinqui* film

Delinquency, sound, sensation

TOM WHITTAKER

Manchester University Press

Published by Manchester University Press
Oxford Road, Manchester M13 9PL
www.manchesteruniversitypress.co.uk

British Library Cataloguing-in-Publication Data
A catalogue record for this book is available from the British Library

ISBN 978 1 5261 3177 5 hardback
ISBN 978 1 5261 7196 2 paperback

First published 2020
Paperback published 2023

Typeset
by New Best-set Typesetters Ltd

Contents

List of figures

Acknowledgements

This book would not have been possible without the time and intellectual generosity of others.

My thoughts on *cine quinqui*, Spanish cinema and sound have been stimulated by many colleagues and friends over the past few years, to name but a few: Dean Allbritton, Ann Davies, Brad Epps, Jo Evans, Sally Faulkner, Julián Daniel Gutiérrez-Albilla, Patricia Hart, Jo Labanyi, Antonio Lázaro-Reboll, Samuel Llano, Abigail Loxham, Steven Marsh, Leigh Mercer, Alberto Mira, Jorge Pérez, Vicente Rodríguez Ortega, Paul Julian Smith, Jon Snyder, Sarah Wright and Kathleen Vernon. I owe a special thanks to Jamie Hakim, Alejandro Melero, Chris Perriam, Davina Quinlivan, Alison Ribeiro de Menezes, Rosi Song, Sarah Thomas, Núria Triana-Toribio, Duncan Wheeler, Andy Willis and Belén Vidal for reading drafts and chapters of this book at its various stages.

Thanks are also due to the University of Liverpool and the University of Warwick for providing me with periods of study leave to work on this book. The staff at the Reuben Library, BFI Southbank never failed to cheer me up when the writing got tough. I am also grateful to Mery Cuesta for sharing some of her *quinqui* films with me. I would in addition like to thank the staff at Manchester University Press for their constant support thoughout this project.

Some of the arguments in this book began in their embryonic form in the chapters 'Mobile Soundscapes in the Quinqui Film', in the book *Screening Songs in Hispanic and Lusophone Cinema* (2013), edited by Lisa Shaw and Rob Stone and 'Sonorous Flesh: The visual and aural erotics of skin in Eloy de la Iglesia's *quinqui* films' in *Spanish Erotic Cinema* (2016), edited by Santiago Fouz-Hernández. I am very grateful to the editors for their thoughtful suggestions.

Last but not least, I am, as always, grateful to Michael, for his unbounded patience and kindness. This book is dedicated to him.

Introduction

A stolen SEAT 124 drives at lightning speed past the police, its engine at full throttle as the tyres skid into the curb. The driver is a 15-year-old delinquent who wears skin-tight denim, a flashy medallion and speaks in slang. He negotiates a hostile physical environment of hastily built tower blocks and squalid reformatories with an almost magical ease of movement. Devoted to instant gratification and the sensuous pleasures of consumerism, he embodies the imperative of accelerated capitalism yet is also excluded from it. To Spanish audiences, this is an instantly recognisable protagonist of *cine quinqui,* a term used to describe a number of films made in Spain in the late 1970s to the mid 1980s which focussed on the theme of juvenile delinquency. His deviance is frequently marked out through sound: the guttural grain of his voice; the ambient noises of gunfire, motorbike engines, arcade games and police sirens; and the music of *rumbas,* songs by popular gypsy groups whose lyrics spoke of police brutality and marginalisation. Living on the margins of the city, the place of the delinquent in *cine quinqui* is marked by its dislocation, one that is both spatial and sonic. Except for in the cinema, where teenage audiences from the suburbs shout, jeer and break into sudden applause as the delinquent actor outwits the police. The voices of the audience resonate and vibrate through the auditorium, fusing into those of the delinquent on screen.

Juvenile delinquency, uneven development and Spanish film

The word 'quinqui' derives from 'quinquillero' or 'quincallero', a derogatory term that was originally used to describe 'mercheros', a nomadic ethnic group from Spain that eked out a living by collecting discarded scrap metal. Ethnically distinct from and more ostracised than gypsies, the *quinquis* were according to Javier García-Egocheaga 'los últimos marginados' (the last marginal people) of Spain (2003). The most famous *quinqui* was Eleuterio Sánchez 'el Lute', an outlaw who escaped from prison numerous times and who featured repeatedly on the cover of *El Caso*, a sensationalist crime weekly. His infamy even inspired the German pop group Boney M to write 'El Lute' (1979), a hit single about his life.[1] As the term *quinqui* gained currency in Spanish media in the late 1960s, it assumed an increasingly vague meaning, being used more generically to describe delinquents and lowlifes regardless of their ethnicity.[2] If the *mercheros* were originally known for their itinerant movement across the country, the term *quinqui* came to be associated with juvenile delinquents who were living more specifically in the outer suburbs of major cities.

In their evolution from nomadic tinkers to urban delinquents, the *quinquis* reflected Spain's rapid transformation from an agricultural economy into an increasingly industrial and consumerist one. The Plan Nacional de Establización Económica (the National Stabilisation Plan) of 1959, a series of measures designed to liberalise the Spanish economy and attract foreign investment, led to a spectacular pattern of growth. While Spain in that year was still classified as a developing nation by the UN, by 1973 it had become the world's ninth industrial power (Hooper, 1995: 18). Spain's so-called 'economic miracle' greatly accelerated the migratory flows from the countryside to its urban centres as people sought employment in the booming service and construction industries. As Inbal Ofer notes, the southern and central regions of Spain – namely Andalucia, Extremadura, Castile-La Mancha and Castile and León – generated 86% of the migration that took place during the regime, with Madrid, Cataluña, Valencia and the urbanised Basque region absorbing almost the entirety of this population (2017: 40). With Spanish cities unable to accommodate this rapid influx of migrants, many of them had no other choice than to live in shanty towns and illegal settlements on the edges of the city, areas of social exclusion that became breeding grounds for petty crime. Attempts by the Franco regime at mitigating the burgeoning housing crisis frequently made matters worse. In a phenomenon known as 'chabolismo vertical' (vertical shanty towns), migrants were rehoused in Unidades Vecinales de Absorción (UVAs), multi-storey tower blocks that were as poorly constructed as they were densely stacked. Too often disconnected from the rest of the city, these new neighbourhoods lacked even the most basic services such as street lights, sewage, green spaces, schools, walk-in clinics, security and street cleaning (Cuesta, A. 2009: 185). The deteriorating material conditions of many internal migrants therefore revealed a rather more complex portrait of Spain's economic miracle. That the term *quinqui* increasingly became associated with this emerging urban underclass reveals the extent to which, according to Pamela Beth Radcliff, inequalities were embedded in the country's new prosperity (2017: 234).

These inequalities were thrown into sharp relief after Spain's economic miracle came to an abrupt end in 1973, when the oil crisis triggered a global recession. The repercussions of the downturn were more acutely felt in Spain than other countries, given that its economy had been particularly reliant on external factors (Lawlor and Rigby, 1998: 101). Unemployment climbed steadily throughout the 1970s, rising from 5% in 1975 to 10% by 1979, before climbing to 15% in 1981 (Holmes, 2001: 68). The threadbare state overseen by Franco spectacularly failed to shield the weakest in society from the economic fallout. Despite its recent economic fortunes, the regime had maintained a very low expenditure on welfare services and social investment (Radcliff, 2011: 37). That crime rates correspondingly rose was therefore unsurprising. Burglary rates swelled between the years of 1977 and 1978 by 87.59% (Sainz Cantero, 1983: 749) while the rate of motor vehicle theft, for instance, doubled between the years 1975 and 1979 (Hernando Sanz, 2001: 266). Significantly, this spike in crime was increasingly linked to teenage delinquency. Felipe Hernando Sanz notes that youths carried out a total of 70% of all car thefts and robberies in 1982 (2001: 266). This in part can be attributed to the fact that Spain's employment crisis bore a disproportionate impact on the young: the high unemployment figures coincided with an ever-increasing percentage of teenagers coming of age in Spain, a result of the fertility boom witnessed in the early 1960s (Gamella, 1990: xxvi). Moreover, while mandatory secondary education had finally been introduced in 1970, children were still nevertheless legally permitted to leave school at the age of 14. Rising crime rates were hardly unique to Spain: the increased ownership of consumer goods in Western countries inevitably brought with it more opportunities for crime. In this respect, Spain's crime rates belatedly followed the dramatic increases in theft and burglary that had previously begun in the United Kingdom and United States in the 1960s.[3] Aside from its belatedness, however, what distinguished the Spanish crime wave from those of other Western countries was its specific coincidence with a tumultuous period of political uncertainty and change.

The death of the dictator Francisco Franco in November 1975 set in motion Spain's transition to democracy, a process that was finally consolidated by the general elections of 1982, which saw the Partido Socialista Obrero Español (Spanish Socialist Workers' Party) gain power. The everyday anxieties and sense of unease felt by much of the Spanish population during these years, as well as the ways these emotions both shaped and were in turn shaped by cultural production, have largely gone unexplored. If the rising crime rates were indeed a cause for concern, the perceived threat of everyday crime was sharply amplified by its unrelentingly sensationalist exposure in the Spanish media, which saw the flourishing of a number of new media outlets during these years. The press frequently reported not only on the delinquent crime waves of Barcelona and Madrid but on the generalised fears and pronounced sense of insecurity of the Spanish population. Moreover, for conservative newspapers such as *ABC*, *El Imparcial*, *Pueblo* and *Ya*, which were in varying degrees nostalgic for the authoritarianism of the regime, juvenile delinquency was held up as both a symptom and symbol of a breakdown of law and order, one that cast doubt on Spain's democratic process. Urban centres became increasingly marked by the auditory presence of terrorist attacks, strikes and mass demonstrations – noises that quite literally undercut the dominant narrative that Spain underwent a peaceful and exemplary process of democratisation. In the face of multiple uncertainties, the diffuse fears of many Spanish people therefore found a more specific expression through the figure of the juvenile delinquent, who emerged as an example of what the criminologists Stephen D. Farrall, Jonathan Jackson and Emily Gray have termed a 'criminal other', whereby crime becomes a 'convenient location for the storing of anxieties' (2009: 109). The moral panic that surrounded youth crime was a vivid example of 'how crime gathers its resonance not from the *meaning* of the event but from wider social change in society' (Farrall, Jackson and Gray, 2009: 27, their emphasis). If the ontological insecurity felt by many Spaniards during these years can be explained through several causes, difficult to disentangle from one another, this insecurity was most clearly articulated through a fear of crime – and in particular the figure of the juvenile delinquent. As such, juvenile delinquency became a powerful cultural symbol during these years, a potent site of meaning and affect whose political currency was frequently more important than the nature of the crimes actually committed.

Just as juvenile delinquents increasingly populated the pages of Spanish newspapers, their images soon enough found their way onto Spanish screens, with several filmmakers quick to capitalise on the nation's growing preoccupation with youth crime. The Barcelona-based director José Antonio de la Loma, in particular, was fascinated by the criminal trajectory of Juan José Moreno Cuenca 'el Vaquilla', who at just 15 years of age had become infamous for escaping from every detention centre in the country. Shot on location in the impoverished *barrio* of La Mina in Barcelona, de la Loma's film *Perros callejeros/ Street Warriors* (1977) was partially inspired by the events of the delinquent's life. In spite of having no previous experience of acting, Moreno Cuenca was asked to play the protagonist – a casting decision that was promptly thwarted by the juvenile courts which prevented him from taking part in the film. As a result, his friend Ángel Fernández Franco 'el Trompeta' subsequently stood in to take the leading role of 'el Torete' instead. *Perros callejeros* was far from the first film to explore the theme of delinquency in Spanish film. The films *Los golfos/ The Delinquents* (Carlos Saura, 1961), *Los chicos/The Young Ones* (Marco Ferreri, 1960) and *El espontáneo/The Rash One* (Jorge Grau, 1964), for instance, explored the relationship between delinquency and marginal space in Madrid, while *Young Sánchez* (Mario Camus, 1964) and *El último sábado/The Last Saturday* (Pedro Balañá, 1967) turned their attention to youth in the suburbs of Barcelona. In their formal experimentation and neorealist-inspired aesthetics, however, these films were primarily aimed at art cinema consumption – and therefore at a public who were evidently distinct from the kinds of marginal subjects depicted on screen. In contrast, *Perros callejeros* more specifically targeted the youth demographic, who recognised their clothes in the way the actors dressed and their own slang in the naturalistic way in which the non-professional actors spoke. If the earlier delinquent-themed films maintained an aesthetic distance from the social deprivation exhibited on screen, *Perros callejeros* fully immersed audiences within it. In its sensuous evocation of movement and thrills, the film

0.1 Ángel Fernández Franco as 'el Torete' in the police station in *Perros callejeros* (José Antonio de la Loma, 1977).

established a close and visceral connection with its audiences, one that signalled a truly popular cinema.

Perros callejeros was produced at a time when the Spanish film industry was undergoing a series of profound transformations. One month after the release of *Perros callejeros* in November 1977, censorship was finally abolished and replaced by a Board of Film Classification, one of several reforms designed to bring the Spanish film industry in line with Spain's emerging democracy.[4] This provided filmmakers with a new-found freedom to show overt depictions of police brutality and corruption, drug taking and other activities that had been strictly taboo during the regime, as well as giving freer rein to representations of nudity and sex, a tendency that had already begun in the final years of the regime. The reforms also led to a greater liberalisation of the Spanish film industry: state funding was reduced for an already fragile industry that was desperately in need of protective measures, and the distribution quota was abolished (Trenzado Romero, 1999: 157). To add to the industry's woes, moreover, Spanish films now found themselves in competition with a backlog of foreign films that had been banned during the regime, whose release began from 1976 onwards (Torres, 1996: 43–44). From 1978, audience numbers began to fall rapidly (from a total of 220 million spectators in 1978 to just 155 million in 1982), while the quota of Spanish films on screens also dwindled (from 29.76% in 1977 to 21.72% in 1982) (Trenzado Romero, 1999: 174). The kinds of narrative films that prospered within this difficult economic climate were politically themed films, the *comedia madrileña* (Madrid-based comedy) and *cine de destape* (cinema containing sex and nudity). As well as these tendencies, the industrial strategy with most success by Spanish filmmakers was the attempt to occupy some of the terrain of American cinema, particularly in its appropriation of the genre film (Hopewell, 1986: 220). In its exciting cat-and-mouse car chases and gritty depiction of criminality, *Perros callejeros* incorporated the familiar generic conventions of the action film and the thriller, but in a novel way that spoke to local audiences. Indeed, the film embodied a spirit of anti-authoritarianism that had rarely been seen in Spanish popular cinema of the Franco period. In its ground-breaking depiction of teenage rebellion and police brutality, moreover, the film powerfully captured the fissures and contradictions of a nation that was on the cusp of youthful democracy on the one hand, while simultaneously hidebound by the authoritarian structures of social control of the regime on the other.

Cine quinqui: between authoritarianism and freedom

The commercial success of *Perros callejeros* brought several delinquent-themed films in its wake, and the subject of marginal youth subculture soon became a regular staple of Spanish film production for the next decade. The moral panic that surrounded the release of *Perros callejeros* no doubt helped to publicise its two sequels, *Perros callejeros 2: Busca y captura/Street Warriors 2* (1979) and *Los últimos golpes de 'el Torete'/El Torete's Last Blows* (1980), again both starring Ángel Fernández Franco. José Antonio de la Loma's later spin-off *Perras callejeras/Street Warrior Girls* (1985) was centred on a group of female delinquents, while *Yo, 'el Vaquilla'/I, 'el Vaquilla'* (1985) was a biopic of Juan José Moreno Cuenca, featuring the real-life delinquent recounting his life story from within prison. Following de la Loma's lead, Ignacio F. Iquino made delinquent-centred films in the suburbs of Barcelona. Iquino was the producer of *¿Y ahora qué, señor fiscal?/And Now What, Dear Public Prosecutor?* (León Klimovsky, 1977) and producer-director of *Los violadores del amanecer/Rapists at Dawn* (1978), films that were more far more reactionary and damning in their depiction of delinquency.[5] While

Barcelona first emerged as the epicentre of Spain's juvenile delinquency crisis, Madrid's crime figures by 1979 had caught up with those of Barcelona (Aguilera, 1979). From 1980 onwards, several *quinqui* films were subsequently located in the outer suburbs of Madrid, starting with Eloy de la Iglesia's *Navajeros/Knifers* (1980). De la Iglesia's film was based on the biography of the most notorious delinquent from Madrid, José Joaquín Sánchez Frutos 'el Jaro'. The non-professional actor José Luis Manzano from Vallecas, Madrid made his cinematic debut in the starring role, alongside the real-life delinquent José Luis Fernández 'el Pirri' who appeared in a minor role. Manzano went on to appear in four further *quinqui* films with the director: *Colegas/Pals* (1982), *El pico/Overdose* (1983), *El pico 2/Overdose 2* (1984) and *La estanquera de Vallecas/The Granny and the Heist* (1987).[6] The theme of juvenile delinquency had long fascinated de la Iglesia, with the subject appearing in his earlier dramas *Los placeres ocultos/Hidden Pleasures* (1977) and *El diputado/Confessions of a Congressman* (1978), as well as his comedy *Miedo a salir de noche/Fear of Going Out at Night* (1980) which satirised the ways in which Spanish media had constructed a moral panic around crime. An active member of the Partido Comunista de España (the Spanish Communist Party), de la Iglesia's films were more explicitly didactic in their politics than the Barcelona-based films of de la Loma. This was influenced by his collaboration with the screenwriter Gónzalo Goicoechea, whose sociological sensibility had been honed through his previous roles as investigative journalist for *Triunfo* and *Interviú*. The figure of the delinquent not only emerged as a site of political contestation for directors on the left but also for those who were rather more sceptical about Spain's fledgling democracy and the subsequent emergence of new civil liberties. As well as the films by Iquino and Klimovsky, Francisco Lara Polop's *La patria de 'el Rata'/No Exit* (1980) and Gil Carretero's *Chocolate/Pot* (1980) – both of which were also filmed on location in Madrid – viewed delinquency as a symptom of the weakness of the Spanish democratic state.

If *cine quinqui* is associated with directors and producers of different ideological stripes, it also signalled a diverse array of production methods and contexts. Carlos Saura and Manuel Gutiérrez Aragón, auteurs who were more readily associated with the mode of art cinema, found new audiences with their delinquent films *Deprisa, deprisa/Fast, Fast* (1981) and *Maravillas* (1981) respectively.[7] Both shot in Madrid in 1980, the contemplative rhythm and poetic sensibility of the films vividly contrasted with the action-driven narratives of the initial flurry of delinquent films. Another take on *cine quinqui* was Montxo Armendáriz's *27 horas* (1986), which was striking for its austere realism and elliptical editing. The film centred on junky teenagers in San Sebastián, the Basque city which was at the centre of Spain's heroin epidemic in the 1980s. Vicente Aranda's *El Lute*: *Camina o revienta/ El Lute: Run For Your Life* (1987) and *El Lute II: Mañana seré libre/ El Lute 2: Tomorrow I'll Be Free* (1988), two handsomely made biopics which chronicled the criminal life of Eleuterio Sánchez 'el Lute', were amongst the final films associated with *cine quinqui*. Through their painstaking attention to historical detail, Aranda's films can also be classified as historical period dramas, their polished production values and sweeping orchestral scores a contrast to the rough-hewn aesthetics of the initial *quinqui* films. As well as film, juvenile delinquency made its way on to Spanish television through *Turno de oficio/In Court Defence* (1986–1987), a highly popular series that was directed by Antonio Mercero and to a lesser degree, *Brigada central/Central Crime Team* (1989–1992).

The narratives of these films were generally focalised through the deviant movement of the delinquent, a dynamic that encouraged the audience to empathise and engage closely with the protagonists. As Mery Cuesta has written, the delinquent constitutes 'la voz principal, el punto de vista narrativo' (the main voice, the narrative point of view) in *cine quinqui*, and not the police – a narrative structure that distinguishes these films from the likes of the crime film (2009: 69). Indeed, in re-enacting versions of their own criminal acts and those of their peers, the *quinqui* voice possessed an almost evidential status, one whose indexical connection to real life brought a documentary-style urgency to the films. The delinquent actors became enormously popular in their own right. Ángel Fernández Franco and José Luis Manzano swiftly made the transition from non-professional actors to magazine pin-ups, their images first appearing in news weeklies such as *El Caso* before moving to 'crónica rosa' (gossip) magazines such as *Pronto, Nuevo Vale, Semana* and *Garbo* (Cuesta, M. 2009: 69).

It is not surprising, then, that these films and actors appealed most of all to young audiences who lived in the kinds of working-class suburbs that were depicted in the films. Out of the four cinemas where *Perros callejeros 2: Busca y captura* was initially exhibited, for instance, three were located in marginal or working-class neighbourhoods in the city: Palacio Balaña in Sants, Pedro IV and Río. While several of these films were resounding commercial hits – in particular *Perros callejeros*, *El pico*, *El pico 2* and *El Lute*: *Camina o revienta*[8] – the official box office figures do not fully reflect the true geographical reach and longevity of the films, given that extended or repeated screenings of films in smaller *cines de barrio* (neighbourhood cinemas) were not included in the statistics. As Mery Cuesta has shown, the majority of the *quinqui* films were shown for only a few days in the main cinemas before they moved on to the *cine de barrio* circuit, where they were continuously shown from eleven o'clock in the morning (2009: 73). From the early to mid-1980s, these films found home audiences through increased circulation of VHS,[9] as well as more commonly through *videos comunitarios* (community video), as Alejandro Melero has noted (2013: 48). *Videos comunitarios* were unofficial cable services located in poorer neighbourhoods in Spain, often where people did not have their own video players, whose programming consisted of a series of films that had originally been obtained on VHS and were illegally transmitted to households for a nominal monthly fee.

Despite reaching large audiences, several of the films associated with *cine quinqui* were critically maligned. To this effect, *cine quinqui* has much in common with several film cycles that were specifically produced for the teenage demographic in the United States, such as the gangster film of the 1930s, the teen pic film of the 1950s and the Blaxploitation film of the 1970s[10] – cycles that, as Amanda Ann Klein has shown, have also been marginalised in critical, popular and academic discourses because of their often deviant subject matter (2011: 6). While *cine quinqui* has often been considered a film genre, following the writing of Klein, it is arguably more productive to describe it as a film cycle – particularly given its association, as we have seen, with a loose and increasingly heterogeneous body of films that was produced over a relatively short time period. One of the ways in which Klein distinguishes film genres from cycles is in terms of their longevity: while film genres draw on a large corpus of films that accumulates for decades, film cycles are financially viable for only five to ten years (2011: 4). This is because film cycles are chiefly defined by their topicality, and as such are only able to court their audiences for so long (Klein, 2011: 14). If several *quinqui* films were similarly shaped by a sense of immediacy and urgency, this was because their narratives so often appeared to be ripped from the headlines.

The directors drew much of their contextual information from news reports and investigative journalism at the time, as well as from the experiences of the delinquent actors themselves. Yet if through their emphasis on testimony and evidence the production method of *cine quinqui* sought to lay claim to the real, the formal construction of the films also emphasised sensuousness and spectacle – characteristics which would appear at first to have more in common with the tabloid media than with the documentary mode.

Ann Klein writes that the creators of film cycles lure moviegoers into the theatres by exploiting their interest in licentious, sensational or even dangerous imagery (2011: 6). As we have seen, in common with much of Spanish cinema after censorship, *cine quinqui* similarly emphasised the spectacle of the forbidden. Yet in its direct appeal to the senses, it also drew influence from the sensationalist press of the time, thereby alerting us to the slippage of meaning between sensationalist and the sensorial. Their use of cinematic techniques – namely mobile camerawork, rapid editing and most crucially sound – emphasised shock, sensation and exhilaration. Rather than undercutting the realism of delinquency on screen, however, the sensuousness of film form served to viscerally convey what criminologist Jack Katz has described as the 'lived experience' of criminality. In exploring the 'seductive qualities of crime', Katz lays emphasis on how it feels, tastes, looks and sounds to carry out a criminal act. Focussing on what he calls the 'seductive qualities of crime' (1988: 3), he explores 'those aspects in the foreground of criminality that make its various forms sensible, even sensually compelling, forms of being' (1988: 3). Katz's writing here correspondingly provides a clue into the popular appeal of the films, whereby delinquents were not presented as mere victims of their geographical surroundings but rather provided audiences with fantasies of spatial mastery and escape, exhilaration and excitement. Jack Katz noted the 'transformative magic' of crime and deviance, (1988: 129) painting the picture of robbery not as a cold and rational act but one that could be spontaneous and hedonistic. *Cine quinqui* similarly alerts us to the sensuous thrills of rule-breaking and transgression, where crime is committed because it is fun.

The cinematic appeal of deviant youth cultures was not limited to Spanish cinema during this period. The controversial British-American film *Clockwork Orange* (Stanley Kubrick, 1971), for instance, whose dystopian scenes of sexual violence led to its withdrawal in the UK, was by far the highest-grossing film in the cinemas of Madrid and Barcelona in 1976.[11] Significantly, the film was a key influence on Eloy de la Iglesia's filmmaking, as seen in particular in *Una gota de sangre para morir amando/Murder in a Blue World* (1973) and *Navajeros.* Other British films that were contemporary to *cine quinqui* depicted the rites and rituals of teenage subcultures such as the mods and rockers in *Quadrophenia* (Franc Roddam, 1979) and punk in *Jubilee* (Derek Jarman, 1978), while *Scum* (Alan Clarke, 1979) chronicled the brutality of life inside British reformatories. While the effects of youth unemployment and the dissemination of hard drugs were felt acutely in Spain, this trend was found in several countries in the West which were similarly experiencing economic stagnation. The German film *Christiane F. Wir Kinder vom Bahnhof Zoo/Christiane F.* (Uli Edel, 1981) depicted the drug scene in West Berlin in the 1980s, while *Pixote* (Héctor Babenco, 1980) provided a quasi-documentary account of street kids in Brazil, starring Fernando Ramos da Silva, an eleven-year-old non-professional actor who would be killed by the police a few years later. The American film *The Warriors* (Walter Hill, 1979), which depicted rivalling street gangs in Brooklyn, became linked to a spate of copycat youth violence which even allegedly resulted in three killings.[12] Yet while youth deviance was indeed a theme that could be found across several national cinemas, these films did not constitute a cycle of films in the way that *cine quinqui* did. Indeed, the Spanish film industry was unique in the sheer quantity of delinquent-themed films during these years, as well as in its creation of delinquent stars. The uniqueness of the Spanish *quinqui* film compels us to consider the specific economic, material and political conditions which shaped the films. These conditions, moreover, can be further illuminated through considering the importance of sound.

Deviant resonance: Sound, sensation and transgression

Accounts of the theatrical experience of *quinqui* films frequently drew attention to the noise of the auditorium, with young audiences shouting, cheering and breaking into spontaneous applause – particularly during moments of resistance and rebellion against the police. The sociologist Jaime Funes, who specialised in juvenile delinquency, was present at a screening of *Perros callejeros* in the marginal *barrio* of San Ildefonso in Barcelona. He observed how 'el cine temblaba' (the cinema shook) that day, characterising the screening as follows: 'Aplausos después de las escenas más violentas, gritos de animación, jaleo colectivo …, todo un hervidero de comunición emocional con la pantalla' (Funes, 1984: 74).[13] Funes then later compared the responses of a group of delinquents watching *Perros callejeros*, to which they responded enthusiastically, with the American film *The Warriors* which they failed to warm to at all (Funes, 1984: 74). Filled with the shouts of the teenagers, the soundscape of the auditorium alerts us to the crucial auditory dimension of the reception of the *quinqui* film. Their enthusiasm at seeing and hearing protagonists on screen was registered through noise.

The noisy reception to *Perros callejeros* can be elaborated through the criminologist Ruth Penfold-Mounce's notion of 'resonance', a sonic metaphor that she uses to describe the relationship between people and criminal celebrities in contemporary society. For Penfold-Mounce, the notion of resonance signals a relationship that goes further than merely identifying oneself with someone or something. Resonance, she writes, presupposes not so much a simple connection to a famous person but a connection which stimulates a response (2009: 63). Resonance, she argues, therefore lays emphasis not on questions of identification but rather to interaction (2009: 63). Funes's account of the exhibition of *Perros callejeros* similarly keenly illustrates a degree of resonance between the *quinqui* actors and the young audiences, while crucially at the same time alerting us to the literal and sonic meaning of the word. The shaking auditorium brings to mind Penfold-Mounce's description of resonance as 'the reinforcement or prolongation of sound by reflection or synchronous vibration' (2009: 64) in its most physical expression. At the same time, *cine quinqui* and the circulation of delinquent stars in the media stimulated a response whose tremors were felt across various sectors of Spanish media and society – a diverse range of responses which ranged from fear and fascination, knee-jerk hysteria to paternalistic compassion. Penfold-Mounce discusses the extent to which resonance 'causes a shake-up' (2009: 65), thereby producing a range of extreme emotions, from fun but also fear, rebellion and horror (2009: 64). As this book shows, *cine quinqui* did not only provide joy and noisy excitement for its audiences; it also triggered a series of debates that entered into political, criminological and political discourses. Providing a mirror onto the injustices of uneven capitalism and the residual authoritarianism of the regime, the films demanded a response that was not only physical but political. Several of the films, such as *El pico 2* and *Yo, 'el Vaquilla'* were exhibited in prisons, with the former followed by a debate on the urgency for penitentiary reform in Spain. Their reception highlighted the extent to which *cine quinqui* could be considered a vehicle for social and political change.

Ruth Penfold-Mounce writes that the key reason that criminals and deviants resonate with society is their potential for transgression. If, she argues, transgression is a central idea of our time in a society created by constraints and boundaries, it is increasingly difficult to determine where these boundaries lie, given that our culture is increasingly uncertain and in flux (2009: 4). She thus writes that 'by focussing on transgression … the search is for limits that are found only by crossing them' (2009: 4). During Spain's transition from authoritarian rule to democracy, the boundaries between criminality and legality were themselves equally in contention and flux. Despite Spain's status as a capitalist liberal economy, a position that was cemented with the Moncloa Pacts of 1977[14] and the Constitution of 1978, its juvenile courts and penitentiary systems had evolved little since the early years of the regime. Spain's slow road to legal reform was most starkly dramatised by belatedness of the democratic Penal Code, which was only finally established twenty years after the death of Franco in 1995. The borders that separated deviance and social control during this period were thus frequently ambiguous and porous, frequently redrawn and reinforced, debated and politicised across the political spectrum. The transgression embodied by the *quinquis* – one whose resonance was felt in the cinemas and which then reverberated across the media and the national body politic – vividly illuminated these shifting borders. As this book shows, thinking sonically enables us to locate where these borders were situated.

If, as the several accounts in this book show, the exhibition of *cine quinqui* generated noise within the cinema auditorium, the on-screen delinquents were themselves a noisy presence – something that was played out on a level that was both simultaneously acoustic and symbolic, material and social. Their deviant slang, obtrusively blaring music and screeching car tyres illustrate G. W. C. Kaye's description of noise as a 'sound out of place' (cited in Thompson, 2017: 20). Unwanted and invasive, their sounds were beyond the realms of social acceptability and found themselves frequently subject to regulation. The saturated and noisy soundtrack of *cine quinqui*, heavy with diegetic and non-diegetic music and sound effects that were registered in auditory close-up, vividly dramatises Kaye's description of noise as 'sound out of place'. The soundtrack of the films provided an authentic reflection of the auditory experience of delinquents and marginal young people on the outskirts of Barcelona and Madrid during this time. At the same time, their noise gave symbolic expression to the social location of the juvenile delinquency, a dissonance alerting us both to their deviance and their subsequent threat to the social fabric. The auditory experience of delinquency often illustrated the extent to which sound is uncontainable and elusive: it is able to move through walls and across borders. If the experience of delinquency in *cine quinqui* was one of walls, both geographical and metaphorical, their noise served to disrupt and transcend the oppressive geographies that contained them. Like soundwaves, they moved between, over and *through*. Yet the noisy interaction of audiences with the delinquents revealed the extent to which sound also established a close community between *quinqui* films, actors and their audiences. Indeed, Marie Thompson has recently nuanced the existing definitions of noise as unwanted sound, arguing that 'what counts as unwanted or non-musical sound can vary drastically according to context' (2017: 1).

While on the one hand, the noise of the delinquents alerted us to their geographical dislocation, it also helped to establish a more resonant interaction and closeness between the films and their audiences, a dynamic that enabled them to carve out their own auditory community, often in environments that were hostile and unforgiving to them. In the soundtracks of the films, this was most vividly borne out through the essential role of music, and in particular the *rumba*. The close synergy established between *cine quinqui* and the enormously popular music of Los Chichos, Los Chunguitos and other gypsy *rumba* groups established an auditory connection to the films that was frequently situated beyond the location of the auditorium, with their soundtrack albums being played on portable radio cassettes. In alerting us to the relationality of sound, *cine quinqui* demonstrates how, as Michael Bull and Les Back write, 'sound connects us in ways that vision does not' (2003: 6). As this book seeks to show, both the production and the reception of *cine quinqui* crucially depended on an intermedial relationship between cinema and sound, music and the media. Unpicking

0.2 The acoustic experience of youth subculture in *Navajeros* (Eloy de la Iglesia, 1980).

the relationship between these different media enables us to explore the close relationship and interaction – or 'resonance' as Penfold-Mounce puts it – between the films and their audiences.

Thinking sonically also enables us to examine the marginal juvenile delinquents in the films as belonging to a subculture in their own right. Dick Hebdige has famously equated subcultures with excess, registering the 'deviance' of a subculture through a range of excessive or exaggerated attributes – instantly recognisable, 'loud' style of dress, slang, modes of consumption – which are in turn contrasted with the measured 'constraints' of normal society (1979). Dick Hebdige writes: 'Subcultures represent noise (as opposed to sound)', in that they constitute 'an interference in the orderly sequence which leads from real events and phenomena to their *representation in the media*' (1979: 90). This conceptualisation of noise as disruptive and disorderly, as something that works as a radical and resistant outside to a system, echoes the writing of the musicologist Jacques Attali, who writes that 'noise ha[s] always been experienced as destruction, disorder, dirt, pollution, an aggression against [the] code-structuring messages' (1985). In placing 'noise' outside the realm of signification and discourse, the writings of Hebdige and Attali alert us here to the sensory and affective dimensions of sound, aspects that shift the focus away from considering simply what their noises meant to how their noises made people feel. This shift subsequently leads us to consider the materiality of sound – its vibrations, its pitch and its flow – and the physical effects they have on the body. Jeremy Gilbert has written, for instance, that 'music has physical effects which can be identified, described and discussed but which are not the same thing as it having meanings' (2004). Through his focus on the non-discursive and non-signifying power of music, Gilbert explores the extent to which sound generates a somatic response. As with other scholars who have addressed the affective dimension of sound, Gilbert is indebted to the work of Brian Massumi, who defines affect as a non-conscious 'intensity' disconnected from signification. Massumi defines affect as 'a state of suspense, potentially of disruption. It is like a temporal sink, a hole in time as we conceive of it and narrativise it. It is not exactly passivity because it is filled with motion, vibratory motion, resonation' (2002: 26). Massumi's writing here brings to mind Penfold-Mounce's notion of resonance established between the criminal celebrity and their fans as that which triggers a shake-up. While Penfold-Mounce does not draw directly on affect theory, her notion of resonance enables us to similarly explore not only what *cine quinqui* meant but what it did. As this book shows, the degree of intensity or resonance produced by the film can be productively examined through paying particular attention to the soundtrack, an approach that moves the discussion of the films beyond questions of representation to consider their broader role among various sectors of Spanish society at the time.

The *quinquis* in contemporary Spanish culture and about this book

Despite its significance to Spanish audiences, *cine quinqui* was critically neglected until the ground-breaking exhibition 'Quinquis dels 80: Cinema, Premsa I Carrer' which took place at the Centre de Cultura Contemporània de Barcelona in 2009, curated by Amanda and Mery Cuesta. The exhibition was accompanied by screenings of several of the *quinqui* films listed above, as well as the publication of an invaluable and meticulously researched volume of contextual essays and photographs (2009). The author Javier Cercas brought the *quinquis* to the attention of the Spanish literary establishment in his novel *Las leyes de la frontera/Outlaws* (2012). Set in a deprived neighbourhood of Girona in the 1980s, the novel was partially inspired by Juan José

Moreno Cuenca and the film *Deprisa, deprisa.* The growing critical attention to *cine quinqui* has coincided with the contemporary cult appeal of the films, with most of the films mentioned above now readily available on DVD and shown regularly on the Paramount channel. *Cine quinqui* continues to resonate with younger generations of audiences, with numerous websites and blogs now dedicated to the cycle and its actors, with ample evidence of online forums in which fans interact with one another and the films. Mery Cuesta, moreover, has noted the YouTube video and audio homages that fans have edited of the films (2009: 101), and true to the deviance of *cine quinqui*, all of the films are available to download illegally. The aesthetic crudeness of the films, moreover, affords pleasures that are specific to contemporary audiences. These aesthetic aberrances are precisely the kinds which resonate with what Jeffrey Sconce, in writing on cult cinema, has termed 'paracinema' (Sconce, 1995). For Sconce, the contemporary cult viewer derives paracinematic pleasure from viewing out-of-date technology, revelling in these moments of stylistic excess which reveal the materiality of the film. Paracinema is 'less a distinct group of films than a particular reading protocol, a counter-aesthetic turned subcultural sensibility devoted to all manner of cultural detritus' (Sconce, 1995: 372). Detritus or trash, of course, is implicit in the original meanings of *quincalla* and *quinquillero,* as discarded pieces of scrap metal and the marginal population respectively who eked out a living collecting it for resale. By analogy, the application of the term *cine quinqui* – a moniker that was conferred on the body of delinquent films some years after their release – similarly evokes a particular reading protocol or sensibility, one in which low-status cultural products that were deemed 'trash' at the time have been re-vindicated and repurposed for contemporary audiences. To this effect, *cine quinqui* can be considered alongside other Spanish popular genres or cycles of films of the 1970s – namely horror (particularly the films of Jesús Franco),[15] *cine de destape* and the *paella* western – whose formal excesses similarly offer up paracinematic pleasures.

The growing interest in *cine quinqui* has been reflected recently in academic scholarship. Juan A. Ríos Carratalá's monograph *Quinquis, maderos y picoletos* (2014) and Joaquín Florido Berrocal et al.'s volume of essays *Fuera de la Ley: Asedios al fenómeno quinqui en la transición española* (2015) are two very useful books on *cine quinqui.* Paul Julian Smith was the first scholar to pay attention to the filmmaking of

Eloy de la Iglesia, through seminal readings of his films through the lens of gender and sexuality (1992, 1998). Alejandro Melero's *Placeres ocultos: Gays y lesbianas en el cine español de la transición* (2010) and Maxime Breysse's *Le Cinéma quinqui selon Eloy de la Iglesia* (2011) have since provided important analyses of de la Iglesia's films from this period, while Eduardo Fuembuena's *Lejos de aquí* (2017), provides a fascinating biography of the actor José Luis Manzano and his relationship with the director. *The Spanish* Quinqui *Film: Delinquency, Sound, Sensation* is the first major study of these films in English, as well as the first monograph of its kind in any language that seeks to theorise the sociological, political and criminological significance of the films. In addition, the book more broadly contributes to a now substantial body of scholarship in Spanish cultural studies that has challenged the dominant narrative of the transition as one of civil liberties and celebration, and that has critiqued the consensual nature of cultural production during this period.[16] To this effect, Florido Berrocal et al. have observed how the history of the *quinquis* similarly illuminates a very distinct portrayal of the transition which has most often been associated with the Movida Madrileña, the counterculture which emerged in Madrid in the 1980s: 'Las historias de los *quinquis* aparecen como un relato alternativo que vuelve la mirada hacia el otro lado de la "fiesta" y explora las "ruinas" humanas que subyacían a la nueva coyuntura política ...' (Florido Berrocal et al., 2015: x).[17]

Where possible, much of this book seeks to situate *cine quinqui* within the broader context of Spain's transition to democracy through a particular emphasis on sound and sensation. Sound is important to my analysis as it occupied an important role in the social formation of youth subcultures during this period. If, as we have seen, their deviance was articulated through sound, the soundtrack of the films also forged a close and affective relationship between the films and their audiences, thereby establishing a sense of community and belonging. In exploring how the soundtrack – in particular, vocal performance, music and ambient sounds – illuminates these questions, this book builds on an approach that has been pioneered in the scholarship of Kathleen M. Vernon, whose work has interrogated the commonly held relationship between the sound and image in Spanish film studies.[18] Alongside Vernon's forthcoming book *Listening to Spanish Cinema*, this book intends to be one of the first monographs that considers the place of the soundtrack in Spanish film. Where possible, this book seeks to acknowledge sound and image together as a dual entity, something that Michel Chion has termed 'the audio-visual contract'. For Chion, in the audiovisual contract, 'the visual and the auditory mutually influence each other … lending each other their respective properties by contamination and projection' (1994: 9). In its emphasis on the broader sonic experience of delinquency and deviance – one that is both cinematic and extra-cinematic (in particular, through the music the *quinquis* consumed and the language they used in everyday life) – the book also seeks to create dialogue with sound studies, a discipline whose influence is now beginning to be felt within Spanish cultural studies.[19] If the material properties of sound are elusive and ambiguous, able to pass across borders and walls, so too are the boundaries of sound studies, which are diverse and interdisciplinary in scope. In exploring the significance of sound and sensation in *cine quinqui,* this book similarly draws on several diverse disciplines – from cultural criminology and sociology to mobility studies and musicology – that have rarely been applied to the context of Spanish film. Through this critical framework, I hope to reveal the ways in which *cine quinqui* can provide a particularly rich conjunctural understanding of its historical period, tracing the way in which its resonance vibrated through and across the various political, criminological, social and economic fault lines of the Spanish transition to democracy. Rather than provide a comprehensive overview of all of the films associated with the cycle, this book instead offers an in-depth analysis of eleven *quinqui* films which stand out as the most commercially and culturally significant, and whose resonance was most keenly felt with audiences, the media and public discourse. As well as providing close textual analyses of the films, the book also considers the social and cultural experience of *cine quinqui*, tracing the consumption, circulation and reception of the films, and their subsequent impact on media, legal and political discourses on delinquency and social disorder.

The first chapter focusses on José Antonio de la Loma's cycle of *quinqui* films – namely *Perros callejeros*, *Perros callejeros 2: Busca y captura* and *Los últimos golpes de 'el Torete'* – which featured the first *quinqui* star Ángel Fernández Franco 'el Torete'. In paying particular attention to the car chases and the significance of stolen vehicles in the cycle, the chapter explores speed and rhythm as a particular site of resonance in the films. While the exhilarating car chases were a source of sensuous pleasure and excitement for audiences, their unruly speed also generated anxieties surrounding the emerging phenomenon of juvenile delinquency that was out of control, with offenders committing thefts at an increasingly young age. Living as fast as they died, the delinquents belonged to a criminal subculture that was marked by its immediacy, yet the depiction of destructive speed in the films pointed to a process of *desarrollismo* (development) that had similarly come about too rapidly, and whose contradictions could not be supported by an authoritarian and poorly funded criminal justice system. The chapter shows how Ángel Fernández Franco's embodiment of deviant speed was not only an integral part of his subcultural appeal and star persona but also a powerful lens through which to explore the rhythmic contours of Spain's recent rapid social, economic and geographical transformations that gave rise to the increase in juvenile delinquency in the first place.

The second chapter explores Ignacio F. Iquino's *Los violadores del amanecer* (1977), Lara Polop's *La patria de 'el Rata'* (1980) and Eloy de la Iglesia's *Miedo a salir de noche* (1980) as three ideologically distinct films associated with *cine quinqui*. Often focalised from the perspective of the victim rather than delinquent, these films respond not only to the increasing crime rates during these years but more specifically to the increase in the *fear* of crime within much of the Spanish population – a theme that specifically gained currency during the general elections of 1977 and 1979. In particular, the chapter examines the home as a site of resonance in the films and Spanish society at the time, whose borders were increasingly reinforced through the rapid spike in investment in home security systems. The soundscape of the home, historically associated with peace and privacy, is depicted as constantly under siege through the voices of delinquents and the noises of alarms, sirens, explosions and other ambient noises. Through its exploration of the resonance of domestic space, the chapter ultimately shows how its acoustic borders reveal anxieties surrounding the shifting understandings of public order in Spain during these years, a concept I show came to be redefined within the new democratic constitution and the subsequent reorganisation of the police force.

The following chapter centres on the *quinqui* films that Eloy de la Iglesia made with the actor José Luis Manzano, focussing in particular on *Navajeros*, *El pico* and *El pico 2*. It explores how the sound in the films contributed towards an aesthetics of shock and sensation, which in turn established a particularly visceral and intersubjective relationship with the audience. A key site of resonance in the films is the fragile body of the delinquent, which is visually and aurally emphasised through the texture of Manzano's skin and the sound of his breath, particularly during moments of drug taking. The chapter explores how the relationship between skin and sound was crucial to the affective charge of de la Iglesia's filmmaking. Through an analysis of haptic sound in particular, the chapter traces the ways in which the film responded to public anxieties surrounding heroin abuse, whose distribution networks found themselves imbricated in the underlying social and political tensions within Euskadi during this period.

The fourth chapter examines the broader social and political resonance of the delinquent voice in *cine quinqui*, through an analysis of *Deprisa, deprisa* and *Yo, 'el Vaquilla'*. The rough-hewn vocal performances of criminal non-actors, many of whom had no prior experience of speaking into microphones, provided Spanish narrative film with a naturalism that had rarely been heard. This chapter explores how the use of direct sound in these films registered the spontaneity of their voices within their immediate geographical surroundings, an effect which also emphasised their agency and testimonial charge of their performances. It further explores how moral panics frequently swirled around the delinquent slang and voice, as well as considering the political function of the voice of Juan José Moreno Cuenca, who became an unofficial spokesperson for mistreated social prisoners in Spain, in addition to being a prominent public voice for penal reform.

The fifth and final chapter addresses the prominent role of *rumbas* – in particular those of Los Chunguitos and Los Chichos – in the films. Coming from similar kinds of marginal spaces as those depicted in the films, the music of these groups enacted a particularly close relationship between geography and sound. It shows how the music of these gypsy groups dramatises a spatial mobility that was similar to that of the delinquents and their families in the films. The chapter explores how the cross-promotion of music and film contributed to the cycle's success, something that was played out through their popular soundtrack albums. The chapter explores the extent to which through sound the delinquents were able to actively produce a space of their own, both inside and outside the film text, something that was aided by the relatively new invention of the radio cassette. The chapter concludes by exploring the influence of *rumbas* on the *rap quinqui* of el Coleta through an analysis of his music videos.

Notes

1 Boney M's song equated el Lute's eventual freedom from incarceration with breaking off the shackles of the Franco regime.

2 As Jesús de las Heras and Juan Villarín wrote in 1974: '¡Quinqui! ¡Quinqui! La calle, desde hace unos años, en España, se ha llenado de esta palabra, de esta especie de grito, expresado unas veces con menosprecio, otras con temor y casi nunca con el sentido exacto de lo que significa' (Quinqui! Quinqui! The streets of Spain in the past few years have been filled with this kind of shout, sometimes expressed with scorn, other times with fear, and almost never with an exact sense of what it means) (1974: 11).

3 For crime rates in the United States see Cohen, Felson and Land (1980). For the United Kingdom see https://www.parliament.uk/business/publications/research/olympic-britain/crime-and-defence/crimes-of-the-century/

4 These reforms were ushered in by the Real Decreto (Royal Decree) of 11 November 1977.

5 Both based in Barcelona, José Antonio de la Loma and Ignacio F. Iquino had collaborated together in the 1950s, and had each since maintained long careers specialising in popular genre films, particularly crime and action films. Vicente Rodríguez Ortega has noted the realist vein in the thrillers produced by Iquino's earlier production company Emisora Films, in films such as *Apartado de correos 1001/P.O. Box 1001* (Julio Salvador, 1950) and *Brigada Criminal/Crime Squad* (Ignacio F. Iquino, 1950), and José Antonio de la Loma's *Las manos sucias/Dirty Hands* (1957) (Rodríguez Ortega, 2014: 266–276). Through their extensive use of location shooting, these earlier films prefigured the emphasis on urban space that would later be seen in *cine quinqui*. The infamous *barrio* of Campo de la Bota, moreover, where 'el Vaquilla' grew up as a child, was a key location in de la Loma's crime thrillers *El último viaje/The Last Journey* (1974) and *Redada/Barcelona Kill* (1973).

6 Eloy de la Iglesia's *La estanquera de Vallecas* was a cinematic adaptation of the theatre play by José Luis Alonso de Santos, which premiered in 1981. See Green and Meyer (2018), whose English translation of the play is accompanied by an excellent introduction which situates the work in its broader context.

7 *Deprisa, deprisa* was the seventh most popular Spanish film in 1981 (749,798 spectators), attracting three times more viewers than Pilar Miró's *Gary Cooper, que estás en los cielos/ Gary Cooper, Who Art in Heaven* (1981),

a canonical film in Spanish film history of the same year (263,981). It was by far Carlos Saura's highest-grossing film to date.

8 According to official filmgoing statistics, *Perros callejeros* was the fifth highest-grossing film in the history of Spanish at the time, with almost 1,900,000 spectators and box office profits of over 170 million pesetas. *El pico* was the second most popular film of 1983 (619,658), attracting more viewers than José Luis Garci's *Volver a empezar/Begin the Beguine*, which was first Spanish film which won the Academy Award for Best Foreign Language Film. *El Lute: Camina o revienta* was by far the most popular domestic film of 1987 with 1,117, 973 spectators, while the sequel *Lute II: Mañana seré libre* was the fourth highest-grossing film of the following year (347,324).

9 *El pico* was reportedly the most popular film on VHS the year after its release (Lozano, 1984)

10 Vicente Rodríguez Ortega (2014: 268) and Rubén Lardín (2006) have argued that *cine quinqui* is the Spanish version of American Blaxploitation cinema, a cycle of films in which music similarly played a central role and which addressed the plight of the marginalised within the city.

11 See 'Clasificación de los estrenos en Madrid año 1976' and 'Clasificacíon de los estrenos en Barcelona año 1976', *Cineinforme*, no. 262, January 1977, 6–7. *Clockwork Orange* had an audience of 618,827 in Madrid that year, and was followed by two other American films: *Alice Doesn't Live Here Anymore* (Martin Scorsese, 1974) (287,544 viewers) and *The Great Dictator* (Charlie Chaplin, 1940) (282,280). The most popular Spanish film in Madrid was *La trastienda/Blood and Passion* (Jorge Grau, 1976) (258,592).

12 See Herman (1979: 18).

13 'Applause after the most violent scenes, animated shouts, collective cheering …, a boiling pot of emotional communication with the screen.'

14 The Moncloa Pacts were a series of agreements designed to curb the high unemployment rate and the ongoing recession.

15 For Spanish horror cinema that can be considered paracinema see Andy Willis (2003: 71–83).

16 See for instance the seminal books *El mono del desencanto: una crítica cultural de la transición española* (Teresa Vilarós, 1998) and *Cultura herida: literatura y cine en la España democrática* (Cristina Moreiras-Menor, 2002). Germán Labrador Méndez's *Culpables por la literatura: Imaginación y contracultura en la transición española (1968–1988)* (2017), Guillem Martínez's *CT o Cultura de la Transición: Crítica a 35 años de cultura* (2012), Luis Moreno-Caballud's *Cultures of Anyone: Studies on Cultural Democratization* (2015), Rosi Song's *Lost in Transition: Constructing Memory in Contemporary Spain* (2016) and Duncan Wheeler's *Following*

Franco: Spanish Culture and Politics in Transition (2020) are more recent examples of this trend.

17 'The history of the *quinquis* appears as an alternative account that turns our gaze to the other side of the "party" and explores the human "ruins" that lurked beneath the new political conjuncture.'

18 See also Vernon (2009, 2016), Gubern and Vernon (2013), Hart (2007), Shaw and Stone (2012), Wright (2013: 23–58), Wheeler (2019) and myself (Whittaker, 2012, 2014) for further examples of the turn towards the soundtrack in Spanish film studies.

19 The work of Ian Biddle (2017, 2019) and Samuel Llano (2019) are key examples of this trend, along with the co-edited special issue on 'Spanish Sound Studies' (Llano and Whittaker, 2019).

1

Unruly speed and sensation in the *Perros callejeros* cycle

While José Antonio de la Loma's *Perros callejeros* (1977) was not the first Spanish film to deal with the subject of juvenile delinquency, it nonetheless became the blueprint for the *quinqui* films that followed it. Its casting of non-professional actors, use of location shooting and its screenplay based on testimonials of underage delinquents and police reports provided the film with a verisimilitude that would be emulated in other *quinqui* films discussed in this book. Most crucially, in the appearance of 15-year-old delinquent Ángel Fernández Franco as the protagonist, the film created the first *quinqui* star, who also went on to appear in two further sequels: *Perros callejeros 2: Busca y captura* (1979) and *Los últimos golpes de 'el Torete'* (1980). As well as their cinematic realism, the films became known for their exhilarating car chases and action sequences, scenes which usually featured stolen SEAT 124 vehicles. While the sensational rush of speed was integral to the pleasures of these films, these sensations also revealed social tensions which surrounded teenage crime and its broader relationship to consumerism during this period.

Through their association with car theft and dangerous driving, Fernández Franco and other underage delinquents at the time embodied an unruly speed and precocity that threatened the established boundaries between youth and childhood. In exploring the significance of cinematic speed and rhythm as a particular site of resonance in the films, this chapter explores the extent to which Fernández Franco 'el Torete''s deviant speed became an integral part of his subcultural appeal. At the same time, it explores the extent to which the production and reception of José Antonio de la Loma's films helped to amplify the public perception that the problem of juvenile delinquency was itself accelerating and becoming out of control, with offenders committing thefts at an increasingly young age. Through a particular sensitivity to the question of temporality in the films, this chapter shows how the unruly speed of delinquency is also a powerful lens through which to explore the rhythmic contours of Spain's social, economic and geographical transformations of the 1960s and 1970, whose rapid unevenness provided the material conditions for the rise of juvenile delinquency and *cine quinqui* in the first place.

José Antonio de la Loma, cinematic speed and delinquency

At the time of *Perros callejeros*, José Antonio de la Loma was an established veteran of the Barcelona film industry, having directed and written the screenplays of popular films for over thirty years. Initially working as an assistant and (frequently uncredited) writer for Ignacio F. Iquino, José Antonio de la Loma emerged from what Ángel Comas has termed 'la otra escuela de Barcelona' (the other Barcelona school), a term he uses to describe Iquino's production company IFI's factory model of production (Comas, 2003). Like Iquino and other directors associated with this school, such as Antonio Isasi-Isasmendi and Joan Bosch, de la Loma specialised in low-budget and commercially dependable films. This school was 'other' to the seriousness of the 'official' Barcelona school, the cosmopolitan film movement which emerged in the 1960s and which was associated with the likes of Pere Portabella and Vicente Aranda. In contrast to the niche audiences of the films associated with the official school, the films associated with Iquino's school were exhibited in *cines de barrio* and popular with working-class audiences, who according to Comas read the kind of pulp novels that were despised by intellectuals (Comas, 2003: 19). Like Iquino, de la Loma's style of production was defined by its speed, economic efficiency and frequently low production values. Most often shot on location, Barcelona featured as a dynamic backdrop to the action of his films, as well as an iconographic marker of the two urban-based genres for which he became most known in the 1970s: crime and action films. These films in particular stand out for their emphasis on kinetic motion, accelerated rhythm and excitement, a vivid illustration of Richard Dyer's description of action cinema as a 'celebration of sensational movement' (2000: 18). Dyer writes that in action cinema, 'extreme sensation is represented as experienced, not within the body, but in the body's contact with the world, its rush, its expansiveness, its physical rush and challenge' (2000: 18). Through the centrality of vehicles in de la Loma's cinema, his films established a close relationship between the human body and the car. As such, his filmmaking not only emphasised speed but an *embodied* experience of speed.

José Antonio de la Loma was one of the first Spanish directors to feature car chase sequences as an integral part of his narratives, an aspect of his cinema that frequently drew comparisons with Hollywood film.[1] The kinaesthetic experience of driving at fast speed, for instance, was central to the pleasures of his Spanish-German-Italian co-production *El magnífico Tony Carrera/The Magnificent Tony Carrera* (1968), a spy film which centres on a race car driver and capitalised on the success of the James Bond franchise. In the 1970s and 1980s, de la Loma would continue to produce commercial films that were not only modelled on American action and crime genres but that explicitly targeted US audiences too, exploiting the low production costs in Spain with the Spanish-US co-productions *La redada/Barcelona Kill* (1973), *Metralleta Stein/Blind Vendetta* (1975), *Goma 2/Killing Machine* (1982) and *Jugando con la muerte/Hit Man* (1984). Made into both Spanish and English versions (and also Catalan, in the cases of *La redada* and *Jugando con la muerte*), all of these films were released on video, with the latter two also gaining a significant foothold with Hispanic audiences in the United States.[2] Significantly, *La redada* also saw the beginning of de la Loma's collaboration with the prominent French stunt co-ordinator Rémy Julienne, who supervised the car chase scenes in the *Perros callejeros* cycle of films. Julienne co-ordinated the second-unit photography of treacherous driving in the films, including scenes which featured sudden handbrake turns, skids and other vehicular stunts. Frequently presented as autonomous to the demands of the narrative, these extended action sequences emphasise the pleasures of 'sensational movement' on their own terms. Yvonne Tasker writes that in being 'deemed noisy and brash', action films have failed to 'meet the markers of aesthetic and cultural value typically applied within contemporary film culture' (2004: 2). The action sequences of de la Loma's similarly connoted excess – an excessiveness that, in common with Iquino and 'la otra escuela de Barcelona', was 'other' to the conventions of good taste. This excess, moreover, was as aural as it was visual: the soundtracks of the films were dominated by the constant throb of the engine and screeching of tyres, noises that emphasise the extreme sensation of dangerous driving.

Described by the director Fernando Trueba, who was film critic at *El País* at the time as a 'película de *consumo* con vocación social testimonial' (film for consumption with a social and testimonial vocation) (Trueba, 1977, his italics), *Perros callejeros* combined the exhilarating speed and the excitement of American action cinema with an explicit concern for contemporary social issues.[3] In addressing the issue of spiralling juvenile delinquency and the outdated youth justice system in Spain, the cycle explicitly intervened in the national debates about criminality that were circulating in the media at the time. Its casting of non-professional teenage actors from La Mina and naturalistic use of location shooting brought a here-and-now urgency to the film, a mode of production that explicitly addressed the delinquent as a subject grounded by its immediate geography and history. De la Loma's interest in the subject of juvenile delinquency stemmed from his early career as a primary teacher in the marginal Barrio Chino area of Barcelona during the 1940s. In order to encourage the children to attend class, de la Loma used to get them to create theatre through making them improvise with the texts they were studying (Anon, 1977a: 41). De la Loma commented that these experiences provided him with his double interest in 'espectáculo, por un lado y la educación por el otro' (spectacle on the one hand, and education on the other) (Anon, 1977a: 41), adding elsewhere that 'en el fondo sigo siendo un maestro frustrado' (I'm still a frustrated teacher deep down) (Mora, 1979). His first-hand experience of delinquent gangs in the *barrio* informed the narrative of his novel *Sin la sonrisa de Dios/Without the Smile of God* (1949), a novel that was similarly set in a primary school and later adapted into a film directed by Julio Salvador (1955). While *Sin la sonrisa de Dios* set a precedent for the film, de la Loma stressed how the causes of juvenile delinquency were clearly distinct in *Perros callejeros.* In an interview for *Fotogramas*, he commented that while the earlier novel depicted a 'delincuencia por hambre' (delinquency of hunger), *Perros callejeros* explored 'delincuencia de la abundancia, el deseo de coches de lujo' (delinquency of abundance, of the desire for luxury cars) (cited in Anon, 1977). The shift in causes of juvenile delinquency reflected the dramatic transformation of Spain's economy during the regime. While the period of autarchy in 1940s Spain was characterised by post-war penury and widespread famine, its economic miracle of the 1960s and 1970s was driven by the spectacle of conspicuous consumption.

In preparation for writing the script of the film, de la Loma carried out a period of intensive research into the causes of contemporary Spanish delinquency, directing his attention to underage car thieves in Barcelona. He obtained police files on the delinquents by getting in touch with members of the Guardia Civil de Tráfico (the Traffic Division of the Civil Guard), the National and Municipal police – a feat that was likely helped by the fact the director came from a military family. A more sympathetic member of the Civil Guard, who maintained a good relationship with some of the delinquents of La Mina, set up a meeting between the director and a group of delinquents from the *barrio* (Galán, 1977: 34) where he met Ángel Fernández Franco (who was known as 'el Trompeta' before he became famous) and Juan José Moreno Cuenca 'el Vaquilla', who were just 15 and 14 at the time. According to the introduction of the script, the director recorded ten hours of interviews with Fernández Franco and el Vaquilla, as well as with Miguel Ugal Cuenca 'el Carica' (the step brother of el Vaquilla), Basilio Fernández Franco 'el Trompetilla' (the younger brother of el Trompeta), el Herra, la Victoria, el Veneno and others. Their conversations provided details of the robberies and the car chases they had been involved in, which he then compared with the police reports that he had received (Galán, 1977: 35). In an interview for *Triunfo*, de la Loma spoke of how their accounts allowed him to make 'una increíble película de acción' (an incredible action film) with Fernández Franco recounting in vivid detail how he had received two gunshot wounds, one in the leg and one in the head; how he had escaped from the police by driving the wrong way down the motorway, and how he and his friends avoided stealing coffee-coloured cars because they knew of four delinquents who had died in vehicles of the same colour (Galán, 1977: 35). For his part, Moreno Cuenca, as we have seen, stood out as one of the notorious delinquents in Spain at the time, and was infamous for escaping from every single reformatory in the country (Silva, 2011: 26).

When it came to casting, de la Loma originally wanted Moreno Cuenca to appear as the protagonist in the film, but the juvenile courts reportedly intervened and prevented his appearance in the film (Mora, 1979). Ángel Fernández Franco was subsequently brought in to replace him. Appearing as el Vaquilla's proxy, the name of his character in the film, 'el Torete' (meaning 'young bull' or 'mischievous child'), was therefore meant to resemble Moreno Cuenca's well-established alias 'el Vaquilla' (which can also be translated as 'young bull' or 'heifer'). Juan José Moreno Cuenca and Ángel Fernández Franco had known each other for several years from hanging around in the streets of La Mina, Barcelona, and would later end up becoming friends after getting involved in a street fight (Moreno Cuenca, 1985: 150). Just as the delinquent Ángel Fernández Franco had substituted el Vaquilla, Ángel's real-life alias 'el Trompeta' soon came to be eclipsed by his more recent cinematic alias, with the Spanish media eventually referring to the actor as Ángel Fernández 'el Torete', or just 'el Torete'.[4] The frequent confusion between subject and its surrogate, the real-life self and its fictional counterpart here only added to the self-reflexive mode of performance for which much of *cine quinqui* would become known. The criminologists Keith Hayward and Jock Young have argued that crime and deviance should be understood in interplay with the proliferation of media images that are associated with them, and that 'every facet of offending is reflected in a vast hall of mirrors' (Hayward and Young, 2004: 259).

As well as living in the same *barrio*, both delinquents developed a passion for fast cars from a young age. Ángel Fernández Franco began stealing cars when he was just ten years old (Corachán and Gasulla, 1991: 33), while Juan José Moreno Cuenca started at the age of nine. Moreno Cuenca was so short that he had to attach bricks or stones onto the car pedals in order to reach them (Arasa, 2014). The journalist Daniel Arasa, who met the delinquent on several occasions, recalls how Moreno Cuenca was renowned for the vertiginous speed with which he drove cars, commenting that 'las persecuciones de las películas americanas quedan cortas a su lado' (the car chases in American films look short compared to his) (Arasa, 2014). Arasa recalls how his son, who worked as a television cameraman at the time, filmed Moreno Cuenca for a documentary as he returned to La Mina during a brief period of leave from a juvenile detention centre. Moreno was filmed as he drove at great speed through the *barrio*, performing wheelies so high that the car almost toppled over. Described by Arasa as an 'exhibición por las calles de La Mina' (exhibition on the streets of La Mina), Moreno Cuenca's driving was eagerly watched by the residents of the neighbourhood, who broke into frenetic applause at the end (Arasa, 2014). Taking place in front an audience of onlookers, his

1.1 El Torete (Ángel Fernández Franco) in a stolen SEAT in *Perros callejeros* (José Antonio de la Loma, 1977).

driving skills here were a spectacle in their own right, one whose display of the sensuous and transgressive pleasures of speed would be recreated through the car chase sequences of *Perros callejeros*.

The attraction of speed to delinquents like Moreno Cuenca and Fernández Franco can be seen as a visceral response to the physical environments in which they grew up. Like the majority of outlying suburbs whose housing comprised *chabolas* and hastily constructed tower blocks, living conditions were cramped and squalid in La Mina. Enrique Martínez Reguera, a prominent psychologist and expert on marginalisation, drew attention to how 70% of all crime in Spain was committed by those under the age of 16 (cited in Torre Iglesias, 1980: 63). He further added that 99% of these delinquents came from poor families with numerous children, living on the outskirts of the cities in homes of 20 square metres or less. He explains how children at five or six years old already experience their own 'cárcel particular' (private prison), as it is common for the mothers to go to work and leave the children locked in their bedrooms. As they reach adolescence, after years of enclosure, they find themselves 'fabulosamente dotados para la fuga y la escalada, para abrir puertas y candados' (fabulously adept at escaping and climbing, at opening doors and locks) (cited in Torre Iglesias, 1980: 63). These skills were alluded to in the aliases el Vaquilla and el Torete, named, as we have seen, after animals known for their restless and uncontrollable movement. As Moreno Cuenca has written, his nickname 'el Vaquilla' had been attributed to him as a young child on account of his naughty and boisterous nature (Moreno Cuenca, 1985: 150).[5]

Perros callejeros: Acceleration, youth and moral panic

After José Antonio de la Loma gained their trust and offered to pay them a salary for three months before the shoot was due to begin, Ángel Fernández Franco and the other non-professional actors agreed to appear in the film (Anon, 1977a: 13). They also signed contracts that prevented them from being arrested by the police during the shoot (Galán, 1977: 35).[6] When it came to production, de la Loma encountered several setbacks which delayed the beginning of the shoot. La Mina had already become synonymous with juvenile delinquency before the production of the film, frequently appearing in the news between 1974 and 1976 with headlines such as 'La Mina, Polígono sin ley' (La Mina, lawless housing estate) and 'Jóvenes delincuentes detenidos en la Mina' (young delinquents arrested in La Mina) (Colomer, 1977: 11). Its neighbourhood association held protests and launched a local media campaign against the production of the film, claiming that de la Loma was perpetuating negative associations with the *barrio* (Colomer, 1977: 13).[7] In addition, the local police reportedly sought to prevent Ángel Fernández and the other delinquents from appearing in the film by telling them that the director was out to exploit them (Anon, 1977a: 13). Movimiento Infantil y Juventil de Acción Católica (M.I.J.A.C.) similarly expressed their concerns about the film and convinced de la Loma, himself a practising Catholic, to make changes to the script. Despite his amendments to the script, M.I.J.A.C. nevertheless remained highly critical of the film, claiming that it failed to explore the motivations behind juvenile delinquency, and that it praised delinquency and created 'modelos de identificación' (models of identification) between young audiences and the delinquent actors (M.I.J.A.C, 1977). De la Loma frequently defended himself against these kinds of charges, commenting in an interview, for instance, that the film provided an important means for the rehabilitation of the delinquents, as well as a source of income, before further adding – somewhat paradoxically – that their performances enabled them to forget about their previous lives (Mora, 1979).

The script went to the board of censors in February 1977 (Anon, 1977a: 41), after which the voiceover during the introduction and other parts of the film underwent modification (Galán, 1977: 34). By the time *Perros callejeros* saw its theatrical release on 24 December 1977, censorship had been finally lifted in Spain, following the legislation that was brought in with the Real Decreto/3071 on 11 November. The director commented that had it not been for the censors, the film would have been 'mucho más fuerte, mucho más dura' (much stronger, much harder) (cited in Anon, 1977a: 41) with many of the testimonials from the delinquents not having made it into the final film (cited in Anon, 1977a: 14). The *Perros callejeros* cycle of films was produced by Profilmes and the director's own in-house production company Films Zodíaco, with José Antonio Pérez Giner as executive producer. Like de la Loma, Pérez Giner had a keen interest in juvenile delinquency and went on to produce Eloy de la Iglesia's *El pico* and *El pico 2*. The advertising campaign for the film centred on a controversial photograph from the film depicting the actor being beaten by a police officer, followed by the words 'El tema de la delincuencia juvenil. ¿Culpables? ¿O víctimas?' (The subject of juvenile delinquency: Guilty or innocent?), as if appealing to the audience for their judgement. In response, accounts of the initial screenings of the film testify to how the audiences unequivocally took sides with the delinquents. As mentioned in the introduction, the sociologist Jaime Funes reported how the 'cine temblaba' (cinema shook) with young audiences who shouted at the screen and broke into applause during the most violent scenes (Funes, 1984: 74). The film's capacity to stimulate a noisy response in the audience was similarly observed by the Movimiento Infantil y Juventil de Acción Católica, who also drew attention to the reception in auditory terms. Their account, in particular, noted the moments of laughter in the auditorium during the shooting of a policeman, and most significantly during the car chase sequences where the delinquents get away (M.I.J.A.C, 1977).

The prevalence of car chases in *Perros callejeros* provoked an altogether more divided response amongst critics, with several criticising the director for inciting crime.[8] Indeed, public anxieties surrounding copycatting – namely, the perceived threat of young people imitating the dangerous driving of the on-screen delinquents – became an integral part of public discourse surrounding the *Perros callejeros* cycle. Sociologists, for instance, pointed to the sharp rise in car theft by delinquents between the ages of 15 and 17 in Barcelona after the film (Collectiu de Ciencies Socials, 1978). In defending his film, de la Loma drew attention to how crime rates in Barcelona actually decreased during the production of the film, as delinquents were busy with the production of the film and 'tratados con afecto' (treated with affection) (Galán, 1977: 35). A similar case can be found when the Guild of Jewellers publicly claimed that his film led to a spike in jewellery store robberies; the director denounced the charge in a letter published in the newspaper *ABC*, stating that police had shown that the rate of robberies had in fact gone down (de la Loma, 1984). In contrast, more positive reviews pointed to the realism of the film provided by the casting of real-life delinquents (Trueba, 1977), as well as its exciting car chase sequences – described as 'la acción mecánica' (mechanical action) (Anon, 1977b) – and as reaching 'cimas de emoción electrizante' (peaks of electrifying emotion) and 'una constante palpitación emocional' (a constant emotional palpitation) (Martínez Tomás, 1977). Alluding here to the thrill of speed through its mechanical and electrical manifestations, these reviews alert us to the affective and emotional force of cars. The depiction of stolen vehicles elicited anxieties and pleasures alike in the critical reception of the film, which on the one hand viewed speed as a site of juvenile deviance that was out of control, and on the other a source of sensuous and exhilarating pleasures.

The script of the film, which can be considered a sociological document of juvenile subculture in its own right, begins with a glossary of the delinquents' slang words and their definitions used throughout the film, many of which are related to cars or car chases. We are told that the words 'un racano' and 'un tegui' both mean car, for instance, while 'una naja' denotes a car chase, and 'el fantasma' a traffic police vehicle. The richness in the vocabulary of cars is testament to the symbolic importance of cars to the delinquent subculture, a dynamic that is played out visually in the film's pre-title sequence, which is accompanied by a 'voice-of-God' narrator. Wide-angle shots of the 'official' Barcelona, represented by Sagrada Familia and Passeig de Gràcia, are contrasted with shots of the margins of the city, depicted through the imposing tower blocks of La Mina, as the narrator says 'Esto es lo que suele llamarse una gran ciudad, tiene sus anchas avenidas, sus casas señoriales, y sus problemas' (This is what they call a big city, it has its wide boulevards, its stately buildings, and its problems).

Despite the images, the narrator is careful not to mention La Mina, Barcelona or indeed even Spain by name – omissions that are likely due to the pressure from both the *barrio*'s residents and the board of censors:[9]

> Por desgracia, no es el problema de un barrio, como algunos pretenden, ni de un distrito, ni siquiera de nuestra ciudad, sino de todas aquellas que sufren los males de un incremento de población acelerado y sin control, de una sociedad lanzada por la pendiente de la vida fácil, del lujo y del exhibicionismo.[10]

Juvenile delinquency is explicitly presented here as a symptom of urban overcrowding and insatiable consumerism, transformations that were ushered in by the Opus Dei technocrats' embrace of modern capitalism and the subsequent process of *desarrollismo*, as Martín-Cabrera rightly points out in his analysis of the film (2015: 113). The voiceover here emphasises the rhythmic shape of modernisation as one of uncontrollable speed, a transgressive velocity that finds its expression in what he refers to as the 'vertiginosa carrera de delitos' (vertiginous career of crime) that is undertaken by a new category of younger delinquents between the ages of 12 and 16. We see a montage of excerpts that have been taken from the film of delinquents engaged in acts of treacherous driving: a getaway car from the site of a bank robbery; a point-of-view shot from within a car as it makes its bumpy ascent on a steep slope; and in what will turn out to be el Torete's death in the final scene, a long shot of his stolen car as it falls down a deep ravine, crashing into pieces as it hits the rocks.

Living as fast as they died, the delinquents belonged to a criminal subculture that was marked by its immediacy and intensity of experience, a dynamic that is formally emphasised through the fast-paced editing and the heavily percussive orchestral score. The dangerous velocity of the car serves as a powerful metaphor not only for the temporality of these ever-younger delinquents but for the process of *desarrollismo* and the destructive effects that followed in its wake. With a social infrastructure and youth justice system unable to keep up with the demands of capitalist development, the effects of Spain's economic miracle are presented as similarly unruly and undisciplined. Like the child delinquent, Spain's embrace of capitalism has grown too fast and spun out of control. With the camera moving from an area of affluence to one of poverty, the opening sequence illustrates how, according to the geographer Tim Creswell, 'mobility is both centre

1.2 El Torete's (Ángel Fernández Franco) car careers off the cliff in *Perros callejeros* (José Antonio de la Loma, 1977).

and margin – the lifeblood of modernity and the virus that threatens to hasten its downfall' (2006: 21). If, as John Tomlinson has written, the 'rhythm of acceleration has been the constant leitmotiv of cultural modernity' (2007: 1), the destructive manifestation of speed in this sequence exposes the limitations of this modernity. As Tomlinson says, 'alongside the reasoned course of velocity-as-progress, there has developed a different imagination of machine speed, associating it with the far less indisputably rational elements of excitement, thrill, danger, risk and violence' (2007: 44). Tomlinson describes this counter-imagination as the 'other unruly child of mechanical modernity' (2007: 44), showing how the culture of youthful immediacy 'overlaps' with the more rational cultural meanings associated with speed and its relationship with modernity (2007: 44). As children of migrants who had settled in the city in the late 1950s and 1960s, *quinqui* delinquents were quite literally the unruly other children of mechanical modernity.

This is established in the following sequence in which el Torete and two members of his gang, el Corneta (Jesús Martínez) and el Chungo (Francisco Javier Sánchez 'el Veneno') are first seen breaking into and hotwiring a SEAT 124. Like the earlier SEAT 600, a car that Tatjana Pavlović describes as a 'symbol of Spain's economic miracle' (2011: 186) and Martín-Cabrera refers to as the 'emblema más visible' (most visible emblem) of Spain's emerging consumerist society

(2015: 114), the SEAT 124 was a hugely popular model in Spain, its high performance and powerful engine also making make it a suitable vehicle for police cars and ambulances. The SEAT 124 in particular would become a totemic image in *cine quinqui,* its constant presence invoking a set of meanings that arguably ran counter to the SEAT 600. If the private ownership of the earlier model, which was introduced to the mass market in 1957, was a 'modern phenomenon that seemed to guarantee unlimited personal freedom and familial mobility, a dream-turned-commodity of personal freedom' (Pavlović, 2011: 5–6), the stolen SEAT 124 was subject to constant surveillance and pursuit, whose freedom is most often ephemeral and illusory. For much of this sequence, delinquents are quite literally framed by the stolen vehicle, as the camera films the actors from within the car as they drive hurriedly to Carretera de Lloret.

Arriving in Lloret de Mar, they drive up to a series of unsuspecting female victims and snatch their bags, a crime that was known as a 'tirón'. The sociologist Felipe Javier Hernando Sanz shows that the rate of motor vehicle thefts doubled in Spain between the years 1975 and 1979, with youths carrying out a total of 70% of all car thefts and robberies by 1982 (Hernando Sanz, 2001: 266). The increase in car-related crime signalled practices of delinquency that were increasingly mobile in nature. A policeman who was also an undercover reporter for the crime weekly *El Caso* claimed that it was common for delinquents to steal vehicles from one city and drive to the next, carry out their crimes, then abandon the vehicle before stealing a new one in order to return home (Seferi, 1976: 21). Cars enabled them to carry out crimes with the greatest impunity and quickly transport their booty from one place to another while avoiding the police (Seferi, 1976: 21). Their criminal practices thus both grew out of and overlapped with the mobility that was ushered in by the miracle years, dramatically exceeding its rhythms through speed. Indeed, delinquents were reportedly choosy when it came to selecting which vehicles to steal, opting for the faster and more powerful models – indicated in the article as the SEAT 850, 1430 and, most crucially, 124 – so as to escape from police and highway controls (Seferi, 1976: 21–22).

As the car accelerates towards a pedestrian, el Chungo stretches out of his passenger seat and snatches a bag from a pedestrian, knocking her to the ground as she shouts ¡ladrón! (thief). As the car brazenly hurtles past police controls, the sudden use of fast-motion photography further dramatises the speed of the delinquents here as deviant and evasive. Their speed, in the words of John Tomlinson, embraces 'a range of transgressive and rebellious impulses chafing the smooth surface order of institutional modernity', in turn forming a 'narrative of speed which is "unruly" both in its orientation and in its expression' (2007: 8). The delinquents are soon chased out of town by Manolo (Victor Petit), an officer from the Guardia Civil de Tráfico, who pursues them until they reach a treacherous mountain country road, their cars snaking precariously from side to side with tyres leaving a trail of dust in their wake. El Torete's skilful driving outmanoeuvres Manolo, whose car falls into a ditch as he shoots at the delinquents as they get away, injuring el Corneta. With some shots orchestrated through the use of stunt doubles, the high-risk car chase establishes the location of the road not as a 'smooth surface' of transportation and connection but as speed's unruly and transgressive other. The location of the road here therefore condenses the themes at play in the *Perros callejeros* cycle: the mobile structures of crime and consumerism, and the tension between evasion and discipline, freedom and danger.

Through emphasising the embodied relationship between the mobile car, body and camera, moreover, the formal elements of the scene work together to privilege the experience of driving as visceral and immersive. In establishing the emotional register of immediacy and thrills for which the *quinqui* film would become known, the car here illustrates how according to Mimi Sheller 'cars are above all machines that move people, but they do so in many senses of the word' (2004: 221).

Between rhythmic dissonance and discipline

El Torete's unruly speed is briefly contained when he is brought to the police station for questioning, where the inspector (Alfonso Zambrano) orders him to take off his clothes in an attempt to humiliate him. Standing naked (albeit with a telephone conveniently hiding his genitals), the fragility of his youth is quite literally laid bare, his small and underdeveloped body a contrast to his display of macho bravado we have seen until now. In spite of censorship, the sheer sadism of the inspector nevertheless signalled a deviation from the moral code of crime films established during the Franco years where, according to Barry Jordan and Rikki Morgan-Tamosunas, 'references to police or government incompetence or corruption were officially banned' (1998: 88). His interrogation is soon cut short by the Chief of Police, who when discovering that el Torete is only 15, orders the inspector to send him to the youth court in haste, given that it was a crime to arrest minors. The judge at the youth court (Florencio Calpe), who mentions previously that he heard elsewhere that el Torete is a skilful driver, orders him to the reformatory (referred to in the film as 'una escuela profesional' [professional school]). The emphasis on the fragility of Ángel Fernández Franco's exposed body illustrates the complex ways in which delinquents under the age of criminal responsibility were not only presented as deviant but also vulnerable and at risk. As juvenile crime rates continued to rise, however, there was also a hardening of attitudes towards the rehabilitation of young offenders, with the sensationalist press criticising the youth justice system as ineffectual. Two years after the release of *Perros callejeros* in 1979, a report in *El Caso* pointed to how if in the past the definition of a precocious delinquent was someone at the age of 16, now it had become just 12 – a problem, it argued, especially given that youth courts were too lenient. Significantly, the report conflated anxieties surrounding speed with those of childhood – or, more specifically, children who have grown up too fast (Aguilera, 1979: 4–5). Describing the recent transformation of the Spanish delinquent from those in the past who stole pears, to those of today who steal cars, the article details their obsession with speedy driving. It writes that while for the rest of the world 1979 is the International Year of the Child (a celebration that was held by the United Nations), Spain instead finds itself celebrating the 'Año nacional del niño delincuente' (the national year of the delinquent child) (Aguiler, 1979: 4–5). Although it was not finally put into legislation, the minority Unión de Centro Democrático (Union of the Democratic Centre) government at this time were proposing a bill that would reduce the penal age to 15 – something that was strongly opposed by many lawyers and sociologists.[11] The demand for greater civil liberties during the early years of the transition to democracy therefore paradoxically also co-existed with an atmosphere which demanded more stringent social control for youths. This contradiction was played out through the temporary repurposing of a section of Zamora prison, known for its incarceration of dissident priests during the Franco years, into a notorious 'cárcel

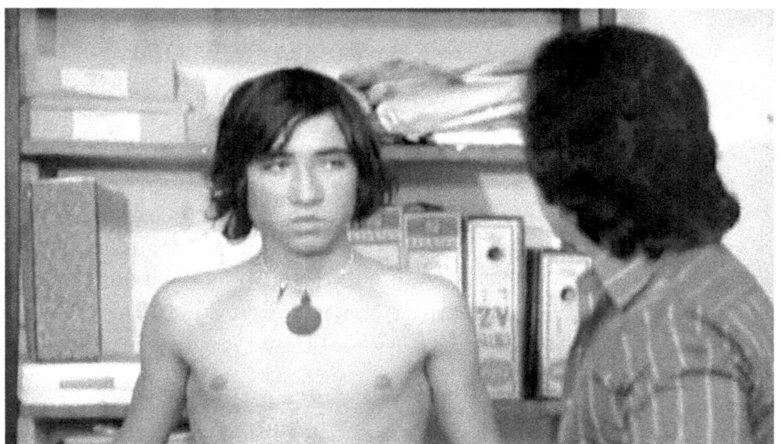

1.3 El Torete (Ángel Fernández Franco) receiving brutal treatment by the police in *Perros callejeros* (José Antonio de la Loma, 1977).

de niños' (children's prison) in 1976. Many of the minors who were considered too dangerous for the youth detention centres were imprisoned here – including Ángel Fernández Franco and Juan Moreno Cuenca, as well as José Joaquín Sánchez Frutos 'el Jaro', whose story was told in Eloy de la Iglesia's *Navajeros* (see chapter 3). With minors imprisoned alongside criminal adults, Zamora prison became a particular site of controversy whose legality was cast in doubt.[12] Also the location of several riots, the prison would later incidentally become the real-life location for prison-based thriller *Celda 211/Cell 211* (Daniel Monzón, 2011), whose narrative hinges on a mutiny over prisoners' conditions.[13]

Poised between childhood and adulthood, el Torete's penal age throughout the film emphasised the contradictory ways in which young delinquents needed to be protected as much as they needed to be controlled. This tension in turn drew attention to the role of the state in its responsibility for the rehabilitation of young delinquents – a subject that greatly concerned de la Loma and was explored in several of the *quinqui* films that followed. The reformatory to which el Torete is sent is run by the well-meaning but ineffectual priest Padre Ignacio (Xabier Elorriaga), an illustration of how the juvenile detention system was mostly run by the Catholic church at the time, dominated in particular by the Capuchin Tertiary Friars, who found themselves ill-equipped when it came to the rehabilitation of prolific offenders.[14] When el Torete is sent to the reformatory for the second time, Padre Ignacio's earlier protective nature shifts to a more punitive and authoritarian stance as he sends el Torete, el Pijo and el Corneta to solitary confinement. Filmed in gloomy low-key lighting, their cells are depicted as dark and oppressive, bereft of proper sanitation or even a bed to sleep on. The damp and discoloured walls have been etched with several pieces of graffiti and drawings, including that of a car in el Pijo's cell underneath which is written 'el Carica' – the real-life delinquent nickname of Miguel Ugal Cuenca, the actor who plays el Pijo. The boys quickly discover that they have been placed next to the cell of el Fitipaldi, a fifth member of their gang who has not been seen until now (played by César Sánchez who, unlike the others, was a professional actor and had not been associated with delinquency in real life). El Fitipaldi has been deprived of food on account of his bad behaviour, and after throwing water in a guard's face, is brutally beaten in his cell. Established during the regime, the notorious punishment of solitary confinement, otherwise known as 'cuarto de hierro' (iron room), led to delinquents being deprived of food for three days – or even five or more in some cases – and continued to be practised even in the years immediately following Franco's death (Goicoechea, 1978: 35). To this effect, the sociologist Enrique Martínez Reguera commented that Spain's youth justice system was 'cada vez más tribunales y menos tutelares' (increasingly more like courts and less like guardians) (cited in Torre Iglesias, 1980: 64). Established in 1948, Spain's youth justice system of Tribunales Tutelares de Menores (youth courts) had become dramatically maladjusted to the social problems of an increasingly urbanised and consumerist society, a failing that was greatly exacerbated by its lack of resources.[15] In interviewing the court staff in preparation for writing the script, the director was shocked to discover how underfunded the Spanish juvenile detention system was, with a budget of ten pesetas per child per day. He commented that there was no money for professionals in the reformatories and that 'por falta de cuidado y posibilidades, son realmente una escuela de delincuencia' (because of a lack of care and opportunities, they are really a school for delinquency) (Galán, 1977: 34). The reformatory in the film merely appears to brutalise and desensitise the delinquents into committing further crimes, each one more dramatic and violent than the last. After the delinquents have escaped from the reformatory in the film, the newspaper *El Correo Catalán* publishes an article on the delinquents being at large. The article includes a statement that Padre Ignacio has given to the newspaper which is heard via a voiceover as Ignacio stands in his office next to a canary cage, an obvious symbol of entrapment. His statement declares that they lack sufficient resources and qualified professionals to deal with the most dangerous delinquents – a comment that was more explicitly echoed in the opening sequence of the original script, in which the narrator condemns Spain's youth justice system as out of date and unfit for purpose. The opening sequence, moreover, contrasts images of speeding cars with a shot of the youth court, the editing here juxtaposing unruly speed with its containment.[16]

In its exploration of urban space, *Perros callejeros* reveals how the *barrio* of La Mina similarly fails to fully integrate its young population. La Mina is first seen as el Torete enters the tower block where he lives under the care of the Fagin-like Casilda (Rebeca Romer), who gives him shelter in exchange for the money that he steals. A backwards tracking shot reveals the geometric rigidity of the building as el Torete approaches its entrance, his body dwarfed by the breadth of the edifice. The script describes the building as 'Un polígono modesto de altos bloques mal acabados' (a modest housing complex with high towers that have been badly finished), situated in an area with unfinished paving and roads full of potholes. The *mise-en-scène* points to the accelerated and unchecked pace with which La Mina was built, a volatility which resonated with its delinquent residents who similarly grew up too fast. La Mina was created as a central part of Barcelona's urban renewal strategy in which most of the shanty towns of the neighbouring Campo de la Bota were rapidly cleared and its residents rehoused in the new area from 1971 onwards. As Monferrer I Celades has shown, however, residents were housed before many of the buildings had been completed (2013: 114). At the time of the film, moreover, the population of the area was overwhelmingly young and unassimilated: 47.3% of the population of La Mina were under 17, with 70% of the families living in the area migrants from Andalucia (Colomer, 1977: 12). Far from eradicating the social problems that were originally associated with shanty towns, the kinds of new housing projects that were depicted in the film only served to reproduce and intensify them.

El Torete is frequently framed on the edges of La Mina, an effect which emphasises his lack of integration within geographical space. He moves between La Mina and a series of stables which lie close by, their informal construction of corrugated iron and plywood resembling the shacks of Campo de la Bota. The stables provide the location for a gypsy criminal network which is presided over by the swarthy el Esquinao (Frank Braña), who exchanges el Torete's stolen dollars and merchandise for pesetas, which he then gives to Casilda so that she can pay the bail money of her husband, el Porro. With horses and ponies as their principle mode of transportation, the gypsies in the film inhabit a slower set of rhythms that contrast with the frantic acceleration of delinquents' cars – a juxtaposition that illustrates Henri Lefebvre's assertion that 'we know that a rhythm is slow or lively only in relation to other rhythms' (2004: 10). Yet the illicit circulation of money here reveals the extent to which these rhythms – both fast and slow, industrialised and nomadic – were dependent on one other. The co-existence and collisions of rhythms in the film reveal the ways 'rhythmic dissonance becomes the symptom of critically examining urban modernity' (Highmore, 2005: 10). This dissonance in particular reveals the uneven temporal development of modern capitalism, a process that much like the tower blocks and the delinquents that they house is frequently depicted as contingent and incomplete.

The rhythmic contrast between the gypsy community and el Torete's gang highlights the broader social and cultural distinctions between the two groups, a tension that is increasingly brought into focus through el Torete's illicit relationship with Isabel (Nadia Windel), the niece of Esquinao, who is engaged to be married to her cousin, el Mosque (Luis Martínez). Isabel soon accompanies el Torete in his stolen vehicles and discovers that she is pregnant. The purity of Isabel's body is strictly policed by the men in her family, who seek to preserve her chastity and the purity of their gypsy blood line from possible miscegenation with *payos* (non-gypsies) such as el Torete. On learning that Isabel has lost her virginity to el Torete, Esquinao furiously promises to take revenge on el Torete for destroying her honour, reminding el Mosque of their gypsy tradition of 'lo limpio por la casa, lo puerco por la calle' (clean at home, dirty in the street). In a scene which most viscerally embodies Fernando Trueba's memorable description of the film as 'tosco, salvaje, animal' (crude, savage, animalistic) (Trueba, 1977), el Esquinao ties up el Torete in the stable and cuts off his penis, the latter's agonising cries of pain heard against the frantic neighing of the horses. To this effect, Martín-Cabrera writes ' "el Torete" es como un animal que hay que doblegar y domesticar' (el Torete is like an animal that must be subdued and domesticated), an excess that needs to be controlled and contained (2015: 124). El Torete's embodiment of speed is thus presented as equally incompatible with Spanish society as it is to the gypsy social order, a disjuncture that is often emphasised through his framing in urban space. For instance, his rhythmic dissonance is vividly displayed in a later scene in which el Torete is sleeping on the streets of La Mina, next to a pony and cart in the foreground, with concrete tower blocks in the background. He is suddenly awoken by Manolo, who has been searching for el Torete since the opening car chase. After taking him to the police station to take his fingerprints, the policeman and delinquent strike up an unlikely friendship. The scene cuts to a bar, where el Torete tells Manolo about his childhood and his criminal education, the actor's face here captured in close-up so as to emphasise the testimonial charge of his words. El Torete's relationship with Manolo is inspired by Ángel's real-life friendship with a member of the Civil Guard who looked out for the delinquents, and as we have seen, was the initial point of contact between the director and actor (Galán, 1977: 34), while his dialogue here draws heavily on several interviews that de la Loma undertook when researching the film. El Torete tells Manolo that when he was born his mother tried to drown him in the river, but that his uncle saved him and brought him to the town of El Prat, where they travelled together in his wagon, stealing chickens and collecting scrap metal.[17] The nomadic pace of his early childhood soon gave way to the velocity of youth, as they moved to Campo de la Bota (and in the original script La Mina) where they began stealing cars and carrying out 'tirones'.[18] The sequence then cuts to Manolo's car, where el Torete explains that he learnt to drive from copying the fastest delinquents, bragging that he is always too fast for the police to catch. As they speak, we hear the constant hum of the engine – an aspect that is further emphasised in the original script, where the delinquent tells him '¿por qué no le zumba más? Suena bien el motor' (why don't you whack up the speed more? The engine sounds good). Recorded in auditory close-up, the ambient sounds of the car engine can be heard most prominently in the final car chase in the film. El Torete avenges his castration by stealing a car and chasing el Esquinao into a wall of car park, where he repeatedly rams the car into his legs, crushing his body with the impact. Pursued by the national police, el Torete drives towards the highest peak of Carretera Garraf, hitting the accelerator so it reaches the highest speed possible as his hands tightly grip the steering wheel. Manolo, who has also been chasing el Torete, sees that he is being pursued by the police and, in a last-ditch attempt to save the delinquent, seeks to intercept the delinquent's path by obstructing the road with his car. As Manolo waves frantically at el Torete to stop, el Torete loses control of his vehicle and drives off the steep ravine – a series of images that, as we have seen, were shown more briefly in the pre-title sequence. As the car tumbles down the steep gorge, we hear Torete's echoing voice defiantly shout 'mierdaaaaa' (shiiiiit), his vocal performance manipulated in postproduction for dramatic effect. Peter Doyle describes the echo in film as 'that which is not the self [that] seems to talk to us with our own voice, using our own sounds' (2005: 39). In reproducing our double, the echo conjures up locations that are uncanny, blurring the spatial cues of nearness with farness, and self with other. Indeed, in the final page of the script, the echo of el Torete's final word is described as: 'El eco, de las montañas, devuelve sin embargo el último grito del muchacho, multiplicado, agresivo, claro, contundente … Su despedida de un mundo que no le quiso, ni quiso tampoco.'[19] De la Loma's description of el Torete's echoing voice as 'multiplicado' (multiplied) brings to mind the descriptions of the noisy reception of *Perros callejeros* and the *quinqui* film more broadly in which the shouts within the auditorium frequently commingled with the soundtrack of the film – an auditory interaction with the actors that illuminates, as we have seen, Penfold-Mounce's notion of 'resonance' with criminal celebrities (2009: 66).

Perros callejeros 2: Busca y captura: Re-enacting speed

With almost 1,900,000 spectators and box office profits of over 170 million pesetas, *Perros callejeros* was a resounding commercial hit and the fifth highest-grossing film in the history of Spanish cinema at the time. The film had an unusually long run in the cinemas, and was still being exhibited over eighteen months after its release in 1979.[20] Much to José Antonio de la Loma's dismay, the protagonist Ángel Fernández Franco did not turn up to the premiere of the film as he was hiding from the police. He would shortly be arrested and wrongly imprisoned for six months for killing a petrol station assistant – an alleged crime for which he was eventually acquitted through the help of de la Loma's lawyer. His imprisonment and release no doubt contributed to the film's continued success at the box-office, and this well-publicised turn of events would feed directly into *Perros callejeros 2: Busca y captura,* produced and released in 1979. De la Loma got around the problem of el Torete's death at the end of the first film by making Ángel Fernández Franco this time quite literally play himself: a delinquent who has recently turned actor, who has missed a premiere of his first film in which he was playing the role of el Torete (who, as noted earlier, more or less serves as a proxy for el Vaquilla) and gets wrongly accused of the petrol station killing and becomes imprisoned as a result.

The film was generally criticised for opportunistically exploiting the success of *Perros callejeros.*[21] *La Vanguardia,* in particular, observed the irony that while the paltry budget for the Protección de Menores (protection of children) has remained the same, the number of delinquents under the age of 21 and the price of cinema tickets have conversely risen (Masó, 1979). Indeed, far more meagre in its construction, the script lacks the sociological context and level of detail that was provided by the first one, and the cast is made up of fewer non-professional actors. As Juan José Moreno Cuenca was again unable to appear in the film, the professional actor Bernard Seray (who, with his blonde hair, bears little resemblance to the delinquent) plays the role of el Vaquilla. Moreno Cuenca's younger brother Miguel Ugal Cuenca 'el Carica' was also meant to appear as himself in the film, but the professional actor Pep Corominas was brought in to play the role of el Pijo, as the brother had also been sent to prison.[22] Nevertheless, in common with *Perros callejeros*, the content of the film appeared to resonate vividly with its young audience, stimulating them into an interaction and noisy response. The critic for *Cambio 16* reported on the 'mayormente agitado y ruidoso' (mostly excitable and noisy) audience during a screening in the Cine Fermina, Barcelona. A delinquent of the name 'el Chino' from the *barrio* of Verneda reportedly jumped up in his seat and asked '¿Ehh, Qué pasa?' (hey, what's up?) when hearing his namesake mentioned by a policeman in the film (Anon, 1979a: 119).

Opening with the final car chase sequence of *Perros callejeros,* the film first appears to suggest that the sequel will pick up where the original film left off. This scene is then revealed to be part of a film within a film: a wide-angle shot shows el Torete's death on a large cinema screen, which is being watched by a middle-aged and moustachioed film director (a thinly veiled surrogate for José Antonio de la Loma), his cameraman and Basilio Martinez Franco, Ángel's real-life younger brother (who played the character el Cornetilla in the first film). The director turns to ask Basilio why his brother did not turn up to the screening, to which the latter replies: 'Pero como anda de busca y captura …' (as he is being chased by the police). A playful wink to the title, Basilio's line is of course also an allusion to the turn of events that resulted in Ángel's imprisonment in real life. Far from a continuation of the narrative of the first film, then, the opening sequence places *Perros callejeros 2* in a meta-textual dialogue with the earlier film, a relationship which further complicates the line between reality and performance, between delinquents and actors. The location of the auditorium, moreover, foregrounds the presence of speed as a theatrical experience, in which its sensuous pleasures and thrills are presented for the audience's enjoyment (the director, for his part,

1.4 The final sequence of the film *Perros callejeros* being shown in the cinema in *Perros callejeros 2: Busca y captura* (José Antonio de la Loma, 1979).

1.5 The film director (Raúl Ramírez) viewing the final sequence of the film *Perros callejeros* in *Perros callejeros 2: Busca y captura* (José Antonio de la Loma, 1979).

appears to be most satisfied with the cut of the film he has just seen). As it would turn out, the delinquent actor's absence, here presented as an ironic re-enactment of what happened during the premiere of *Perros callejeros*, would also prefigure the well-publicised non-attendance of other *quinqui* actors at their own screenings due to run-ins with the police – namely *Deprisa, deprisa* (José Antonio Valdelomar) and *El pico* (José Luis Fernández Eguia 'el Pirri').

The scene that follows is a car chase sequence between Ángel and the policeman Fernando (played by Mexican actor Raúl Ramírez), as they race down Barcelona's Gran Vía. The scene rapidly cross-cuts between the points of view of Ángel and Fernando respectively, so that the densely congested road ahead can be seen through their windscreens. The frame-within-a-frame of the cinema screen in the pre-title sequence is thus now replaced by the frame of the windscreen, an effect that bears out Paul Virilio's famous assertion that '(w)hat goes on in the windscreen is cinema in the strict sense' (cited in

Wollen, 2002: 88). The use of editing and camerawork here establishes an even more immersive and visceral relationship with the car, an effect that is heightened through the prominence of the acoustic environment of the road on the soundtrack, with its enveloping noises of engines and car horns. Unlike the car chase at the beginning of the first film, where el Torete's movement was established within the community of a gang, Ángel is here introduced as a lone individual, forced to fend for himself. In his pursuit of Ángel, Fernando seeks to exact his revenge after the delinquent's car ran into him, leaving him with an injury. Fernando's hunt for Ángel continues into the *discoteca* Zafiro, wherein Ángel successfully hides himself in a cubicle in the woman's toilet – all while simultaneously seducing a girl. Recognised by girls wherever he goes, Ángel enjoys the recently found fame that starring in a film would appear to bring. His individuality would therefore also appear to point to his new status as a celebrity, self-consciously drawing on the recent media exposure that the actor had received in real life.

Around the time of the film's release, Ángel Fernández Franco was interviewed by Maruja Torres for *Fotogramas*. As the title of the interview suggests, 'Ángel Fernández: "el Torete": "Me arrepiento cantidá"' (I regret it a lot), the interview reveals the unvarnished sincerity and vulnerability that were arguably key to his star appeal. He says that now that he is famous, police nevertheless find ways of blaming 'el Torete' (referring here to his cinematic moniker) for crimes, even though he no longer steals cars. He has taken to cutting himself in response, so that he is sent to the hospital instead of the police station. While Fernández lives off earnings made from the films, Torres draws attention to how fast his money goes, emphasising how a structure of immediacy and contingency continues to define his day-to-day existence (Torres, 1979).[23] Accompanied by a series of photographs in which Fernández looks seductively at the camera, Torres also noted how much he enjoyed posing for the shoot, and showing off his right wrist which revealed his homemade tattoos and scars. The actor claims female admirers throw themselves at him, and does not fully deny a rumour that fans have even offered to pay him for sex (cited in Torres, 1979). These kinds of comments are reflected in the script of the film, when, for instance Ángel boasts to Verónica (Verónica Miriel) that 'Desde que hice la peli, ya es demasiao ... Me esperan en la puerta con las bragas en la mano' (Since I made the film, it's too much ...

They wait for me at door with their panties in their hand). If his naked body in *Perros callejeros* articulated anxieties around questions of youth, risk and responsibility, here it is unequivocally positioned as the object of the gaze. First introduced in the script as 'Ángel con un par de años más, alto, espigado' (Ángel, a couple of years older, tall and slim), his body is now notably broader and more developed, his toned chest partially revealed through the half-unbuttoned shirt which he wears underneath a flashy medallion. The use of lighting often bathes his lustrous black hair and the contours of his body in a soft halo-like glow, particularly in the erotic scenes that take place in the shack of his occasional lover Gumer (Grace Renat), where he stays along with Gumer's younger sister Charo (Teresa Giménez).

Ángel exploits the erotic potential of speed when, in an early scene, he uses the act of stealing a vehicle as a means of seducing Veronica. In a covert attempt to break into a Chrysler – a faster and more modern model of car than the SEAT 124, but also one that is more difficult to

1.6 Ángel (Ángel Fernández Franco) and Verónica (Verónica Miriel) in *Perros callejeros 2: Busca y captura* (1979).

steal – he asks Veronica to lean against the car door as they embrace, her body serving to conceal his hand as he unlocks the vehicle with a filed-down key.[24] Tony (Reyes Poveda) and el Chino (José Fobles) then use the car as a getaway vehicle for a robbery; with Ángel refusing to get involved, they get el Choto (César Sánchez), a slightly older and more sinister delinquent whom el Chino (José Febles) describes as 'una bestia al volante' (crazy at the wheel), to drive the car. This sets in motion a close recreation of the tragic turn of events that led to the actor's real-life imprisonment. As Tony, el Chino and el Choto stop to fill up the tank at a petrol station, the attendant recognises el Choto's face from a previous robbery and drags him out of the car; as the scuffle escalates, el Chino panics and shoots the attendant dead. After capturing el Chino, the police are intent on blaming Ángel as his accomplice, having found his fingerprints on the car, despite el Chino's assertions that he was not with them at the time. Charo warns Ángel that the police are after him for murder, and that his photographs and reports of his pursuit have appeared in the paper. Furrowing his brow and biting his lip with worry, Ángel says 'Quieren buscarnos la ruina' (they will be the ruin of us) before driving away at haste. The noise of his screeching tyres gives way to the machine rhythms of the newspapers being printed on a conveyor belt in the following shot: a cut that links deviant speed with its subsequent mediatisation. The script here appears to draw directly on a comment that Ángel made to *Interviú* in an article entitled '¿Qué queréis, buscarme la ruina?' (Do you want to cause me problems?) shortly after his release from prison (Gracia, 1978). In the article, Ángel Fernández Franco explains in great detail to *Interviú* his alibi during the night of the shooting (Gracia, 1978) – events that are closely reconstructed in the film. After Ángel calls the director to plead for his help, the director hires a lawyer and asks him to come to his apartment. Looking at his watch, the director waits impatiently as Ángel turns up late to his home. Ángel then explains his precise whereabouts of that night, whose images are depicted in flashback as he speaks.

The unfolding of events that follow provides a fascinating insight into the entanglement of speed, celebrity and cinema in the lives of the delinquents during this period in Spain. On the same day that the petrol station shooting occurs, Ángel hears that *Perros callejeros* has been released for three or four weeks in Zaragoza before Barcelona. So eager is he to watch the film that he drives (in a different car to the one that was used in the robbery) to Zaragoza to catch the matinee that day, accompanied by el Chelo and el Pijo (here as a proxy for el Carica). Ángel's voice again takes on a testimonial charge in the film, as his words are spoken over a re-enactment of the precise route taken by the three friends, depicted in flashback: their car as they approach the city, with its famous *mudéjar* cathedral El Pilar seen through their windscreen on the horizon; the fish restaurant which they visited for lunch, and their entry into the cinema Coliseo. The film, we assume, has been a success in Zaragoza as Ángel and el Pijo are treated like celebrities wherever they go, and people approach them for their autographs. Slightly later in the film, Charo is called to provide further evidence, where she admits that after the *discoteca*, the three of them stole another car and hurriedly drove back to Barcelona. As Charo describes the road as narrow with curves, her voice is accompanied by a POV from Ángel as he drives rapidly down a treacherous stretch of the road. Ángel loses control of the vehicle and crashes into a stationary car, where the force of his body slamming into the wheel leaves him with a minor injury in his chest.

Despite providing the judge with evidence of the X-ray scans of his chest and various statements from witnesses (José Antonio de la Loma reportedly took out an advert in the *Heraldo de Aragón* to appeal for witnesses who saw them in Zaragoza that day (Gracia, 1978: 91)), Ángel is nevertheless sentenced to prison along with el Pijo, on account of the fingerprints he left in the Chrysler from when he and Veronica had sex inside the car. In the original script (but not in the final film), the judge tells the director, who is dismayed by the sentencing, that 'la ley de enjuiciamiento criminal, se nos ha quedado antigua … como muchas cosas en este país, es del siglo pasado' (The Code of Criminal Procedure is now too old for us … like many things in this country, it's from the last century). La Modelo prison is depicted as authoritarian and overcrowded, its infrastructure woefully ill-adapted to the mounting social problems of an increasingly urbanised and socially unequal Spain. During the six months of his sentence, the actor consistently bore witness to violence from other prisoners and staff, claiming for instance that the prison guards accused him of selling heroin and beat him repeatedly so that he would confess to it (Gracia, 1978: 91). Now that he is over the age of 16, Ángel is incarcerated along with the other adult prisoners, most of whom appear conspicuously more dangerous and older than el Pijo. One of the prisoners is Sebastián

(Antonio Maroño), el Pijo's moustachioed older brother, who brutally rapes el Chino out of revenge for the imprisonment of el Pijo and Ángel. Sebastián leads a mutiny in the prison gallery, in which he is able to slip past the guards in disguise and escape from the prison. Sebastián's role here mirrors that of el Carica's/el Pijo's older stepbrother Julián Ugal Cuenca, who was known for his prominent role in prison rebellions as well as his involvement in COPEL (Coordinara de Presos en Lucha), a grass-roots activist group that was established in 1977, whose aim was to demand rights for prisoners and do away with the Criminal Procedure Law (Cañellas et al., 2000: 290).

In its disruption of the strict carceral schedule, the mutiny which Sebastián triggers illustrates how, according to Henri Lefebvre and Catherine Regulier 'the citizen resists the State by a particular use of time. A struggle therefore unfolds for appropriation in which rhythms play a major role. Through them, social, therefore, civil time, seeks and manages to shield itself from State, linear, uni rhythmical measured and measuring time' (2003: 190). A handheld camera weaves itself through the chaotic scrum of prisoner and guards, its spontaneous and shaky movement further emphasising the rejection of the fixed rhythms and routines of the prison. Shouting 'Libertad, libertad' (freedom, freedom), prisoners throw their mattresses and other pieces of everyday furniture from the galleries onto a makeshift bonfire in the patio below, while others hurl stones at the anti-riot police who arrive at the scene. Although Ángel attempts to keep out of the melee, he nevertheless ends up beaten by one of the police officers in the scene, the colour of his blood matching that of his bright red jumper – a beating that mirrored what happened to him in real life (cited in Torres, 1979). The mutiny prefigured the sharp increase of prison rebellions and escapes across Spain in 1978: after Ángel's release from La Modelo in March of that year, the prison would become the site of two rebellions during which two prisoners would escape in April, and most notoriously, 45 would escape in June.[25]

Ángel's stubborn resistance to synchronise with the regulatory rhythms of the prison continues right until his release, which is depicted at the end of the film. Pepe, Charo, Basilio and a delegate of reporters and a photographer eagerly await Ángel's release opposite the prison gates. When Ángel fails to appear at the scheduled time of his release – and in so doing standing up the director for the second time – everyone goes home except for Charo, who dutifully waits all night for him. When Ángel is finally released in the early hours of the morning, he runs across the road to greet Charo and is killed by a speeding hit-and-run car, whose driver is concealed from the viewer. Unlike much of the rest of the film's narrative, which conforms closely to events that have taken place in Ángel's life, the depiction of Ángel's death here appears to conform instead to the generic conventions of the *quinqui* film, which frequently ends with the tragic death of the delinquent. El Torete lives for speed and is finally killed by speed – their unruly rhythms cannot be assimilated into the narrative of the films. Ángel Fernández Franco's real-life release from La Modelo, in contrast, was rather more auspicious, and was attended by reporters from *Interviú*, who observed that the majority of the two or three dozen fans waiting for him lived in 'chabolas tercermundistas' (third-world shanty towns) from the outer suburbs of Barcelona, living without running water (Gracia, 1978: 91). The crowd of onlookers reported by the article here reflects the extent to which audiences committedly followed the vicissitudes of Ángel Fernández's criminal life both on screen and in real life.

Los últimos golpes de 'el Torete': Parodying speed

After the commercial success of *Perros callejeros 2*, de la Loma made *Los últimos golpes de 'el Torete'* in 1980, the third and last instalment of his *quinqui* films starring Ángel Fernández Franco. While the film featured the high-speed car chases and robberies for which the cycle had become known, its style was markedly different from the previous two films. The director described the film as a 'comedia de acción' (comedy action film) (Crespo, 1981), and the comic mode drives the freewheeling and whimsical narrative of the film, where the characters find themselves in a series of increasingly outlandish and farcical situations. The commercial success of *Perros callejeros* and its sequel had led to a flurry of other delinquent-themed films by a range of different directors – a trend that in particular gathered momentum and diversified in 1980, with the productions of auteurs such as Carlos Saura's *Deprisa, deprisa* and Manuel Gutiérrez Aragón's *Maravillas* also under way that year. In contrast to the seriousness of these films, however, *Los últimos golpes de 'el Torete'* broadly works as a parody of the *quinqui* film. In its self-conscious exaggeration of the tropes of *cine quinqui*, its main referents are not so much urban space and the prison as they are the cinematic construction of the delinquent actor and his 'performance' of delinquency. The comedic elements of the film were poorly received by *El Correo Catalán* (Ruiz, 1980), and *ABC* criticised it for its incoherent and muddled structure and clichéd use of dialogue, adding that its sole saving grace was found in the car chases directed by Rémy Julienne (Crespo, 1981), who also appears as a cameo in the film.

The promotional poster presented Ángel as el Torete and Bernard Seray as el Vaquilla 'solos, frente al peso inexorable de la ley' (alone, facing the inexorable weight of the law), without their respective gangs, accompanied by the image of two SEAT cars driving side by side in a duel. While the character el Torete was killed off at the end of *Perros callejeros,* Fernández Franco's reappearance as el Torete in *Los últimos golpes* was not out of keeping with the parodic mode of the film. Besides, as we have seen, Ángel was now commonly known in the media as el Torete anyway, and this blurring between actor and character, delinquent and celebrity provided the film with a rich seam of humour throughout. The blurring of these lines in turn illuminates how cultural criminologists seek to 'make sense of a world in which the street scripts the screen and the screen scripts the street' (Hayward and Young, 2004: 259).

The theme of performance is self-reflexively invoked in the opening sequence in which el Torete and el Vaquilla are introduced wearing thinly veiled disguises. El Torete is first seen wearing thick black sunglasses and a reversible raincoat, attempting to hold up a branch of Santander on Barcelona's Plaza de Cataluña at gunpoint. He is interrupted by the sudden arrival of el Vaquilla, who, wearing a rubber mask and brandishing a gun, has also coincidentally come to rob the very same bank. El Vaquilla says 'Qué casualidad' (what a coincidence), before asking el Torete to reveal his identity. When the bewildered cashier asks el Torete to whom he should give the money, he retorts that 'el atraco es mío' (the robbery is mine) and that he came first. When an elderly lady, unintimidated by the pair of thieves, refuses to lie on the floor for cover, he shrugs his shoulders and carries on with the robbery regardless. Dan Harries writes that 'film parody has long been associated with the recitation and violation of rules: rules of character, rules of setting and rules of narrative – in essence, the rules of genre' (2002: 281). Right from the outset of the film, the conventions and iconographic tropes of the *quinqui* cycle are similarly broken and repurposed for comic effect. The usually rough-hewn and naturalistic style of acting associated with the genre, for instance, is here replaced by broader and more stylised performances, whereby sincerity and selfhood have been substituted by impersonation and masquerade. El Vaquilla's gun – a crucial prop to *cine quinqui* – is revealed to be a toy replica (which el Torete refers to as 'chunga' (dodgy)) and the usual fast-paced action of a high-stakes robbery and getaway is instead here drawn out and deferred for comic effect. In playfully pointing to its own construction, the self-reflexivity of the scene illustrates the way in which, according to Harries, parody 'conducts its meta-commentary on the genre through a process of recontextualisation that operates on the simultaneous creation of similarity to and difference from the targeted text' (2002: 283). In particular, this difference is created through a number of comic strategies, which include 'exaggeration, extraneous inclusion, literalisation, inversion and misdirection' of the conventions of the genre (2002: 283). Comic inversion and exaggeration, in particular, are used throughout the film. As the police approach the scene of the crime, el Torete runs for cover into another bank with his reversible jacket folded inside out so that its checked inner lining can be seen, with a conspicuous wad of stolen cash sticking out of his pocket. An affable bank manager warns him that there are an increasing amount of thieves around, and offers to deposit his money in an account. El Vaquilla later asks: '¿lo atracaste?' (did you rob the bank?) to which he replies, 'no, metí dinero' (no, I deposited money). Much of the humour of the film to come will, moreover, derive from the exaggeration of the longstanding rivalry between Ángel Fernández Franco 'el Torete' and el Vaquilla, a tension that is frequently literalised through the significance of speed in the film.

In the car chase that ensues, el Torete exhibits his mastery of speed with a relaxed and amused expression as he looks back through the rear window emblazoned with a SEAT sticker to see the hapless policeman Perales (played by veteran actor Fernando Guillén) trailing behind. On a country road, el Torete once again encounters el Vaquilla driving a stolen vehicle, their cars close to each other, sometimes competing for speed as el Torete dodges Perales's poorly aimed bullets. The two cars then tailgate Perales from each side, taking it in turns to bump into his vehicle until his police car loses control and careers off the road, rolling down into a ravine. Here, the space of the road

1.7 El Torete (Ángel Fernández Franco) and el Vaquilla (Bernard Seray) in disguise while robbing a bank in *Los últimos golpes de 'el Torete'* (José Antonio de la Loma, 1980).

dramatises the relationship between Ángel Fernández Franco and Juan José Moreno Cuenca in real life, whose criss-crossing paths provide a metaphor for the parallel and often intersecting biographies that were observed by the press.[26] Their converging motion on the road points to their complicity and camaraderie, something that was fostered through growing up together in La Mina against the repressive agents of the law. This relationship, however, was also complicated by bitter rivalry, particularly on Moreno Cuenca's part. As the real-life el Vaquilla, Moreno Cuenca expressed his resentment in an interview that while others had financially profited from his life story, he had not yet received a penny – in spite of de la Loma paying for his lawyers and bail money (Gracia, 1980a: 91).[27] At the end of the interview, the journalist Vicente Gracia concluded that 'el Vaquilla continúa sólo frente a un incierto futuro' (el Vaquilla continues alone faced with an uncertain future) (1980a: 91) – an observation that was ironically close to the standfirst on the promotional material for the film. In Bernard Seray's brief appearance as el Vaquilla in *Perros callejeros 2,* he churlishly tells Ángel that the starring role of *Perros callejeros* should have belonged to him. His comment takes place shortly before snatching woman's bag from a stolen vehicle, a robbery which is suddenly thwarted by the police vehicle, which obstructs el Vaquilla's path. In a desperate bid to avoid capture, el Vaquilla accidentally reverses his car into the woman, who dies from the impact with the vehicle – a turn of events that in part led to his arrest in real life and subsequent inability to appear in the film.[28] The rivalry between el Vaquilla and el Torete in *Los últimos golpes* is brought into further relief through the character of Berta, Vaquilla's girlfriend (played by Berta Cabré, who also appeared in a string of erotic films during this period) who also attempts to seduce el Torete. While the depiction of Berta is far from progressive (her purpose in the scenes in which she appears naked is merely to provide titillation), her character is nevertheless presented as freewilled and sexually autonomous, and is seen to challenge el Torete's misogynistic and traditional views on women.

That the Spanish media frequently discussed el Torete and el Vaquilla in the same breath is parodied in the film through the appearance of the roving radio reporter Begoña (Isabel Mestres), whose show reports on the social problems faced by those on the margins in Barcelona. Begoña's empathetic stance on juvenile delinquency is placed in contrast with that of Quique (Simón Andreu), a reporter from a struggling rival station whose view is altogether less forgiving. The *mise-en-scène* of Quique's claustrophobic and spartan studio is juxtaposed with that of Begoña, whose walls are adorned with posters of countercultural rock groups such as Guadalquivir and where her colleagues smoke while they work. Railing against Begoña's 'falsos paternalismos' (false patronising attitudes) and her constant criticisms of the police and government, Quique is quite literally presented as the mouthpiece of the conservative alarmism that surrounded delinquency, a stance which was most embodied through the political campaigns of the Alianza Popular and the conservative press of the period (see chapter 2) – publications that were also highly critical of José Antonio de la Loma. As Begoña recounts the story of Torete growing up in La Mina, her voice is accompanied by scenes from the first *Perros callejeros* film, as she explains to her listeners that el Torete was wandering the streets of La Mina at just nine years old, given that nurseries and schools could not be built in time. She reassures her listeners that while the actions of el Torete and el Vaquilla may well be dangerous, 'nunca han dejado de ser niños' (they have never stopped being children). Buoyed by hearing his life story on the radio, el Torete calls into the radio station to promise Begoña that he and el Vaquilla will redeem themselves and find a job.

While they seek to become integrated into society through employment, poor working conditions and the temptation for unruly speed soon lead them astray. Finding positions as trainee mechanics, they work under the supervision of their cigar-smoking boss Mariano, who refuses to let them go for lunch until they have finished their work. Played by Florencio Calpe, who also appeared in the role of the judge in the first two films, the casting of the actor here establishes a continuity between the authoritarianism of the youth justice system and the exploitative and non-unionised employment practices of young people – something that is further emphasised through his use of a cigar as a prop in both roles. El Torete and el Vaquilla decide to break with the gruelling and monotonous rhythms of their work by testing one of the sports cars that is currently being fixed in the garage. Careering down a country road, el Vaquilla attempts to carry out a dangerous ski stunt, so that the car is driven while precariously balanced on its two side wheels. After losing his balance, the car becomes stuck on its side; managing to clamber out of the front window of the vehicle, el Vaquilla and el Torete light up cigarettes and accidentally set fire to it. The upturned vehicle is literally an inversion of the generic function of the car in the *quinqui* film, usually presented as a getaway vehicle which provides accelerated movement and mastery of urban space. The humour of the scene here relies not only on what Harries describes as the 'spectatorial activity that accompanies the watching of film genre' (2002: 282) but on the audience's extra-textual knowledge of el Vaquilla's real-life passion for dangerous vehicular stunts, in particular wheelies. On discovering that SEAT is holding auditions for stunt drivers for the launch of their 'car of the year' – the script specifies that the new model is called 'Ritmo' (rhythm) – el Torete and el Vaquilla go along to try their luck. Denied entry into the SEAT headquarters, they climb over the security fence and sneak onto the racing circuit. Commandeering two rally cars, they race around the tracks wearing motorcycle helmets so that no one recognises them.

1.8 El Torete (Ángel Fernández Franco) performs a dangerous stunt in *Los últimos golpes de 'el Torete'* (José Antonio de la Loma, 1980).

After technicians attempt to stop them as they speed past the controls and ram into a wall of tyres, the police start shooting at el Vaquilla's vehicle; demanding that he takes off his helmet, they then exclaim 'pero si es solo un crío' (but he's just a kid).

Significantly, the judge of the competition is none other than Rémy Julienne, who was playing a quasi-fictional version of himself. The casting here is an example of what André Bazin once called 'doubling' – which, as James Naremore explains, is the 'casting of a player in a fiction that parallels his or her public life' (1988: 269). The 'doubling' here also extends more literally to the cinematic construction of speed and sensation in *Perros callejeros,* given that Rémy Julienne choreographed the stunt doubles for el Vaquilla and Ángel/el Torete in the films. Julienne is later interviewed by Begoña in front of an assembly line where the SEAT Ritmo is being built, where he expresses his amazement at the delinquents' driving skills. Against the diegetic sounds of machinery and hammering, he comments into a microphone that 'no me explico cómo pueden conocer nuestros trucos ... Hicieron cosas que yo mismo no puedo superar' (I can't understand how they can know our tricks ... They did things that I can't do better). Describing their driving skills as 'algo sensacional' (something sensational), Julienne's comments also bring to mind the somatic pleasures of action cinema, which is described by Richard Dyer, as we have seen, in its 'rush and its challenge' as a 'celebration of sensational movement' (2000: 18). The location of the SEAT headquarters here therefore ironically points to the correspondence between automobile speed and cinematic speed – a relationship that, as we have seen throughout the chapter, has been physically embodied through the transgressive body of the delinquent. Located in Martorell, in the province of Barcelona, the SEAT assembly line – here depicted as running with a highly disciplined and fast-paced efficiency – also resonates with the factory-style production of the so-called 'otra escuela de Barcelona'. In common with SEAT, de la Loma, Ignacio Iquino, and Antonio Isasi-Isasmendi oversaw standardised products – namely genre films – that were made swiftly for the mass market. The parallel here between the cinematic production of speed and the material production of vehicles therefore illustrates the transgressive pleasures of de la Loma's filmmaking, one which demonstrates, in the words of Mimi Sheller, that 'there is a crucial conjunction between motion and emotion, movement and feeling, autos and motives' (Sheller, 2004: 226).

Conclusion

The final scene of *Los últimos golpes de 'el Torete'* sees el Vaquilla dying in el Torete's arms, after being shot by the police. In real life, however, Juan José Moreno Cuenca would outlive Ángel Fernández Franco by two years. Despite returning for a brief cameo appearance in *Yo, el Vaquilla* (José Antonio de la Loma, 1985) (see chapter 4), Fernández Franco failed to make more films in the 1980s and died of an AIDS-related illness in 1991 at the age of just 31. In a newspaper report that provided an obituary of his life, the headline wrote: 'Una vida pisando al acelerador' (a life with a foot on the accelerator) (Corachán and Gasulla, 1991: 33) – a biography of life that was lived out with a rapid intensity, which, as this chapter has shown, found its expression in the kinaesthetic force and rhythm of de la Loma's filmmaking. Despite the director's help, Fernández Franco would go on to spend much of his young adulthood in prison. He found himself reunited with Juan José Moreno Cuenca and his brother Miguel Ugal Cuenca 'el Carica' in court in 1984, where the three were sentenced for violent robbery and carrying arms for an alleged crime that dated back to 1978 (Anon, 1984b). For his part, Moreno Cuenca would finally appear as the narrator in a film about his own life, *Yo, el Vaquilla* in 1985 – albeit while appearing behind bars – before dying in 2003 of cirrhosis of the liver. In the same year, his brother Miguel was killed in a car crash during a police chase – another victim of unruly speed (Montaout, 1985: 1). As this chapter has shown, the embodied motion and speed of both the cinematic body and the delinquent alike bore witness to the temporal unevenness of modernisation, where unfettered capitalist development rubbed up against a decaying and authoritarian criminal justice system. These social and economic contradictions would similarly inform the depiction of delinquency in several other films of the *quinqui* cycle, as the rest of the book will show.

Notes

1 See for instance Crespo (1981).

2 See Peiró (1983).

3 Fernando Trueba would go on to win the Academy Award for Best Foreign Language Film with *Belle Époque* in 1994.

4 See, for instance, the famous interview with Maruja Torres 'Ángel Fernández: "El Torete": "Me arrepiento cantidá"' (1979: 3–7, 33). The origin of the name El Trompeta or El Trompetilla (trumpet or horn) might originate from his childhood habit of putting his hand to his ear in order to hear better. See Marchena (2014).

5 In a rather less auspicious account, the nickname 'el Vaquilla' may also have originated from when he was a baby. On observing the great size of the baby's excrement, one of his uncles, who was later shot dead by the police, reportedly commented that 'parece mierda de vaca' (it looks like cow's shit). See Marchena (2014). In the early 1980s, the delinquent Juan Carlos Delgado 'el Pera' from Getafe in Madrid similarly became known for his speedy driving, and years later, as a reformed criminal, taught the police how to chase cars. El Pera did not feature in the *quinqui* films, though *Volando voy/My Quick Way Out* (Miguel Albaladejo, 2006) later presented a biopic of his life. For a history of el Pera and *Volando voy*, see Ríos Carratalá (2014: 151–174).

6 Ángel Fernández Franco was already familiar with the director's films, and commented in an interview that he had seen *Metralleta Stein* and

Razzia, the latter shot on location in his neighbourhood, La Mina (Anon, 1977a: 13).

7 The director later commented that, after convincing the residents that he was not exploiting or corrupting the delinquents, they dropped their complaints against the film. See Masó (1979).

8 See for instance Jímenez (1978), who in an interview sums up the negative critical response to the film as follows: 'Algunos críticos han dicho de "Perros callejeros" que es una invitación, un canto a la violencia' (some critics have said that *Perros callejeros* is an invitation, a song to violence).

9 In the original script submitted to the Biblioteca Nacional de España in October 1976, it contains an entirely different pre-title sequence which is far more violent in tone. The voiceover depicts the deaths of four delinquents under the age of 16 – el Pacorro, el Loquillo, Pepe el Majara and el Maito – all of whom were reportedly shot dead by the police.

10 'Unfortunately, it is not a problem of one *barrio* in particular, as some claim, or of a district, or even of our city, but of all those who suffer the ills of an accelerated and out-of-control population growth, of a society intent on an easy life of luxury and exhibitionism.'

11 See Lahera (1980: 60), who reports that the El Colegio de Abogados in Madrid opposed the bill. See also Torre Iglesias (1980: 64) for an interview with the sociologist Enrique Martínez Reguera, who pointed to several problems with the proposed bill and the punitive approach towards delinquency more generally. While the criminologists Esther Fernández Molina and Cristina Rechea Alberola do not specifically mention the discussion of the proposed bill in their overview of Spain's juvenile justice system, they write that: 'With the enactment of the 1978 Constitution, there began a period of debate and reflection about the role of the state regarding delinquent children. But this debate, held among professionals, did not have an effect at the legislative level' (2003: 390).

12 Ángel Fernández Franco commented that he had spent time in Zamora, along with el Vaquilla and other delinquents Pedro el Loco, el Clemén and el Mario. The journalist asked Fernández Franco if he knew that the prison was officially illegal (cited in Anon, 1977: 14).

13 For an excellent discussion of the film and a history of Zamora prison see Woods Peiró (2015).

14 See Goicoechea (1978).

15 The Ley de Protección de Menores (The Law for the Protection of Minors), enshrined in law on 2 July 1948, was brought in by Javier

de Ybarra, who was kidnapped and assassinated by ETA in 1977. See Goicoechea (1978).

16 It is significant, then, that the character el Fitipaldi, named after the Brazilian automobile racing driver Emerson Fittipaldi and known within the *barrio* as the fastest driver around, helps el Torete to escape from solitary confinement. The modern speed he embodies cannot be assimilated into Spain's outdated youth justice system whose punitive approach only serves to further brutalise its subjects.

17 The town and municipality of El Prat de Llobregat is famous for its breed of chicken, known as Catalana del Prat.

18 The original script makes explicit how his involvement in stealing cars began after the shanty towns of Campo de la Bota were removed and they were rehoused to La Mina. The reference to La Mina did not make it into the final version of the film, most likely owing to the demonstrations carried out in the neighbourhood.

19 'The final shout of the boy, multiplied, aggressive, clear, overwhelming, can be heard echoing from the mountains … His farewell to a world that did not love him, which he did not love either.'

20 Statistics show that two years after its 1979, *Perros callejeros* picked up 199,336 viewers and was the 38th highest-grossing film of that year. As mentioned in the introduction, however, these statistics do not include smaller *cines de barrio*.

21 See for, instance, *Cambio 16* (Anon, 1979a: 119).

22 The original script refers to the character as Carica, but his name has been changed to el Pijo in the film. Miguel Ugal Cuenca 'el Carica' was with Ángel Fernández Franco the night of the petrol station shooting and was arrested as an accomplice and also sent to prison. While Ugal Cuenca had been released from prison when José Antonio de la Loma wrote the script for the film, he was arrested again before the beginning of the shoot. He was therefore replaced by the professional Pep Corominas, and the character's name somewhat confusingly reverts back to el Pijo(!), the character Ugal Cuenca plays in the first film.

23 Maruja Torres further observes: 'Vive en la provisionalidad, incluso ahora, porque su realismo de chaval de alcantarilla no le impide ser un perfecto ingenuo, uno que hoy cree en esto del cine y la fama sin preguntarse qué va a ocurrir después. Tampoco le importa demasiado el futuro, acostumbrado como está a vivir al día …' (Even now, he lives for the present, because his lad-from-the-gutter realism doesn't prevent him from having the naivete of someone who believes in cinema and fame, but without ever asking himself what comes afterwards. He's not

too worried about the future, as accustomed as he is to living from day to day …) (1979).

24 Ángel in *Perros callejeros* similarly carries around a set of 'espadas', a word he uses to describe keys which have their ridges shaved down so as to fit into multiple car doors and ignitions.

25 See for instance Anon (1979b).

26 As borne out, for instance, by Pereda's article for *El País* (1984).

27 Moreno Cuenca had been released from prison on 18 July 1980, two months before the interview.

28 Moreno Cuenca frequently expressed regret for the accident, which took place on 5 December 1976 when he was 15 years old. See Gracia (1980: 92).

2

Soundscapes of anxiety: Civil insecurity, democracy and the home

The figure of the delinquent during the transition to democracy frequently articulated the general anxieties and fears of the public. Many ordinary Spaniards were more concerned with rising crime rates, unemployment and the threat of political violence than they were with the subject of democratic consensus, an illustration of Antonio Sánchez-Gijón's claim that the '"political country" seemed to be far away from the "real country" during these years' (1987: 130). This social malaise was vividly captured in the films *Los violadores del amanecer* (Ignacio F. Iquino, 1978), *La patria de 'el Rata'* (Lara Polop, 1980) and *Miedo a salir de noche* (Eloy de la Iglesia, 1980). The films not only responded to the problem of crime but more specifically the *fear* of crime that resonated in the national consciousness during this period – a fear that while not completely unfounded was not always proportional to the actual rates of victimisation. This malaise gained particular intensity in the wake of the new democratic constitution of 1978 and the reorganisation of the Spanish police force, which was subsequently decoupled from the military. For the criminologists Stephen D. Farrall, Emily Gray and Jonathan Jackson, the fear of crime becomes a problem within society 'when its citizens lose faith in the structures of social control' (2009: 3). If anxieties around crime and public disorder in Spain found their expression through the demonisation of the delinquent, they also spoke to more diffuse and underlying fears in the face of rapid social change.

In exploring the cinematic responses to these everyday fears, this chapter seeks to examine how the process of democratisation was felt from below rather than above, from the level of ordinary citizens rather than the political elites. In so doing, this chapter places the focus on the depiction of the home and everyday spaces in *cine quinqui*. In *Los violadores del amanecer*, *La patria de 'el Rata'* and *Miedo a salir de noche*, for instance, domestic space is presented as under siege by the threat of delinquency. As this chapter shows, these depictions more broadly reflect the extent to which the home became a particular site of resonance during the transition to democracy, one whose walls became increasingly reinforced through the rising popularity of home security and surveillance. In particular, the chapter explores how the soundscape of the home, historically associated with peace and privacy, was threatened through the deviant sounds of delinquents, as well as through the noises of alarms, sirens, explosions and other ambient noises. Through exploring the acoustic borders between inside and outside, private space and public space, this chapter ultimately aims to show how the films revealed public anxieties around the subject of public order during these years, a concept that came to be radically reconfigured within Spain's new democracy.

Victimhood, insecurity and the soundscape of the home

If *Los violadores del amanecer*, *La patria de 'el Rata'* and *Miedo a salir de noche* emphasised the vulnerability of victims of crime, this more broadly reflected the extent to which the subject of victimhood and public insecurity increasingly figured in Spanish popular culture and the press of this period. Spain's bestselling novelist at this time, for instance, was Fernando Vizcaíno Casas, whose alarmist narratives both reflected and fed on these public fears. Nostalgic for the regime and markedly sceptical about the process of democratisation, several of Vizcaíno Casas's novels were adapted into films directed by Rafael Gil, such as *La boda del señor cura/Father Cami's Wedding* (1979) and *Hijos de papá/Daddy's Children* (1980). The priest-turned-novelist José Luis Martín Vigil, moreover, wrote a number of gritty and curiously salacious 'social problem' novels for the teenage market. His delinquent-themed novel *¿Y ahora qué, señor fiscal?* was adapted into a film directed by León Klimovsky (1977), while the novel *La droga es joven/Drugs Are Young* formed the basis for the screenplay of the film *Chocolate* (Gil Carretero, 1980). While articles and news reports on the threat of crime first gained popularity through the crime news weekly *El Caso* in the 1950s and 1960s, the subject became particularly prominent during the transition to democracy, which saw the emergence of a number of new media outlets that were sensationalist in tone. The press frequently reported not only on the delinquent crime waves in Spain's urban centres but on the generalised fears and ontological insecurity of the Spanish population. These fears arguably brought in their wake a turn towards a pronounced responsibility of the self and the household – something that found its physical manifestation in the increased fortification of the home.

These years witnessed a spike in the use of home security and surveillance devices in Spain, with much of the population investing in the defence of their property and their possessions. Spaniards rapidly acquired what David Garland has termed 'security consciousness', a pattern of responses where individuals take more routine precautions against crime (2001: 161). Home security would prove to be big business during these years: the sale of antitheft systems in Spain soared considerably between 1975 and 1979 (Hernando Sanz, 2001: 266), while insurance companies capitalised on the public fear of crime, running a number of advertising campaigns urging people to secure their property (Huertas et al., 1978: 88). Spanish businesses of varying sizes were also investing in security. There were some 300 companies devoted to private security in Spain by 1984, none of which were older than 15 years, with a growing industry responsible for employing 10,000 people. Security doors, safety vaults, bomb detectors, alarms and fire protection systems – these were amongst some of the products that these new companies specialised in, with several also offering the service of armed guards for banks and other institutions (Anon, 1984a: 24).

The pervasive fear of crime and disorder similarly disrupted the use of public space, having an impact on the everyday journeys and routes taken by Spaniards. Christopher Hewitt observes how between 1975 and 1984, Spain saw a 29.3% and 27.8% decrease in the public use of Metro and the bus respectively, along with a 9.4% fall in railway use (1993: 35). The fortification of private spaces served to demarcate and reinforce the borders between the inside and outside in Spanish cities, borders that were perceived to be increasingly permeable and under threat by criminals, whose vulnerability was accentuated by the growing perception that the state was ineffectual in its attempt to stop crime. According to Alison Blunt and Robyn Dowling, the home is not only a 'material dwelling' but an 'affective space', it is 'both a place/physical location *and* a set of feelings (2006: 22). The *quinqui* film frequently revealed the extent to which the cultural imagination of the home during these years was reshaped by feelings of anxiety. The home in these films is presented as a defamiliarising space under the constant threat of siege or invasion. Just as security systems and surveillance increasingly demarcated and territorialised the home as a threshold and fortress, the perceived threat of social disorder that lay beyond it similarly assumed a particular urgency.

These reinforced boundaries ironically served to protect that which the new liberal democracy had guaranteed to safeguard. As Elías Díaz notes, the Spanish Constitution of 1978 gave total supremacy to the principles of private enterprise and property, the market, and the interests and values of capital in general (1999: 29). The pronounced discursive focus on ownership coincided with new considerations of how the concept of public order – upheld as instrumental in maintaining peace under the regime – should now be defined, given that it was placed within the broader structure of a constitutional democracy. The term 'orden público' (public order) had become strongly tainted with the authoritarianism of the regime, which had ensured that law and order were upheld through the Fuerzas de Orden Público (Forces of Public Order) and repressive apparatus such as the Tribunal de Orden Público (Public Order Court, established in 1963). The Spanish Constitution of 1978, however, significantly changed the structure and role of the Spanish police force. Their official title was changed to Corps and Forces of Security (Cuerpos y Fuerzas de Seguridad) and they were uncoupled from the military. The removal of 'Public Order' from their title more broadly reflected the wording of the new democratic constitution, where 'orden público' was therefore scarcely mentioned and the terms 'seguridad pública' (public safety) and 'seguridad ciudadana' (literally translated as 'citizen safety') were used instead (Hurtado Martínez, 1999: 27).[1] These constitutional changes were accompanied by an increasingly diverse range of public attitudes towards law enforcement, whereby the subject of public safety became a highly contested and fraught site of meaning.

The first national crime survey in Spain, published the same year as the constitution in 1978, provides a window onto just how divergent public attitudes were towards public order at this time. Carried out by the Centro de Investigaciones Sociológicas (CIS), whose recently acquired name had replaced the original Instituto de la Opinión Pública which had been established in 1963, the survey represented a significant advance for empirical sociology in Spain – a nascent field that, emerging only recently from the shadow of dictatorship, had meagre resources during the early years of democracy.[2] Unsurprisingly, the data provided by the survey revealed that differences in public perceptions to crime and risk frequently ran across lines of political affiliation. The responses to the question as to whether levels of security were worse now than they were in the past were markedly different depending on the political inclination. Perhaps unsurprisingly, those who voted for Alianza Popular, the right-wing party established by Manuel Fraga, stood out as the most pessimistic, with 26% who agreed with the statement (compared with 14% and 13% of voters of the UCD and PSOE respectively). When asked to consider the causes of the perceived increase in crime, the differences were even more starkly delineated. 48% of Alianza Popular voters attributed the increase to too much freedom and a lack of authority, while just 19% believed that unemployment was the main cause. In contrast, just 13% of PSOE voters blamed freedom and lack of authority, and 38% unemployment, while the picture for UCD voters was more mixed, with 25% and 34% respectively (CIS, 1978: 225). While fewer Alianza Popular voters considered unemployment to be a pressing issue, they were also most likely to be amongst the sectors of the Spanish population to be the most comfortably off. The survey showed, for instance, that the perceived risk of insecurity was highest amongst those who had higher levels of education and paid the highest rate of rent (CIS, 1978: 224). Most significantly, the survey indicated that the pronounced fear of crime amongst the right was not always commensurate with the actual risk of victimisation. Just 11% of AP voters had actually reported having been a victim of crime – a rate that was similarly low amongst UCD (11%) and PSOE (12%) (CIS, 1978: 252).

The fear of victimisation during these years was arguably a symptom of a more diffuse social malaise about the deterioration of public order and social change, something that was as commonly linked to the rapid increase of terrorist attacks as it was to robbery. As is well known, Spain's transition to democracy unfolded against a backdrop of high levels of terrorist violence whose gathering intensity during these years threatened to derail the process of democratisation. Between the years 1975 and 1982, there were 504 fatalities due to non-state violence: the majority (71%) of these were perpetrated by ETA and its various splinter groups, while far-left and far-right groups were responsible for 13% and 15% respectively (Aguilar and Sánchez-Cuenca, 2009: 435). As Christopher Hewitt has shown, 'more important than the direct effects of terrorism and rioting are the fear and increase in insecurity that they produce' (Hewitt, 1993: 32). In political campaigning, delinquency and terrorist attacks were often highlighted together in the same breath as a threat to personal safety, an effect that arguably bestowed on them an equivalency that only served to engender more fear and paranoia. Again, this was most keenly borne out on the right: the political programme of the Alianza Popular in the 1977 elections sought to counter feelings of insecurity, for instance, through establishing 'peace, order and the unity of the Patria as its main objectives' (Aguilar, 2001: 251). The burgeoning pressure to ameliorate public safety even led the ruling coalition government UCD to declare 'UCD, vota por la seguridad ciudadana, contra la delincuencia y el terrorismo' (vote UCD for public security against crime and terrorism) as part of its 1979 manifesto[3] – despite the fact that the rates of both delinquency and terrorism had only increased during their administration.

The generalised structure of insecurity felt by much of the population brought with it a retreat into the private sphere. Antonio Sánchez-Gijón writes that in neglecting important aspects of social life, the process of democratisation led Spanish people to 're-privatise their lives' (cited in Sánchez-Gijón, 1987: 130). Within these broader social, economic and political contexts, the home became an especially dense node of affect and meaning during the transition. Not only did it serve as a sanctuary or buttress from the perceived collapse of social order outside but it demarcated the boundaries of private property and capital that were kept within, aspects which, as we have seen, assumed a renewed symbolism in the constitution. The home in several *quinqui* films was staged as a site of auditory conflict which dramatised the threshold between outside and inside, sonic disorder and tranquility. As Marie Thompson has recently argued, 'domestic spaces are particularly sensitive to noise given their cultural associations with peace, privacy and intimacy' (2017: 19). She writes that 'within the private home, order is equated with quiet, and the maintenance of domestic order with audible regulation. Noise as a sonic intrusion from the outside world marks a transgression of the domestic order' (2017: 22). She further writes that 'noise, when it breaks the quiet of the orderly home, works to blur liberalism's carefully constructed separation between private and public spheres – the "internal" home and the "external" world' (2017: 22). The peace of the home in the films is frequently broken through the voices of delinquents, alarms, sirens and other urban ambient sounds, and in the case of *Miedo a salir de noche*, terrorist explosions. Far from being a site of stability and comfort, the sonic environment of the home in these films articulated fears of victimisation and insecurity. That these borders were politicised in various opposing ways, I show, bears testament to the fractionalisation of political viewpoints that were debated during the transition, whose diverse and often conflicting ideologies were often articulated through the theme of public order.

Los violadores del amanecer: Erotic cinema and the violation of the home

In its depiction of the deterioration of public order, Iquino's *Los violadores del amanecer* arguably stands out as the most alarmist of *quinqui* films. Through the figure of the delinquent rapist, Iquino's film combines the visual iconography and themes of *cine quinqui* with the aesthetics of erotic cinema. The film was produced during a moment of transformation for the Spanish film industry. As Duncan Wheeler notes, Iquino's film was 'one of the last films to be passed (unanimously) by the censorship board prior to its institutional dissolution' (2019), while also being one of the first Spanish films to capitalise on the financial opportunities of the new 'S' rating. As Daniel Kowalsky shows, the 'S' rating was allocated to products whose theme and content might offend the sensibility of the spectator (2004: 188). Frequently (although not always) attached to erotic films that embraced the kinds of explicit themes that had only recently been taboo in Spanish film, 130 Spanish productions or co-productions received the 'S' rating between the years 1978 and 1982 (Kowalsky, 2004: 188).[4] At almost 70 years of age, Iquino was part of an older generation of directors (along with Rafael Gil and Pedro Lazaga) that had been active since 1940s who now somewhat cynically embraced the new climate of permissiveness, often despite their reactionary political views. After *Los violadores del amanecer*, for instance, Iquino would go on to direct other key 'S'-rated films such as *Emanuelle y Carol/Emanuelle and Carol* (1978) and *¿Podrías con cinco chicas a la vez?/Can You Be with Five Girls at the Same Time?* (1979). The film was produced by IFI (named after his own initials), a Barcelona-based company established by the director/producer himself, specialising in the production of commercially minded genre films. Active for 34 years, the longevity of IFI owed itself to its remarkably swift and efficient turnover of productions, as well as a knack for tailoring its output to the changing tastes and sensibilities of Spanish audiences (Comas, 2003: 19) and Iquino had collaborated with several directors of commercial cinema, such as José Antonio de la Loma (see chapter 1). Iquino had specialised, for instance, in religious films of the 1950s and *paella* westerns in the 1960s, while earlier in the 1970s his filmmaking turned to moralising 'social problem' films with the commercial success of *Aborto criminal/ Criminal Abortion* (1973). After the recent commercial success of de la Loma's *Perros callejeros*, whose production and cast were similarly based in Barcelona, Iquino cannily turned to the theme of delinquency. He had recently produced *¿Y ahora qué, señor fiscal?* (1977), a Mexican co-production that was directed by León Klimovsky. Filmed on location in Barcelona, the film hinged on the social conflict arising from the unlikely relationship between José (Valentín Trujillo), a delinquent from the wrong side of the tracks, and Paloma (Leticia Perdigón) who belongs to a wealthy family. After Paloma falls pregnant, José burgles a house belonging to one of her relatives. Through José's penetration of bourgeois domesticity, the film articulated the anxieties surrounding the violation of private space, fears which would resurface in an even more extreme expression in *Los violadores del amanecer.*

Los violadores drew on some of the same locations as de la Loma's film (namely the *barrio* of La Mina), as well as a cast of actors who also collaborated with José Antonio de la Loma. Bernard Seray (who plays Rafi), Daniel Medrán (Quinto) and César Sánchez (Caña) as well as Linda Ley (María) were actors in the *Perros callejeros* cycle. While these were professional actors who had not been associated with criminality, the promotional material that accompanied the film knowingly drew on the way in which *Perros callejeros* blurred the boundaries between real-life crime and its fictional representation. A newspaper advert for the film mimicked the format of a crime news report, with police-style mugshots of the five actors under the heading 'Han sido detenidos' (Arrested).[5] Underneath the date of the 'news report', which doubles up as the date of the film's release, the text describes the film's narrative in the register of a sensationalist news article: 'una banda de indeseables violadores atacan a indefensas mujeres' (a gang of undesirable rapists attack defenceless women). Yet in its foregrounding of delinquents as a predatory gang, the film diverges considerably from de la Loma, whose depiction of criminality is individualised through the sympathetic character of el Torete. Indeed, the camera frequently frames the delinquents in *Los violadores* together as an indissoluble group, whose unencumbered movement through the city is emphasised through the film's use of the Vistarama widescreen picture ratio. The unrelentingly negative characterisation of the delinquents, whose actions appear to be motivated only by sadistic impulses, was amply observed by critics at the time. In a review for *Vale*, a critic wrote not without irony that viewers of the film will find that the death penalty would be 'poco castigo para estos jóvenes desalmados' (scant punishment for these heartless youngsters), and that after watching the film, they will be scared every time a young person in jeans approaches them to ask the time (cited in Comas, 2003: 301). With the exception of Rafi's character, who has a troubled relationship with his father, the film rarely presents the psychological motivations behind their actions, nor does it explore the structural causes that have led them to criminality. The sociologist Stanley Cohen has recently shown that, over the past five decades, crime has been increasingly portrayed in the media as a pervasive threat to ordinary people. This perceived threat is subsequently exacerbated '[i]f the offenders' background, motivation and context become less salient so they are easier to demonize' (Cohen, 2011: xxx). The withholding of psychologisation and background similarly serves to further vilify the figure of the delinquent in the film, a strategy that could also be located in the conservative press at this time in newspapers such as *ABC* and *El Imparcial*.

The theme of public disorder is emphasised from the outset of the film, whose opening pre-title sequence presents streets of Barcelona as lawless and dangerously beyond the control of the authorities. Filmed on location at night, the scene introduces us to the gang of five delinquents. The sole female member of the group, the heavily pregnant Lagarta (played by Alicia Orozco, an actress who was pregnant in real life) seduces a slow-witted policeman, while the others force themselves on him and snatch away his gun. They proceed to carjack a stationary vehicle at gunpoint, violently interrupting the couple who are kissing inside. As opening titles appear over a black screen, we hear the cries of pain of one of the rape victims in a voiceover, repeatedly asking for help, followed by the sounds of gunfire and the ignition of a car engine. While the disembodied voice here foreshadows the sequence of violent rapes the delinquents will carry out during the film, it also suggests that the narrative will be focalised through the experience of the rape victim – despite the fact that, as we will see, the editing and camerawork will ensure that the focus will be channelled instead through the sadistic pleasures of male rapists. The episodic narrative that follows hinges on a series of protracted rape scenes, each more gruesome and outlandish than the last, calculatedly designed to display the vulnerable naked female body in an increasing variety of scenarios. Despite Iquino's surface condemnation of rape, the film's prurient fascination with the tortured female body – whose depiction, we have seen, was facilitated through the film's 'S' classification and the liberalisation of censorship – also serves as a vehicle to criticise the deterioration of public order and the apparent weakness of the post-Franco state. Iquino therefore draws on the aesthetics of *destape* to articulate an agenda that is reactionary and populist, reflecting a nostalgic political worldview that was most clearly aligned with the politics of the right at the time. Made at a time when, according to Manuel Palacio, 'vectores "liberales europeos"' (liberal and European vectors) had become hegemonic, Iquino's filmmaking can also be seen as part of a lingering tendency – embodied, as Palacio notes, by the directors Rafael Gil and Mariano Ozores – that continued to be wedded ideologically to the symbolic values of the regime, and whose films achieved a certain degree of box-office success into the early 1980s (Palacio, 2011: 9).

While rape is presented in the film as an urgent issue that the state needs to address – as most clearly played out in the depiction of a mass demonstration held after the death of the underage rape victim Elisa (Eva Lyberten), demanding more severe legal action against rapists – its conflation with the theme of juvenile delinquency appears to be little more than opportunistic. Indeed, in the same year as the film, Josep M. Huertas et al. demonstrated that juvenile delinquents were not the most frequent offenders of rape in Spain (1978: 63), and that most rapes were carried out by men who already knew the victims (1978: 65). That the rape victims in the film are school children also arguably reflected broader underlying social anxieties around schools in the 1970s. Secondary education in Spain was not made compulsory for all children until the Ley General de Educación (The

Education Act) of 1970, which was an attempt to modernise the structure of schools.[6] The bill led to the makeup of schools becoming progressively mixed as the decade wore on, as middle-class children in urban schools found themselves in classrooms alongside the children of illiterate rural-to-urban migrants. These anxieties find their expression in the film's *mise-en-scène,* where the borders of the home and the school are presented as porous and easily penetrated – even during the hours of daylight. As the film's title suggests, the delinquents frequently attack their victims at dawn in plain sight, leading to their nickname in the press as 'Los violadores del amanecer'. They are frequently depicted as loitering on the threshold between inside and outside, waiting for their victims as they leave or enter buildings. The first rape scene begins with María (played by Linda Ley) getting ready for school in her bedroom, as the gang lie in wait for her outside on a piece of disused wasteland. As she leaves her building, the gang hide behind a car, spying on her through the vehicle's windows, while the camera voyeuristically lingers on her movement from behind the branches of a tree. She is taken to Rafi's grandfather's large country house, which is replete with a grandfather clock and other heavy mahogany furniture. Before preparing to rip off María's clothes, Rafi puts on a radio cassette on the portable stereo player, playing the funk-inflected music that was initially played non-diegetically in the first sequence that was filmed at night on location on a shady street. In the repurposing of the opening music which is now used as the diegetic accompaniment to her rape, the soundtrack brings the threat of nocturnal urban space inside the sunlit house, thereby threatening the sanctity of domestic space. The instrumentation of funk guitars and Hammond organs, while broadly typical of the orchestral scores of American urban crime and action films, also here resembles the *caño roto* style of rock music that became popular during the mid 1970s in Spain. Named after the eponymous band from the crime-ridden *barrio* of Caño Roto (see chapter 5) in Madrid, the repeated use of the music throughout the film – in both its diegetic and non-diegetic source – serves as a crude *leitmotif* of their marauding deviance. Their penetration of the otherwise peaceful bourgeois home, an invasion which is further enacted through sound, parallels the repeated penetration of the female body throughout the film.

Dana (Mireia Ros) is similarly kidnapped in the morning on the steps to her private Catholic school. In another scene, the delinquents

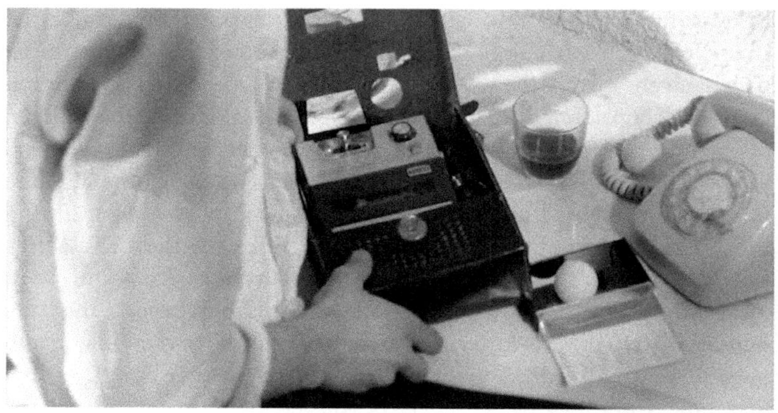

2.1 Rafi (Bernard Seray) puts on music before raping María in *Los violadores del amanecer* (Ignacio F. Iquino, 1978).

2.2 Rafi (Bernard Seray) and his delinquent friends rape María (Linda Ley) in *Los violadores del amanecer* (Ignacio F. Iquino, 1978).

rob unsuspecting hotel guests by pretending to be police officers and demanding they open the door. One guest mutters under her breath: 'Con los atracadores sueltos y encima la policía viene aquí' (with thieves on the loose and to top it all police come here). Her comment here reflects the lack of public confidence in policing and its ability to tackle the issue of public disorder at a time when the structure of the Spanish police force was itself in flux, so that it could be aligned to the constitutional democracy. No longer officially recognised as 'Fuerzas de Orden Público', the police are either conspicuous by their absence in the film, or else hamstrung by their inability to punish the delinquents because of their status as minors. Confronting Comisario Vives (Joan Borrás) after her rape, Dana accuses the police of being too soft on delinquents, saying that they will be sent to a reformatory only to be released soon afterwards, when they will only attack again. Picking up a newspaper, she contrasts Spain's criminal justice system with that of France, showing the headline of the recent execution by guillotine of a man who raped three women at the behest of the law-and-order French president Valéry Giscard d'Estaing.[7] When Vives later arrests the delinquents, who at this point are living together in a cramped bedroom, Lagarta responds mockingly: 'somos menores' (we are minors). Caña mocks the policeman, telling him that he was sent to a reformatory once but that he escaped – here a clear reference to the portrayal of underage delinquents in *Perros callejeros*. The *mise-en-scène* of the bedroom, whose walls are covered entirely with dozens of pages that have been ripped from porn magazines, establishes a causal link between Spain's new-found civil liberties and its corrupting influence on young delinquents. At the same time, however, the tatty images of female nude models, crudely assembled together to form a collage-like montage, provide a materialised extension of the aesthetic of 'S'-classification film. The walls therefore present the contradiction at the heart of Iquino's erotic films, whose simultaneous fascination and repudiation of the new permissiveness in Spain also provided a spectacular vehicle for critiquing what many on the right saw as a deterioration of law and order in the country.

La patria de 'el Rata': Democracy and the failure of the state

Produced two years after *Los violadores del amanecer*, *La patria de 'el Rata'* also reflected public sensations of fear and panic around law and order. While Francisco Lara Polop's film is less reactionary than Iquino's, *La patria de 'el Rata'* nevertheless critiques the weakness of the Unión de Centro Democrático (UCD) in their inability to stem terrorist and delinquent violence. The film closely follows José Moya Merino (also known as 'el Rata' [the rat]), who is played by Danilo Mattei, a petty delinquent who gets mixed up with the FRAP (Frente

Revolucionario Antifascista y Patriota [Revolutionary Antifascist Patriotic Front]), the revolutionary organisation deemed by the Franco regime to be a terrorist group. Imprisoned for his alleged involvement in a terrorist attack against two police officers, Moya is released along with several other political prisoners following the passing of the amnesty law of 1977. As the film suggests, Spain's political classes are, however, more concerned with the greater project of national reconciliation than addressing the material problems of youth unemployment and public insecurity. On its release, Lara Polop was keen to stress that his ambivalence about the newly installed democratic system should not be confused with nostalgia for the regime. 'Yo creo en la democracia, en la libertad de expressión, pero también en el orden,' he said, adding that however 'eso no se da en esta especie de democracia parlamentaria que estamos padeciendo' (García, F. 1981: 38).[8] While he claims that his political stance is 'antipartidista' (non-partisan), his assertion was arguably disingenuous in retrospect, given that all references to terrorism in the film are revolutionary in nature (mostly FRAP but also GRAPO [Grupos de Resistencia Antifascista Primero de Octubre] in a couple of scenes) while fascist violence is conspicuous by its absence – despite the fact that, as we have seen, Spain was afflicted by both far-left and far-right violence to an equal degree during this period.

Francisco Lara Polop was primarily a commercially minded director with an eclectic and often irregular output, something that was clearly borne out in *La patria de 'el Rata'*, which drew on a number of different influences. Like Iquino, Polop had recently specialised in erotic cinema, with his recent films *Climax* (1977) and *Historia de S* (1977) designated with the 'S' classification. In its sustained critique of Spain's fragmented political landscape, however, *La patria de 'el Rata'* was a rather more ambitious and serious offering, particularly when taking into account his collaboration with the established auteur Manuel Summers, who wrote the script, and the production company Kalender Films, both of which brought 'quality' credentials to the film. Polop and Summers had studied together at Spain's official film school during the regime, Instituto de Investigaciones y Experiencias Cinematográficas (renamed Escuela Oficial de Cinematografía in 1962), with Summers going on to direct *Del rosa al amarillo/From Pink to Yellow* (1963) and *La niña de luto/The Girl in Mourning* (1964), two key films of the short-lived art cinema movement the Nuevo Cine Español.

In the 1970s, Manuel Summers collaborated regularly with Kalender Films, which produced *Adiós, cigüeña, adiós/Goodbye, Stork, Goodbye* (1972, directed by Summers) and, more significantly, *La patria de 'el Rata'*.[9] Established by Antonio Cuevas, Kalender films was strongly associated with the *tercera vía* (third way) trend of filmmaking (Pavlović et al., 2009: 112) which took hold in Spanish film in the early 1970s. According to Casmiro Torreiro, *tercera vía* cinema distanced itself from both 'coarse commercial cinema and more voluntarily auteurist and metaphorical cinema' (cited in Faulkner, 2013: 121). While the film's explicit engagement with party politics and social issues suggested a similar mode of address to that of the *tercera vía*, it also drew on several of the formal elements of *cine quinqui* and *cine de destape*, in particular through its inclusion of exciting car chases and graphic scenes of sex and violence. Indeed, Lara Polop's overall conception of the film was motivated by a commercial imperative where he defined his filmmaking in an interview against 'cine elitista que últimamente se viene rodando en España' (elitist cinema that has been directed recently in Spain) claiming that it was one of the first films directed in Spain to have an international appeal (García, F. 1981: 38). While Summers was similarly non-committal about his politics, he would become a regular writer and cartoonist for the arch-conservative newspaper *ABC*, where he would become, according to Manuel Palacio, part of the publication's 'violenta campaña' (violent campaign) waged against the socialist government (Palacio, 2011: 25) which would be voted in in 1982. After his collaboration on *La patria de 'el Rata'*, Manuel Summers would also return to the theme of delinquency as the writer of the nihilistically violent film *Coto de caza/Hunting Ground* (Jorge Grau, 1983), also produced by Kalender, a film which depicted delinquents as dangerous predators.

If the film depicted the contemporary sense of social discord, these public anxieties also resonated across both production and exhibition of the film. Panic broke out amongst residents of the neighbourhood where they filmed a hostage scene which sees the confrontation between a number of policemen and the delinquent. Passers-by were reportedly unsure as to whether the hostage scene was happening for real, despite the presence of numerous film lights and cameras. The actor José Luis Martín Álvarez blamed the confusion on the circulation of the news of the arrest of the real-life delinquent actor José Antonio Valdelomar in *Deprisa, deprisa,* which had taken place recently in the nearby district of Villaverde (García, F. 1981: 38). On the film's release, Lara Polop said that *La patria de 'el Rata'* was his 'película más conflictiva' (most conflictive film) to date, and the immediate reception of the film was hugely divisive. The screenings of the film across the country initially polarised audiences, with Lara Polop in an interview calling attention to the noise within the cinema auditorium. He recalled that some in the audience were clapping while others were booing and whistling (García, F. 1981: 38).

The film's distinctive title sequence similarly presents Madrid as a city gripped by the fear of crime, where apprehension and panic are further conveyed through the soundtrack. A bank robbery is depicted *in media res* through a series of photographs, revealing in close-up the terrified faces and bodies of customers frozen in motion with their hands in the air. The intertitle 'Madrid, un sábado por la mañana' (Madrid, one Saturday morning) provides a tellingly vague temporal frame for the robbery, as if to suggest that violent crime has become a habitual occurrence in the city, fear an integral part of the texture of everyday life. Further images partially reveal the parts of the robbers' faces and guns, including those of the protagonist Moya, though their identities are initially hidden by their balaclavas. The soundtrack draws attention to itself through the use of complete silence during these images, whose effect serves to convey the muteness of the victims who are speechless with fear. The silence is broken by the high-pitched sound of a whistle gradually building in volume and intensity; the sound stops abruptly at the end of the title sequence, with the static photographs suddenly giving way to the moving image of the film. The use of sound here generates a particularly immersive effect, where the play between silence and the noise of a tinnitus-like whistle suggests the auditory point of view of the victims, whose hearing has been impaired by the noise of gunfire. As anthropologist Stefan Helmreich has written, tinnitus is a 'moment when hearing and listening break down' (2007: 629). If the soundtrack here alerts us to the act of listening – or rather, not listening – it also foreshadows the confrontations that Moya will encounter with a series of political representatives in the film, who each in turn fail to listen to his concerns. The invasion of the bank, moreover, a key location in *cine quinqui*, foregrounds the heightened significance of private property and capital during these years.

That Moya is first introduced to the viewer in a static photographic image, wearing a balaclava and carrying a gun, freezes and fixes his

2.3 A bank robbery in *La patria de 'el Rata'* (Francisco Lara Polop, 1981).

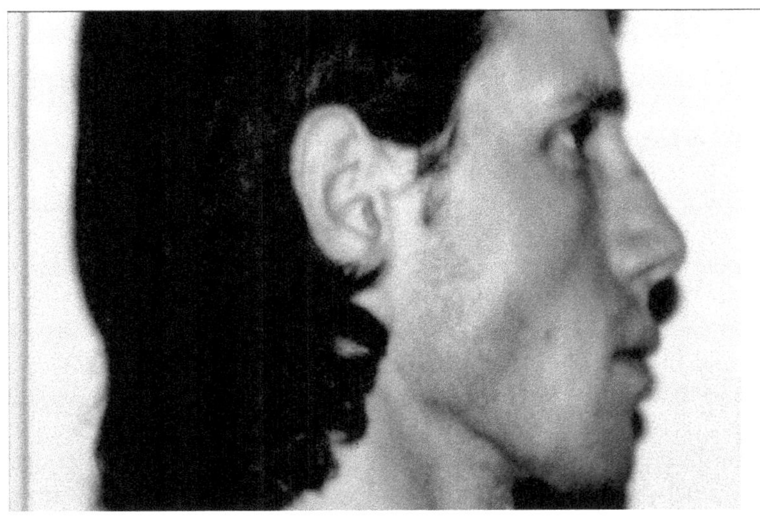

2.4 A police mugshot of the delinquent José Moya Merino 'el Rata' (Danilo Mattei) in *La patria de 'el Rata'* (Francisco Lara Polop, 1981).

identity in place as a criminal. After leaving the bank, an extended chase scene ensues in which he and his two accomplices are pursued by the police. After a violent shoot-out in which his accomplice is killed, Moya shoots two police officers in self-defence with a submachine gun before violently commandeering a man's car and driving haphazardly to the periphery of the city. He abandons the vehicle in Quinta de la Paloma (a marginal *barrio* which, straddling the side of the M-30 ring road, was redeveloped soon after the film's production), before breaking into the first house he can find. To his surprise, he encounters a young girl (played by child actress Elena Rivera) by herself in the house and reluctantly holds her hostage. As the police surround the house, an officer addresses Moya by his alias 'Rata' through his loudspeaker: 'Entrégate Rata ... Nadie te ayudará! Siempre has sido un vulgar chorizo' (Hand yourself in, Rata! No one will help you! You've always been a common thief). A close-up of the actor's face dissolves into a series of black-and-white mugshots of his face; the images are accompanied by an expositionary voiceover, describing Moya's criminal career to date from petty theft at the age of nine to his later involvement with FRAP. A second dissolve then signals a flashback three years earlier to winter 1977, when Moya is being released from Carabanchel following the Ley de Amnistía. The voiceover asks in a demagogic tone: '¿Acabará así el terrorismo? ¿Serán capaces la amnistía y la democracia de terminar con esta amenaza?' (Will terrorism now end? Will amnesty and democracy be able to end this threat?).

The flashback structure serves to underline the fatalism of Moya's situation, where despite his several attempts at social integration he can never escape his identity as the criminal depicted in the photographs. The film therefore situates Moya within a deterministic world whereby any attempt at exercising free will will be impeded by forces beyond his control. Despite protesting that his real name is Moya, figures of authority repeatedly continue to address him by his criminal alias 'Rata'. The editing hereafter cuts between two planes of action – the home as a site of the hostage and subsequent penetration of domestic space on the one hand, and the amnesty and release from prison on the other – which intersect by the end of the film. As implied by the English translation of the title *Exit: Dead End*, the narrative structure thus suggests that far from offering freedom, democratic reform has only compounded the plight of petty delinquents such as Moya, whose physical incarceration in prison runs parallel to their broader structural incarceration within a cycle of unemployment and violence.

Moya's recourse to crime is most explicitly blamed on the political figures in the film. Moya seeks help from his former inmate Richi from FRAP, who has similarly been released. Meeting in the iconic Café Comercial (whose atmosphere is described contemptuously in the script as 'tiene el inconfundible aspecto de reunión de izquierda snob' [having an unmistakable look of a snobbish left-wing meeting]), Richi tells Moya that the only job he can offer is to place him within a clandestine cell, telling him that they should all fight together for a shared ideal and for freedom. Moya responds that he has no interest in politics, and that he would be better paid committing robberies. In two further unlikely scenes, he visits representatives from the Partido Comunista de España (against whom the FRAP at this time were rebelling, since the organisation believed that its leader, Santiago Carrillo, had sold out and made too many concessions during the Moncloa Pacts) and the PSOE, both of whom dismiss him without offering help. These scenes point to the disjuncture between 'real country' and 'political country', as mentioned by Sánchez-Gijón (1987: 130), that was perceived by many during the transition. Ignored by political elites of all stripes, Moya chooses self-preservation over collective action and rejects the various ideologies for a misplaced form of radical individualism.

The political party for which the film reserves its most explicit criticism, however, is the UCD. As the hostage scene continues into the night, a television crew arrive at the scene in eager anticipation of the arrival of José Luis Salgado (played by José Luis Martín Álvarez), a fictional minister for the UCD. As he alights from his car, the director tells a cameraman to film the politician in close-up. One neighbour asks why a politician like him would turn up at a hostage scene, to which his friend responds cynically: 'joder, votos' (votes, damn it). Salgado is positioned centre-frame in a wide-angle long shot standing in front of the police and the onlookers as he attempts to establish dialogue with Moya. Wrongly believing that Moya is still associated with the FRAP, he beseeches Moya to leave behind his revolutionary tendencies so that he may, in his words, 'contribuya a construir ese sólido edificio que todos queremos para nuestro pueblo' (contribute towards the construction of this solid building that we all want for our people). Speaking in a grandiloquent tone, his speech is clearly made for the benefit of the camera and journalists that stand on the sidelines, as well as the audience of onlookers behind, whose sizeable presence is registered through a tracking shot. The portrayal of the politician, whose measured and glib speech contrasts with the spontaneous dialogue of Moya, is a possible satire of the media savviness for which the UCD, under the auspices of its leader Adolfo Suárez, had become known. Prior to entering Franco's government, Suárez was Director General of Radiotelevisión Española (the Spanish Radio and Television Corporation) and was subsequently known as a consummate media operator. That the actor José Luis Martin Álvarez was also more widely known for his work as a radio presenter at the time is thus perhaps significant, with the insincerity of his performance further compounded by the fact that his voice was dubbed in postproduction by another actor (García, F. 1981: 38). The general elections of 1979, which saw a dramatic drop in turnout and waning enthusiasm for the UCD, marked the beginning of the collapse of the political party. E. Ramón Arango argues that the electorate were resentful of what they perceived to be UCD's condescension, writing that 'the governing elites of the UCD, although democratically elected, continued to treat the electorate disdainfully, in a manner reminiscent of that embraced by the Francoist elites, seemingly ignoring their voices' (1995: 134). Moya replies angrily through the window of the house that every political party that is helping to construct the great building of democracy ignored him when he sought help, shouting that 'la derecha, la izquierda, el centro y los de atrás … sois unos chorizos' (the right, the left, the centre and those from behind … you're a load of thieves).

If consensus and national unification have been achieved in the name of the 'patria' (homeland), which is evoked in the film's title, it has come at the price of growing public insecurity that has been persistently ignored by what Polop considers to be the country's elites. The UCD's words do little to assuage Moya, who communicates with the politician and the police through the bars of the window of the house that he just broke into. As in *Los violadores del amanecer*, the presence of the delinquent destabilises the borders between public and private space, so that the space of domesticity becomes a site of anxiety and violation. This is heightened by the presence of Elena, whom Moya has taken hostage, who is separated from her mother throughout the film. Standing alongside the policemen outside, the tearful mother informs Moya that Elena has chronic diabetes, and

2.5 The hostage scene featuring 'el Rata' (Danilo Mattei) in *La patria de 'el Rata'* (Francisco Lara Polop, 1981).

2.6 The politician José Luis Salgado (played by José Luis Martín Álvarez) responds to 'el Rata' in the hostage scene in *La patria de 'el Rata'* (Francisco Lara Polop, 1981).

must therefore receive regular injections of insulin. Like the doors and walls of the house, the skin marks another intimate border, one that is emphasised through the subsequent extreme close-up shot of the needle penetrating Elena's skin, as Moya tenderly administers her injection. The presence of the sick girl mainly serves as a crude melodramatic device in the film, whose vulnerability brings out a hitherto unseen caring and tender side to Moya. Through having to care for Elena, Moya is offered a chance of redemption in the film. After seeing a sensationalist news report of Moya's robbery and escape from the police on the television, the girl turns to tell him 'no eres malo' (you're not bad), a comment that she repeats several times in the film. Within the confines of the house, both Elena and the audience are afforded a privileged glimpse into the 'real' Moya, a delinquent who has been misunderstood and unheard by the institutions of the politicians, the police and the media that lie in wait for him outside.

Moya escapes from the house early the following morning by carrying Elena into a car at gunpoint. Travelling north of Madrid into the heart of Castile, the depiction of rural landscape provides a striking contrast to the oppressive *mise-en-scène* of the city that has otherwise dominated the film until this point. The frequently large depth of field here presents the countryside as a liberating space, whose vibrant palette of blue and deep greens harmonises with the colour of his green jacket. As the car speeds down a country road, the camera lingers on a pastoral scene of a herd of cows, the gentle sounds of their bells a contrast to the strident alarms, sirens and loudspeakers of the city. Moya's escape is derailed, though, when he realises that he has forgotten to bring Elena's insulin. Leaving her on the roadside, he drives into a village pharmacist where he demands insulin at gunpoint before frantically returning to Elena's side to administer an injection for one last time. In an echo of the final iconic scene of *Bonnie and Clyde* (Arthur Penn, 1967), a slow-motion sequence captures Moya being repeatedly shot by police who have been lying in wait for him behind trees. The use of slow motion here presents the choreography of his death in a spectacular fashion, his body held in suspension as it is riddled repeatedly with bullets. As Moya collapses into Elena's tiny arms, the camera pulls back to provide a valedictory long shot of their embrace, his body stretched out on Elena's lap like Jesus on the Virgin Mary's in the *Pietà*. The final image of Moya's body places the delinquent as the unlikely moral centre of the film, one whose sacrificial redemption contrasts with the depictions of the cynical politicians and the uncaring state.

Miedo a salir de noche: Satirising the fear of crime

Released a few months before *La patria de 'el Rata'*, Eloy de la Iglesia's comedy *Miedo a salir de noche* emphasised a markedly different take on the theme of public order. The film centres on Paco (played by de la Iglesia regular José Sacristán), a cautious and mild-mannered banker whose family and colleagues become increasingly gripped by a fear of crime. The various terrorist attacks which took place in 1979 serve as a backdrop to the narrative action, an effect that further amplifies the panic of the characters and drives their need to fortify their apartment and belongings with security devices. Through the use of satire and comic exaggeration, de la Iglesia reveals the ways in which the pervasive fear of crime and urban space was primarily manufactured by conservative politicians and the sensationalist media, as well as by the alarmist films directed by the likes of Iquino and Lara Polop. Filmed entirely on location in Madrid over a period of six weeks (Gracia, 1979: 13), the premiere of the film sought to present a corrective to recent media and cinematic depictions of the city as lawless and dangerous. Indeed, Enrique Tierno Galván, who had recently been appointed socialist Mayor of Madrid, attended the well-publicised premiere of the film, along with several other delegates of the municipal government. After the screening, a special event was held in homage to the municipal workers who worked nightshifts in the city, where they handed out commemorative plaques (Gracia, 1980a).

The comedic mode of *Miedo a salir de noche* signalled a change in direction in Eloy de la Iglesia's more controversial filmmaking. Unlike his previous films, *El diputado* (1979) and *El Sacerdote/The Priest* (1979), which although they were not conceived as erotic films were nevertheless unintentional recipients of the 'S' classification, *Miedo a salir de noche* is much lighter in tone and has a more episodic shape, one that is driven by a loose series of comic scenarios rather than clearly defined linear plot. De la Iglesia has commented that he was influenced by the *sainete* (Aguilar, 1996: 145), a Spanish tradition of comedy whose cinematic expression was most famously found in the films of Luis García Berlanga, Marco Ferreri and José María Forqué in the 1950s and 1960s. As in the *sainete*, characterisation in the film is primarily articulated through external means – accentuated gesturality, iconographic costumes and settings, stereotypical 'types' of characters – rather than by means of inner psychology. The most recognisable 'types' in the film are illustrated in particular by the more elderly characters, Don Cosme (played by Antonio Ferrandis), who plays a former Republican prisoner who exudes optimism about Spain's democratic future, and Paco's mother, Doña Claudia (Mari Carmen Prendes), a devoted Catholic who is deeply nostalgic for the Franco regime. The Manichean contrast between 'las dos Españas' (the two Spains) is mediated through the protagonist Paco. His pragmatic politics and profession as a bank manager arguably align him with the centre-right and business-friendly UCD. Sacristán's somewhat stiff performance as Paco tends to be reactive rather than active, a passive witness to a number of events over which he seemingly has no control – a dynamic that further suggests a parallel with the position of the minority government, whose leadership under Suárez at this time was viewed as increasingly ineffectual and rudderless.

In common with the *sainete*, the film centres on the everyday locations of home and work (and the neighbourhood association) and its frequent use of long shots serve to frame large ensembles of actors within groups, a type of framing that Steven Marsh has shown was typical to what he calls the 'popular' (Marsh 2003) filmmaking of Berlanga. The familiarity of these locations, however, is rendered unfamiliar by a series of disruptive and often surreal fantasy sequences and improbable plot twists. These departures from reality are combined with scenes that are dominated by real-life news footage of terrorist attacks that are seen on the television of Paco's house. In the film's tension between the absurd and the real, the uneasy combination of registers work together to erect a critical distance from the news footage of civil disorder. The different style of the film also owes itself to the collaboration with Roberto Bodegas, who co-wrote the script with de la Iglesia. Indeed, the film at first appears to have more in common with Bodegas's earlier *Españolas en París/Spaniards in Paris* (1971) and *Los nuevos españoles/The New Spaniards* (1974) – films that, according to Sally Faulkner, 'gently question contemporary concerns' through the 'unchallenging, and light-hearted manners' of melodrama and comedy respectively (2013: 122) – than de la Iglesia's usual filmmaking. Like the directors José Luis Garci and Antonio Drove, and producer José Luis Dibildos, Roberto Bodegas was associated with the *tercera vía* (third way). As Faulkner has convincingly shown, the *tercera vía* of this period forms part of a broader 'middlebrow' trend of Spanish film which appealed to Spain's increasingly populous urban middle classes (Faulkner, 2013: 121). José Sacristán starred in several of the films associated with the *tercera vía*, including *Los nuevos españoles* and *Asignatura pendiente/Unfinished Business* (José Luis Garci, 1977), roles that led to his star persona as the everyman of the Spanish transition. Like *Asignatura pendiente*, much of the narrative in *Miedo* similarly hinges on the social tensions and unmaterialised hopes of adapting to life under democracy.

The film's composer's Carmelo Bernaola was similarly associated with the films of the *tercera vía*, and had provided the orchestral scores for *Españolas en París* and *Los nuevos españoles.* The opening credits begin with a song whose lyrics repeat the phrase 'que viene el lobo, que viene que viene' (the wolf is coming, he's coming), an allusion to the predatory archetype of the Big Bad Wolf frequently found in fairytales. The song then leads into the light-hearted and jaunty type of melody that was characteristic of Bernaola's scores, orchestrated with strings and woodwind. The upbeat music establishes a tone that appears to be at odds with the content of the images. In the film's opening sequence, for instance, the music accompanies a series of animated black-and-white photographs of newspaper reports that flash onto the screen, either moving over or dissolving into blood-red background. The first headline, 'Cientos de personas abandonaron la ciudad huyendo el caos y la inseguridad' (hundreds of people abandoned the city fleeing chaos and insecurity), immediately establishes the urban setting of the film, which is swiftly followed by a number of other sensationalist news stories, such as 'Atracadas' (Mugged), 'Cunde El Pánico' (Panic Spreads) and 'Confesó su crimen' (He Confessed to the Crime), appearing in extreme close-up, alongside advertisements for security doors. The credit sequence cuts abruptly to the opening scene of the film, which begins with a disorientating close-up of a television screen. A news report shows images of the ETA attack which took place on 25 May 1979 in Madrid, where the army chief of personnel and two high-ranking officers were assassinated, followed by a long shot of a middle-class family sitting around the television set. As both the establishing shot and the focal point of the scene, the television dominates the *mise-en-scène* of the apartment, framing the experience of domestic space. After hearing reports of the increasing wave of terrorism and crime, the protagonist Paco (José Sacristán) gets up to turn the television off. The explicit centrality of news media at the beginning of the film here recalls a 1983 interview with Eloy de la Iglesia which has been observed by Paul Julian Smith, where the director called for a cinema that would be 'like a newspaper' (cited in Smith, 1998: 217). Smith subsequently writes that the model of the newspaper in his films 'suggests actuality, the immediate irruption of the real into the text' (1998: 217). While the tightly woven interplay between film, newspaper and television news – a characteristic shared by other *quinqui* films in this book – gives urgent expression to the contemporary issues of Spain that year, it also more specifically alerts us to the causal link between the fear of crime and its frequently distorted representation in the media. It is significant, here, that two very different forms of criminal violence – the terrorist acts reported on the television, and several newspaper articles on felony and other petty crimes in the newspapers – are both established simultaneously as the causes of the perceived breakdown of public order in the city. This illustrates that, although unrelated, Spanish people conflated the two types of crime as both being symptoms of the broader lack of security at the time.

2.7 Opening credits of *Miedo a salir de noche* (Eloy de la Iglesia, 1980) depict the growing civil insecurity in Spanish cities.

His mother, Doña Claudia (Mari Carmen Prendes) picks up a copy of *El Imparcial*, reading out headlines such as 'Miedo en Madrid' (Fear in Madrid) and 'Niña violada en el Barrio del Pilar' (Girl raped in the *barrio* of Pilar) in a dramatic fashion. López Pintor notes that the newspaper *El Imparcial*, which had begun publishing just one year before the production of the film in 1978, became the 'standard bearer of *golpismo*', writing that 'rarely did it fail to emphasise violence by terrorists, by the police or by criminals in order to show how poorly the country functioned under democracy' (1985: 267). Indeed, the mother says 'Con El General no pasaban esas cosas' (These things didn't happen with the General) – referring, as the joke transpires, to the earlier dictatorship of General Primo de Rivera rather than that of Franco – claiming that in those days you could walk in the Retiro park without the fear of being raped. Although presented in typically broad strokes, Doña Claudia's nostalgia for authoritarianism, emphasised through her choice of newspaper, points to how much of the older population blamed the perceived increase in violence on democratic reforms.

Her anxiety surrounding rape is also shared by Paco's younger colleague Loli, with whom Paco has an affair. Loli confides to Paco that she was recently raped by a taxi driver who resembled an American actor. As she does so, her words accompany a comic flashback in which Sacristán is reimagined as the driver, sporting a virile-looking moustache, as he attempts to rape her. In reducing the experience of sexual violence to erotic male fantasy and comic titillation, the scene parodies the function of the kinds of rape scenes found in *Los violadores del amanecer* and other 'S'-rated films of the period. She later confesses to Pablo in her bathroom to having fabricated the story of the rape in its entirety. The sequence cuts to a brief flashback of what really happened, filmed at night with noirish high-contrast lighting, which shows her taxi breaking down on a deserted road. The 'real' taxi driver, here depicted as a cheerfully harmless man, offers to share a cigarette with Loli as he fixes the engine. As she makes her confession, Loli is filmed in a medium shot looking into the bathroom mirror, so that the scene depicts both the actress and her reflection. As well as deflecting the gaze and emphasising Loli's duplicity, the centrality of the mirror to the *mise-en-scène* also brings to mind Jeff Ferrell's writing on the deeply woven interplay between crime and media images of criminality in which 'every facet of offending is reflected in a vast hall

2.8 Paco (José Sacristán) is depicted as Loli's rapist in a comic flashback in *Miedo a salir de noche* (Eloy de la Iglesia, 1980).

of mirrors' (cited in Hayward and Young, 2004: 259). When Paco asks Loli why she lied, she ruefully likens her fabricated story to being in a film in which she was the protagonist, intimating that 'es que nunca he sido protagonista de nada' (I've never been the protagonist of anything). Loli's fantastical story demonstrates how in the interplay between crime and its endless mediations, 'the line between the real and the virtual is profoundly and irrevocably blurred' (Hayward and Young, 2004: 259).

The recent constitution of 1978 had confirmed women's legal re-entry into the public sphere in Spain, whose article 32 recognised equal rights for women, and whose article 34 enshrined in law the right for both sexes to work. That the rape story should revolve around Loli in this immediate context is therefore arguably significant. As the sole female character in the film associated with the sphere of work and other public places, Loli is presented as a newly democratic female citizen, one whose independent movement is placed in contrast with the immobility of Claudia and Begoña. Her particular association

2.9 Loli (Tina Sáinz) as a rape victim in a comic flashback in *Miedo a salir de noche* (Eloy de la Iglesia, 1980).

with rape within the narrative therefore appears to articulate broader underlying anxieties in response to sudden social change. The increased public fear of rape – and in particular rape taking place in public spaces – found its expression in a spike in sales of illegal anti-rape sprays during these years. A *Diario 16* article from April 1980, for instance, reported that 13,000 anti-rape sprays had recently been confiscated (cited in Martínez Reguera, 1982: 83). A pharmacist convinces Doña Claudia to buy one of the sprays through recounting a story about young girls at a convent school who were raped in broad daylight. Claudia gives the bottle to her granddaughter, who after being approached innocently by a group of young boys in the playground, sprays it in their faces, resulting in them collapsing to the ground. In the following scene, a policeman reprimands a distraught-looking Claudia, who is accompanied by Paco and the granddaughter. The policeman reminds them that the sale of the sprays is illegal, before softening his stance to add wistfully that 'tantas cosas eran ilegales hasta hace poco' (so many things were illegal until recently).

Paco asserts himself, stating to the commissioner that as the head of the household he assumes full responsibility. Despite the fact that women had achieved legal equality with men, the film reveals the extent to which their cultural and social recognition as equal citizens lagged far behind.

Soundscapes of fear

The auditory presence of sirens – heard frequently from within the domestic setting of the home – serves as an all too constant reminder of the crime on the streets of the city below. In the opening sequence, for instance, the oscillating signals of the sirens compete with the sound of the dialogue, creating disharmony within the scene. Along with the other off-screen sounds that often punctuate the narrative, namely gunshots and alarms, the sirens are here an example of what Michel Chion refers to as 'acousmatic sound', a sound whose source is not visualised or immediately apparent (1994: 71–73). The unclear location of the sound, whose spatial coordinates are heard as constantly shifting, creates a particularly acousmatic effect during the film. Writing on Chion's definition of 'acousmatic sound', K. J Donnelly argues that 'there is an essential ambiguity to such sounds … In psychological terms, such sounds are perceived as a potential threat in that they hang in uncertainty for the perceiver' (Donnelly, 2016: 76). Encroaching on the borders of the walls and windows of the apartment, the diegetic source of the siren penetrates the soundscape of the home, unsettling the relationship of tranquil privacy that is usually associated with the domestic sphere. The siren therefore sets up both a sonic and spatial division between inside and outside – a theme that will be employed to comic effect during the film. As the film shows, the everyday rhythms of middle-class Madrid are constantly disrupted and reorganised through the sonic persistence of the sirens, an effect which further terrifies and stymies the movement of its characters. As the sirens sound, Begoña (Claudia Gravy) asks Paco how he can dare to leave the house after hearing the news headlines, while Doña Claudia becomes so frightened that she refuses to leave the apartment during much of the whole film. As the narrative progresses, Paco observes a terrible smell emanating from within his mother's bedroom. While she insists that the smell comes from the street below, Paco finally forces her to open her wardrobe, where it is revealed she has been storing food supplies that have become rotten. As he angrily confronts his mother, the tight framing of the grandmother's body in this scene emphasises her entrapment, as she explains that he couldn't begin to imagine the hunger that they endured during the Civil War, comparing their present situation with that of 1936. The grandmother's anxieties surrounding a return to the conflicts of the past were shared by many in the Alianza Popular and on the right, whose misgivings about the transition to democracy became compounded after the legalisation of the Communist Party in 1977.[10] With its heavy mahogany furniture, religious ornaments and candles, the *mise-en-scène* of the grandmother's bedroom provides a repository of the past, a site of contamination presented ironically as far more oppressive than the space of the city.

The division between public and private becomes reinforced through the increasing presence of home security and surveillance during the film. In response to the increasing sense of public disorder, the neighbourhood association enlists a company to replace all of the doors with strong security doors. In a clear satirisation of the opportunism of the booming home security industry during these years, a smooth-talking young salesman, dressed in a flashy blue suit and fashionable dark glasses, shows Begoña the function of a security lock on one of these doors, claiming that it is as strong as a 'caja fuerte' (safe). Yet their frantic attempts to keep criminality at bay only serve to isolate them further. The locks on the reinforced door are so strong that Paco's family finds themselves incarcerated in their own home. Paco comes home from work only to encounter firemen rescuing Begoña and his daughter after climbing up several storeys to their window. The camera tilts upwards to show the mother at the window announcing that she would rather die in her bed than come down, before slamming down her bedroom shutters. The neighbourhood association also hires a private security guard called Agapito (whose name comically alludes to the Spanish boxer Agapito Gómez at the height of his fame at the time of the film), who thereafter protects the building armed with a gun. Towards the end of the film, Agapito mistakes Paco's neighbour, Don Cosme, for an intruder and shoots him. Significantly, it is the sound of an alarm that leads to his untimely death. Paco agrees to lend Don Cosme his car, though he remembers too late that he has forgotten to turn off his newly installed car alarm. On hearing the alarm, the security guard panics and takes aim at Don Cosme before he manages to clearly see him. The alarm in this scene plays a similar role to the sirens which have been heard throughout the film. Writing on the soundscape of London after the 2005 terrorist bombings, Les Back states that the sound of sirens 'create an imminent threat in which dread and alarm are mutually enhanced' (Back, 2007: 121). The increasing sound of police surveillance created a 'soundtrack of the war on terror' in which the pervasive paranoia and fear on the streets resulted in the 'creation of a climate of misrecognition', whereby innocent people such as the young Brazilian Jean Charles de Menezes were shot mistakenly by the police (Back, 2007: 125). In the frequent sounds of the sirens, gunshots – and in this particular scene, car alarms – the soundtrack of the film betrays a similar function, one that creates an atmosphere of panic that leads to Cosme's untimely death. In hospital, Don Cosme reassures Paco that he isn't to blame for the shooting, and that blame lies squarely with el 'lobo feroz', here a possible allusion to the tendency to 'cry wolf' and give false alarm.

This act of misrecognition, in which danger is persistently heard rather than seen, and in which innocent people are mistaken for criminals, recurs frequently throughout the film. Of the several headlines the grandmother reads out in the opening scene, the most dramatic is that of a recent robbery at a petrol station, whose four bearded suspects have become known to the police for a string of other crimes. As Paco walks into a bar, we hear the song 'Mala ruina tengas' by Los Chichos played non-diegetically. After ordering his drink, he looks over to see four bearded young men whom he wrongly believes to be the suspects. As discussed in depth in chapter 5, Los Chichos and other similar *rumba* groups such as Los Chunguitos were strongly associated with *cine quinqui*, and their lyrics about criminal transgression and marginalisation had a clear resonance with urban youth subcultures at the time. Presented here as a *leitmotif* for Paco's irrational fear of delinquency, the function of the *rumba* in the case of *Miedo* is ironic rather than an authentic reflection of marginality. Indeed, nearly every time the four men appear in the film, Los Chichos is played non-diegetically over the action, an effect that will signal a shift into Paco's subjective world of paranoid fantasy. In another scene in the bar, in which the four bearded men are seated in the same location, Los Chichos' song 'Vivía errante' (He led a wandering life) can be heard. The barman animatedly mentions to Paco a rumour about an incident in which four criminals held up a married couple at gunpoint at night, taking all of their valuable possessions and money. The barman's story continues off-screen, as we hear it accompany a series of shots in which Paco and Begoña re-enact the roles of the married victims, while the bearded men from the bar act as the criminals. In a clear disruption to the otherwise conventional visual style of the film, the frontal framing and symmetrical compositions alert us to the artificiality of the performances. After handing over their possessions, one of the bearded men violently removes Begoña's bra and proceeds to twist her nipple until it bleeds, an act that is shown in a fetishistic and strikingly graphic extreme close-up. In a scene which takes place in Paco's bank, his colleague Barroso tells Paco and a crowd of other employees a different version of the rumour which, rather than ending in sexual violence concludes with the couple calling the police, who subsequently refuse to help due to their lack of resources. Paco and Begoña again re-enact the roles of the married couple, but this time the voices of the criminals are provided by Barroso's voice (and subsequently dubbed by the actor), as he recounts their dialogue in reported speech. The conspicuous use of dubbing here, in which Barroso literally projects his voice onto the criminal, serves to uncannily blur the identities between the self and the criminal 'other'. Its disorientating effect serves to illustrate how concerns about crime were a projection of a range of social anxieties during that time, whose cause, the film suggests, was self-compounding.

The scene illustrates the film journal *Contracampo*'s interpretation of the key message of the film, whereby 'las principales víctimas del terror nocturno las provoca nuestro propio miedo' (the main victims of our nighttime terrors are created by our own fear) (Fernández Torres, 1980: 80). The blurring of the self into the criminal other can be found in the illustrated promotional poster of *Miedo a salir de noche*. Here, the delinquent takes the shape of a distorted black silhouette holding a gun at cartoon versions of José Sacristán and Antonio Ferrandis. Towering over the actors, the sinister outline of the body of the delinquent appears both larger than life and distorted. Yet in casting a shadow that bleeds into that of Sacristán's feet, the poster suggests that the shadow belongs not only to the criminal but to the character of Paco himself. The ghostly shadow here represents how, in the words of a journalist Fernando Gracia, the film sought to show how 'muchos españoles padecen la psicosis de un miedo fantasmal' (many Spaniards suffer from the psychosis of a phantom fear) (Gracia,

1979: n.p.,), a fear that was intrinsically as much a product of the imagination as it was a rational response to actual threats.

The characters' inability to disentangle fact from fiction intensifies as the circulation of rumours gathers apace in the narrative, an aspect that is in turn emphasised through other disruptive aspects of the film's sound design. As Barroso recounts the story to Paco, he attracts an increasingly numerous crowd of colleagues who gather around them to listen to the story. After criticising the ineptitude of the police, his colleagues respond by shouting over one another in indignation and panic. The scene is then suddenly played in fast motion, with the pitch of the actors' voices becoming comically high for humorous effect. In its description of the scene, the script says 'arrecia la avalancha de voces. El caos sonoro llena la banda sonora. Aunque todos hablan el mismo idioma aquello parece la torre de Babel' (the avalanche of voices intensifies. The sonic chaos fills the soundtrack. Although everyone is speaking the same language, it appears as if it is the Tower of Babel). The use of sound here illustrates the ease with which people, particularly within the broader context of media-generated moral panics, can swiftly succumb to the herd mentality of irrational fear and panic. As Barroso tells his story, the panic swiftly spreads from him to his employees. In the cacophony of overlapping multiple voices that ensues we no longer hear particular actors, or even pieces of dialogue or fragments of words, but the sound of the crowd in its entirety, a chorus of voices that would appear to speak as an unwieldy group rather than as a set of individuals. The 'caos sonoro', or sonic chaos, ironically dramatises the sheer contagiousness of anxiety and fear in Spain during the transition, serving as a sonic *mise en abîme* for the film's broader exploration of moral panic explored throughout the rest of the film. The sound design here thus appears to bear out Stanley Cohen's famous notion of a 'deviance amplification spiral', where the exaggerated portrayal in the media of deviant and criminal behaviour leads to greater public concern and sensitisation around the issue (2011: xii). As the police and the courts increasingly respond to the issue, so the perceived threat of deviant behaviour becomes further amplified, so that the overall perception is that the problem is getting worse (Cohen, 2011: xii). Like the deviance amplification spiral, the circulation and looping back and forth of fearful rumours in this scene lead to an echo chamber where the real event and its distorted retellings blur into one another.[11] As de la Iglesia has commented on his film, 'El miedo está demostrado que no produce más que más miedo …' (Fear has proved that it produces nothing more than more fear …) (Gracia, 1980a: n.p.).

Conclusion

As this chapter has shown, *cine quinqui* was frequently informed as much by the fear of crime as it was about the actual threat of crime. Despite the official narrative of democratisation as one of consensus and national unity, *Los violadores del amanecer*, *La patria de 'el Rata'* and *Miedo a salir de noche* all attest to how the everyday experience of the transition for many was one of great uncertainty and social malaise. As we have seen, these anxieties were frequently displaced or re-articulated onto broader underlying fears of public disorder, bringing in their wake a subsequent retreat into the domestic space of the home. In showing the distinct ways in which these fears were articulated across three films, this chapter has sought to provide a more nuanced understanding of the diversity of cinematic practices and politics that have become associated with *cine quinqui*. Through their interaction with the erotic cinema, *tercera vía* and the *sainete* respectively, the films provided distinct and diverging imaginations concerning the causes of delinquency and the subsequent role of the new democratic state in imposing social order. In particular, the chapter has explored the home as a particular site of resonance in the three films, whose soundscape is threatened by the perception of social disorder and noise from the outside. Through exploring the shifting acoustic borders between interior and exterior space in the films, this chapter reveals the extent to which the cultural imagination of the home during these years was reshaped by feelings of uncertainty.

Notes

1 The earlier 1959 law, María del Carmen Hurtado Martínez shows, first and foremost prioritised the protection of institutions over the individual rights of people (1999: 32–33). In its emphasis on the protection of individual freedoms and the inviolability of property and belongings, she argues that the wording and content of the constitution is in diametrical contrast to the earlier Ley de Orden Público. She observes, moreover, that in Article 104, the new constitution no longer prioritised

the protection of public order as much as the 'protection of exercise of rights and liberties and the guaranteeing of the safety of citizens' (Hurtado Martínez, 1999: 31).

2 See Stangeland (1995: 82). Per Stangeland also argues that in this first national survey, and the four that subsequently followed in 1980, 1981, 1991 and 1992, 'the training of the interviewers, the way the sample was drawn, and the actual wording of the questions was rather improvised' (1995: 82).

3 For an example of the advert containing this slogan, see Unión de Centro Democrático (1979: 27).

4 While the majority of 'S' films were erotic in nature, Daniel Kowalsky notes that a small number of them were also deemed offensive on account of their political or violent nature. The most famous example of this was *El crimen de Cuenca/The Cuenca Crime* (Pilar Miró, 1979).

5 See for instance the image provided by the blog Proyecto Naschy, https://proyectonaschy.com/2014/12/29/los-violadores-del-amanecer-contra-violacion-castracion/.

6 For an overview of how the Ley General de Educación constituted an important turning point in the history of the Spanish education system, see Pamela O'Malley (1995: 25–31). O'Malley notes that before the passing of the bill, the school system in Spain had remained basically unchanged since the Education Act of 1857 (1995: 30).

7 The report refers to Hamida Djandoubi, the last person to be executed by guillotine in France, after the rape and brutal murder of Elisabeth Bousquet. France would in fact abolish capital punishment in 1981, three years after it was banned in Spain.

8 'I believe in democracy, in freedom of speech, but also in order, and we don't get this in the parliamentary democracy that we are having to endure.'

9 Other production companies involved in the production of the film were Ogro, Eva Films and Paraguas Films, a company that was set up by Summers himself.

10 Paloma Aguilar writes that 'at the First National Congress of Alianza Popular, 1977, shortly after the PCE had been legalised, [the politician Gonzalo] Fernández de la Mora equated Marxism with "terror"' (2001: 252).

11 The inability here to separate individual dialogue from the shouts of the crowd, or actual meaning from both the physical and metaphorical noise of hearsay, also intriguingly illuminates the etymology of the word 'rumour'. Rumour is derived from the Latin *rumorem,* whose meaning not only denoted hearsay and common talk but also noise and clamour. Both of these meanings co-exist in the Spanish word *rumor.*

3

Sound and skin in the *quinqui* films of Eloy de la Iglesia

After *Miedo a salir de noche*, Eloy de la Iglesia made five delinquent-themed films, all of which starred the actor José Luis Manzano as the protagonist: *Navajeros* (1980), *Colegas* (1982), *El pico* (1983), *El pico 2* (1984) and *La estanquera de Vallecas* (1987). With his chiselled features and distinctive curly locks, José Luis Manzano was the most striking cover boy for the *quinqui* subculture. Youthful, smooth, taut yet fragile, the surface of Manzano's skin emerged as a crucial motif in these films, one that, as this chapter shows, brought into play a tactile and sensory engagement with cinema. The fragility of his skin was particularly emphasised in *El pico* and *El pico 2*, films which depicted heroin addiction with a striking directness. Through alerting us to texture and skin, these films emphasise the slippage of meaning between sensationalism and the sensorial. The visceral aesthetics of these films had a powerful affective charge – one that, to borrow the words of Steven Shaviro, shows how the cinematic body is able to 'confront the viewer directly, without mediation' (1993: 26).

In focussing in particular on three of the most commercially successful de la Iglesia/Manzano films, *Navajeros*, *El pico* and *El pico 2*, this chapter explores how the body of the delinquent was a particular site of resonance in *cine quinqui*. It examines how the fragility of Manzano's body was visually and aurally emphasised through the significance attributed to texture in the films and the physiological sounds of his breath. Through my analysis of *Navajeros*, a film which was inspired by the life of the famous delinquent José Joaquín Sánchez Frutos 'el Jaro', I explore the extent to which the film reflected the intermedial nature of his celebrity, particularly through his depiction in popular music and the media. Like el Jaro's depiction in the media,

Navajeros similarly pursues a sensationalist aesthetics in order to interrogate the complex ways in which cultural understandings of delinquency were frequently shaped and distorted by the sensationalism of the press. My analysis of *El pico* and *El pico 2* traces the ways in which the films responded to public anxieties surrounding heroin abuse, whose distribution networks were bound up with the underlying social and political tensions within Euskadi during this period. As skin is frequently damaged, distressed and punctured in the films, its troubled surface provides an eloquent example of how, in the words of Bryan S. Turner, 'dominant concerns and anxieties of society tend to be translated into disrupted, disjointed and disturbed images of the body' (2003: 1). The disturbance of skin, which is emphasised in the films through sound design and texture, illuminates the broader concerns around the role of police repression which was increasingly used to tackle Spain's heroin epidemic, something that in turn disrupted the narrative of social progress that was associated with the newly elected socialist government of 1982.

Navajeros, el Jaro, and the sensation of delinquency

While de la Iglesia's films frequently enjoyed commercial success, they nonetheless drew a less than favourable treatment from critics. Like many of the other films associated with the *quinqui* cycle, de la Iglesia's filmmaking was primarily one of shock and confrontation. As Steve Marsh writes, 'de la Iglesia's raw style has been labelled *tremendista*: sensationalist, populist and lurid' (2013: 157). Yet in an interview in *Triunfo* in 1979, de la Iglesia not only defended his cinematic excesses – described here by the journalist as 'sensacionalista' (sensationalist), 'melodramática' (melodramatic) and 'panfletaria' (propagandistic), terms that are frequently associated with his work in the Spanish media – but commented that he actively sought to encourage them in his filmmaking (Galán 1979). The hallmarks of his style are well known: Manichean structures of morality, in which the marginalised victims are dialectically pitted against their exploiters; rapid, shock cutting which underscores contrasts and correspondences between images and themes; a hyperbolic *mise-en-scène,* whose use of décor, costumes and props serves as heavy-handed indexes for characterisation. But most of all, his filmmaking is marked by its fascination with the fragile glamour of male youth, an aspect which is most strikingly borne out in his *quinqui* films. Indeed, several of his scenes feature the naked or semi-naked flesh of José Luis Manzano and other teenage boys, creating a visual surface that Manuel Hidalgo at the time dubbed an 'estética de calzoncillo' (aesthetic of the underpants) (1983: 38). The male erotic imagery of his films has subsequently drawn comparisons with Pier Paolo Pasolini and Rainer Werner Fassbinder, gay directors who similarly had a fascination for the vulnerability of youth and masculinity. Yet through his crude aesthetics, de la Iglesia also crucially distinguished himself from the formal rigour and art-house credentials of these directors, whose filmmaking frequently maintained an aesthetic distance between spectator and subject. If Pasolini's filmmaking offers a poetic meditation on lumpen youth, and Fassbinder diffuses the erotics of the male body through Brechtian distanciation, then de la Iglesia provides a far closer and more sensorial engagement with its subject matter. De la Iglesia has argued that this directness is crucial to his particular invocation of what he terms 'cine popular', allowing the films to reach as broad an audience as possible. In an interview that coincided with the release of *Navajeros*, the director commented that 'ese contacto tan directo con el público que tienen muchas de mis películas es la verdadera base de su comercialidad' (Llinás and Téllez, 1981: 30).[1] In its power to arouse and touch the viewer, his filmmaking created a palpable, visceral response from its audiences.

This physical directness can be felt in the opening sequence of *Navajeros,* for instance, which establishes a striking parallel between the human body and the cinematic body. Just as the film's title appears, an animated image of a knife can be seen cutting across the screen in a diagonal motion, bisecting the image in two. If the wounded screen here foreshadows the violence of the film, where the human flesh of the delinquent is similarly presented as damaged, the aesthetic of surface here – emphasised sonically through a sudden ripping sound – establishes the tactile structure of spectatorship encountered in de la Iglesia's *quinqui* films. The title 'Navajeros' appears in a mechanical typewriter font, which in common with *Miedo a salir de noche*, emphasises the intermedial and reactive relationship between the Spanish press and his filmmaking. José Sacristán appears as a journalist at the typewriter, writing an article about el Jaro as he lists in a voiceover all the crimes the delinquent had committed before turning 16. Indeed, it was a news article on el Jaro's untimely death in February 1979 that provided de la Iglesia with the nucleus for the screenplay of the film (Mauri, 1998: 62).[2] In a vivid example of how

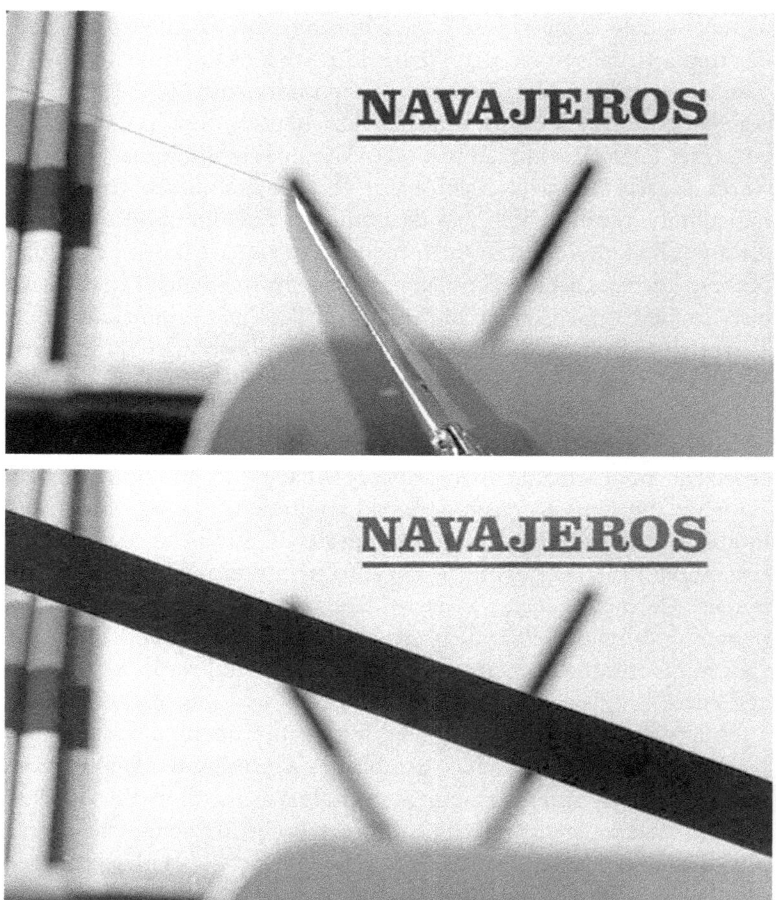

3.1 and 3.2 The 'wounded screen' in the opening credits of *Navajeros* (Eloy de la Iglesia, 1980).

cine quinqui not only reflected reality but shaped it, Mery Cuesta shows that el Jaro had reportedly learnt how to steal through watching *Perros callejeros* (2009: 79). The mediated nature of el Jaro's criminal identity is something that de la Iglesia was particularly attuned to in his film, especially as he was still in the process of completing *Miedo a salir de noche* – which, as chapter 2 shows, critiques the role of the media in amplifying the risk of crime – when he began working on the script. Eloy de la Iglesia was struck by how el Jaro's death had been at the hands not of the police but of an ordinary citizen who was protecting his property with a gun (Martínez, 1980), another example of how domestic space was becoming increasingly fortified during these years. Further inspiration came a few months later from the rock singer Joaquín Sabina, who wrote the song 'Qué demasiao' which was inspired by el Jaro's life and death (Mauri, 1998: 62–63). The song's description of el Jaro as 'Macarra de ceñido pantalón, pandillero tatuado y suburbial' (Thug in tight trousers, a tattooed and suburban gangster) is brought to life through Manzano's costume of body-hugging blue jeans and a tattoo on his biceps. The final line of the song invokes el Jaro's imagined last words (¡Qué demasiao, de esta me sacan en televisión! [How awesome, this will get me on the TV!]), where he fantasises about how his death will be mythologised in the media. Like the delinquent el Lute before him, el Jaro's ascent to fame can be attributed to his frequent appearances in *El Caso,* a weekly newspaper that specialised in reporting on crime with lurid and sensory details. In its aim to shock and amaze its readers, the front covers of *El Caso* were known for being violent and bloody, often featuring photographs of corpses, an aspect that led to the popular saying that its covers 'chorreaban sangre' (dripped blood) (Rodríguez Cárcela, 2012: 230–231). Two months after his death, it ran a special issue on el Jaro described as a 'niño convertido en leyenda a los 16 años' (a boy turned legend at 16 years old) with 32 illustrations recounting his life, including one on the front cover of his injured body.[3] In the months following el Jaro's early death, his celebrity had circulated across a number of media and sources, whose cross-fertilisation emphasised the multi-sensorial articulation of his deviance. Sonic, textural and visual, el Jaro's celebrity thus alerts us to the slippage of meaning between the sensational and the sensorial – a relationship that found an especially rich expression in the formal elements of *Navajeros.*

In search of an actor who could authentically embody el Jaro, de la Iglesia placed adverts in the newspapers announcing the casting call for the role. De la Iglesia recalls how hundreds of teenage boys turned up for the auditions, leaving the employees of the production company aghast at the sight of the outline of knives in their skin-tight jeans and the discarded spliff butts on the stairs (Mauri, 1998: 64). The director was unable to find a boy with the right face and physicality for the role, so he asked one of his collaborators to go out and find José Luis Manzano, whom the director had met the year before. Manzano and de la Iglesia had previously had sexual relations – a fact that, given Manzano was 16 at the time, was omitted in the official narrative provided for the press, which claimed that José Luis Manzano was offered the role after attending the audition.[4] His scriptwriter and collaborator Goicoechea more recently commented that they met many of their teenage actors because they were the rent boys they visited at the time, boys who also dealt in drugs on the side (cited in Melero 2013: 49). While Manzano was not actually a delinquent himself, he nevertheless lived in Villa de Vallecas, a district of Madrid where unemployment and crime were rife. With his slight and nimble frame, pale skin, and curly auburn hair, Manzano also looked the part of el Jaro (the word 'jaro' means blonde or chestnut-coloured) – whose appearance is correspondingly described in the script as 'Menudo. Pálido. Rubiasco. Los ojos tristes y agresivos' (Slight. Pale. Fair-haired. Sad and aggressive eyes).

Like the other boys in the film – together with whom Luis Fernández Eguía 'el Pirri' would also make his cinematic debut – Manzano had no previous acting experience. Nevertheless, the director commented that the young cast, and in particular Manzano, possessed 'una intuición milagrosa para la interpretación' (a miraculous intuition for acting) (Mauri, 1998: 81). The realism of the criminal acts performed on screen – some of which stand out for their technical precision – can be attributed to the pains to which de la Iglesia went in researching and preparing for the shoot. He reportedly asked delinquents to explain to him how to commit crimes such as hot-wiring a stolen vehicle, getting money out of a phone box and snatching a bag (Gracia, 1980b). As it transpired that Manzano could barely read and write, de la Iglesia hired a teacher to help him with literacy skills until he could he could read the script properly (Fuembuena, 2017: 154). Much to

Manzano's own consternation, his voice was finally dubbed in post-production by the actor Ángel Pardo (who had incidentally also appeared as a delinquent character in de la Iglesia's *El diputado* (1978) and *Los placeres ocultos* (1977)), as de la Iglesia declared himself unable to understand his vocal delivery (Fuembuena, 2017: 195–196). The spontaneity of Manzano's and el Pirri's performances largely contrasts with that of their co-stars, such as the classically trained Mexican actresses Isela Vega and Verónica Castro. As a co-production with the Mexican company Producciones Fenix, their appearance was essential to the film's economic viability in the Mexican market, where it was released as *Dulces navajas/Sweet Knives*. Manzano was reportedly paid 300,000 pesetas – an amount that was ten times less than that of Isela Vega, who in the role of Mercedes, el Jaro's much older girlfriend and surrogate maternal figure, only features in a handful of scenes (Fuembuena, 2017: 144). While the reviews of the film were typically negative, *Navajeros* was commended for the authenticity of its dialogue [5] – an aspect that was most likely helped by the director recording twenty hours of conversations of delinquents so that he could reproduce their slang in the script (Gracia, 1980b), as well as the fact that Manzano corrected some of the dialogue to make it sound more natural (Martínez, 1980).[6]

Eyewitness accounts of the theatrical experience of *Navajeros* testify to the visceral resonance between the film and the audience, something that was clearly played out through the sound of the auditorium. Described in the press as 'una balada dinámica, ruidosa y violenta antiautoritaria' (a dynamic, noisy and violently anti-authoritarian ballad) (Anon, 1980a), the film's strident soundtrack correspondingly elicited a noisy response from its audience. One journalist noted, for instance, how the teenagers in the audience booed when the police appeared (Anon, 1980a), while de la Iglesia commented that the public during its release in Madrid shouted in support of the delinquents (Anon, 1980b). In particular, audiences reportedly started to shout and applaud during the scene in which el Jaro and his gang violently confront a group of fascists in the Retiro park (Martínez, 1980). Eduardo Fuembuena notes that despite packing out cinemas, however, *Navajeros* could have fared better at the box office, having reached an audience of 807,001 spectators. After five weeks of selling out in Cine Fuencarral in Madrid, for instance, the film would be removed from the programme, no doubt owing to the fact that many boys from the peripheral suburbs were seen to be creating a nuisance of themselves in the city centre (Fuembuena, 2017: 216). Here, the moral panic surrounding *cine quinqui* extended from the film to the space of the cinema itself, whose programming in this case served to regulate and exclude the noisy excesses of working-class teenagers. The reception of the film, moreover, illustrates how the screen might be considered an affective interface in which the noise of the soundtrack and the noise of the audience, the cinematic body and the human body, momentarily dissolved into each other. Indeed, this found its most literal (and violent) expression at a screening of the film one year later in a *cine de verano* (outside screening) in Getafe, Madrid: the young audience reportedly started throwing bottles at the screen, with some of them even tearing it with their own hands, during the scene in which el Jaro's friend Chus is shot down by the police (Fuembuena, 2017: 216). Aural, physical and kinaesthetic responses such as these emphasised the intersubjectivity of Eloy de la Iglesia's filmmaking. In sensuously implicating the young audiences in the film, his cinema blurred the separation between viewer/auditor and image, subject and object. This blurring was crucial to the 'contacto tan directo' (such direct contact) between film and audience that was integral to Eloy de la Iglesia's practice of filmmaking.

The sonic orchestration of the delinquent body

Focalised through el Jaro and his gang, the narrative foregrounds the experience of delinquency from the perspective of the delinquent. On the film's release, the director commented that while films on juvenile delinquency are always 'condenada a ser una historia moralista' (doomed to be a moralistic story), his intention when making *Navajeros* was precisely the opposite, instead telling the story between police and thieves but with the usual values associated with them reversed (A.S.H., 1980). To this effect, he said the film avoided the 'tono paternalista' (paternalistic tone) adopted by José Antonio de la Loma in the *Perros callejeros* cycle. Stating his allegiance to Jaro and his gang, the director commented that he himself was also 'poco delincuente' (a bit delinquent) (Martínez, 1980) – here a reference to his dissident position as a queer director and Communist Party activist. The clear-cut morality of the film, where police are presented as sinister aggressors and the delinquents their victims, was criticised as overly simplistic and demagogic by much of the press.[7] While this is a fair argument, it overlooks how the cinematic aesthetics of *Navajeros* operate on a more elemental and visceral register, which far from seeking to flesh out the moral psychology of the characters, tends to emphasise the bodily and sensual experience of delinquency. De la Iglesia's filmmaking illustrates the extent to which, as Laura Marks has written in *The Skin of the Film*, 'film is grasped not by an intellectual act but by the complex perception of the body as a whole' (Marks, 2000: 145). The audience's alignment with el Jaro and his gang derives not merely from his sympathetic treatment in the film but from the way in which the audience affectively engages with the actors at the level of the body. Presented in a series of physically strenuous and often dangerous scenarios which emphasise his athletic agility, Manzano is frequently seen to be climbing and jumping off walls, driving motorbikes, running from the police and getting into scraps. His actions are given further momentum through the fast-paced editing used throughout, providing the film with a frenetic rhythm and pace that lay emphasis on the human body in constant motion. The danger and risk brought about by these physical activities are made manifest through the depiction of the vulnerability of his body, which as the narrative progresses is increasingly seen as bleeding, damaged and penetrable. Some time after el Jaro robs the drug dealer El Marqués (Enrique San Francisco) of his supply of hash, El Marqués takes his revenge by getting his henchmen to strip him from the waist down, and then ordering his burly henchman Kid Merino (who is described in the script as having an 'aspecto de boxeador sonado' [appearance of a punch-drunk boxer]) to rape him. With his naked buttocks on display, el Jaro is visibly humiliated. After el Jaro is injured by the bullets during his escape in the aforementioned botched burglary scene, in which Chus is also shot by the police, he wakes up in the penitentiary hospital and discovers that he has had one of his testicles removed. As well as alluding to the symbolic wounding of his masculinity, the scene illustrates how, according to Jennifer Barker, the bodily encounter between film and spectator 'occurs not only at the skin or the screen, but traverses all the organs of the spectator's body and the film's body' (Barker 2009: 2). As he says 'me han copado, me han copado' (I've been castrated), Manzano's humiliated and distressed expression is registered close-up, the physical proximity to the actor further emphasised by the fact that de la Iglesia was able to salvage Manzano's original voice in the dub for these few moments (Fuembuena, 2017: 196).

The film's alignment with the body of the delinquents is further emphasised through its sound design, particularly through the physiological sounds of el Jaro's body. After being injured, el Jaro is on the verge of slipping out of consciousness as he waits to be admitted into the hospital emergency ward. As the police arrive on the scene, the echoing internal diegetic sound of el Jaro's heartbeat can be heard in auditory close-up, a sound effect that is also heard in *El Pico* and *El Pico 2* to convey the slowing of the heartbeat after he takes heroin. El Jaro struggles to hold his body up, moving his head out of frame so that the tattoo of his name 'Jaro', emphasised through the high cut of his T-shirt sleeve, can be seen in a lingering close-up. The sound of his heartbeat becomes amplified as the police approach him, their image focalised through the blurry POV of the protagonist, who then collapses on the ground. In foregrounding the physical proximity of his body, the immersive cinematic aesthetics of this scene illustrate the ways in which, according to Laura Marks

> Haptic images are erotic regardless of their content, because they construct an intersubjective relationship between beholder and image. The viewer is called upon to fill in the gaps in the image, engage with the traces the image leaves. By interacting up close with an image, close enough that figure and ground commingle, the viewer *gives up her own sense of separateness from the image.* (1998: 341)

As we have seen, however, the intersubjective relationship here is created not only visually but aurally as well, through the physiological sounds of el Jaro's body whose heartbeats similarly create a commingling closeness with the audience. If, as Laura Marks writes, the viewer is called upon to engage with the 'traces the image leaves', the lingering trace of the tattoo also has a crucial auditory dimension. The tattoo here was also inspired by the physical description of the delinquent as a 'pandillero tatuado y suburbiano' [tattooed and suburban gangster]), immortalised through the lyrics of Joaquín Sabina's song.

Another of el Jaro's tattoos appears earlier on in the film, after he lies naked in the bath and dries himself in front of Mercedes. With the light reflecting off the toned contours of his wet body, which is framed by the door of Mercedes's bedroom, he shows her a tattoo

3.3 El Jaro's (José Luis Manzano) tattooed and naked body in *Navajeros* (Eloy de la Iglesia, 1980).

on his hand composed of a pattern of five dots. The scene cuts to an extreme close-up of the tattoo in shallow focus, as he explains that the tattoo means 'Muera la policía, viva la golfería' (death to the police, long live delinquency), a symbol of transgressive defiance. In what is a rather more literal illustration of Marks's 'visual erotics', cinematic touch is again given further expression through the soundtrack. In the next erotic scene that takes place in her apartment, el Jaro and Mercedes have sex, their moans of pleasure conveyed through post-synch sound. Jacob Smith draws on the writing of Linda Williams to show how 'post-synch "sounds of pleasure" have a certain clarity that makes them seem to come from very close up' (cited in Smith, 2012: 46). Following Williams, Smith shows that this not only lends 'a certain ambiguity as to the performer's position in space (a sense of "spacelessness") but porno-performativity also provides an index of intimacy' (2012: 47). The sense of spacelessness to post-synch sound can also be clearly felt in the moments when the sounds of el Jaro's breathing can be heard, particularly in scenes of action and violence. Regardless of his proximity to the camera, his breathing is frequently recorded in auditory close-up – a technique of vocal performance which similarly creates an intimate connection with his body. In the scene in which el Jaro is humiliated and raped, for instance, the quick and irregular pace of his breathing can be heard against the threatening words of El Marqués. Later on, when el Jaro gets into a knife fight with his mother's pimp, we hear only the sound of el Jaro's breathing and not that of his adversary. As el Jaro slashes Seba's face, a cutaway to the crowd of onlookers shows an elderly lady shouting 'navajeros, navajeros' (knifers, knifers), words that allude to the title of the film. In both scenes, the sounds of el Jaro's breathing not only foreground his subjectivity aurally within the scene but underscore the vulnerability of his body, here shown when it is most under strain or under threat of penetration. Breathing is therefore emphasised as an embodied sound at the very moments when the body is in crisis, when its skin is subsequently presented at its most porous and vulnerable.

In her exploration of the place of the breath in film, Davina Quinlivan builds on Laura Marks's model of haptic viewing and extends her work into an audiovisual context. If, as Quinlivan argues, Laura Marks tends to privilege the image over sound, Quinlivan's work explores how the embodied exchange between viewer and film can also take place in the soundtrack through what she calls a 'breathing encounter'. For Quinlivan, this encounter 'envisages the point of contact according to the ways in which breathing unsettles the borders between inside and outside' (Quinlivan, 2012: 20–21). Through addressing the soundtrack in her analysis, Quinlivan's writing prompts a 'shift away from haptic visuality towards "haptic hearing", reconciling the act of listening to the proximal gestures of touch which pervade Marks's thinking' (Quinlivan, 2012: 21). Through the close miking of breath, the two scenes here might be said to similarly disturb the border between inside and outside, moments that generate particularly intense intersubjective encounters with the film. That the 'haptic hearing' should be emphasised through the presence of the knives is significant. Like images of the tattoos, the knife alerts us to the surface contact of skin, whose tear we also saw in the opening sequence.

Navajeros is the most musical of all of de la Iglesia's *quinqui* films, and the director has said that when Goicoechea and he were devising the script, they wanted to achieve a 'copla popular de niño bandido' (popular *copla* of a young outlaw), which was constructed 'casi con ritmo de tebeo' (almost with the rhythm of a comic) (A.S.H., 1980).

Several songs by the *rock urbano* band Burning can be heard non-diegetically in the film, including 'Una canción dedicada al Jaro' (A song dedicated to el Jaro), which was composed especially for the film. A genre of rock music to emerge from Madrid from the early to mid-1970s, *rock urbano* combined the Anglo-American sounds of hard rock and blues with lyrics that dealt with social problems within Spanish cities. Described in the script as 'Comienza a sonar, a todo volumen, un rock and roll. Música dura, urbana, proletaria' (Rock and roll starts to be played at full volume. Hard, urban and proletarian music), we first hear the music non-diegetically in the opening title sequence, after the journalist lists el Jaro's criminal record to date. As well as providing further exposition for the protagonist, the song ties the noise of the music thematically to his deviant status as an outlaw. In addition to the music of the group Burning, el Jaro and his friends are depicted listening to the *rumbas* 'Vivía errante' by Los Chichos and 'Ya no te quedan lágrimas' (You have no tears left anymore) by Rumba Tres. As chapter 5 will also show, *rumbas* had become an enormously popular genre of music with marginal teenagers in Spain at the time, and was associated in particular with the district of Vallecas where Manzano grew up. In particular, two scenes which take place in Almudena Cemetery emphasise their shared listening of the music as a transgressive act, with the diegetic source of the stolen radio stereo conspicuously placed in the foreground of the *mise-en-scène*.

The popular music of *rumbas* and *rock urbano* is contrasted with the pieces of classical music by Tchaikovsky and Chopin which are also used in the film. Tchaikovsky's 'El Vals de la Bella Durmiente (Act 1 No 5)' from *Sleeping Beauty* is played non-diegetically over three extended montage sequences in which el Jaro and his gang carry out a series of different crimes. The use of classical music here echoes that of *Clockwork Orange* (Stanley Kubrick, 1973), a direct influence on Eloy de la Iglesia's earlier shlock-horror film *Una gota de sangre para morir amando/Murder in a Blue World* (1973), in which pieces of Beethoven, Elgar and Rossini perversely work in rhythmic parallel with the orchestration of violence depicted on screen. The first of these sequences begins as el Butano (Jaime Garza), Jonny (Pep Corominas) and el Chus meet el Jaro outside an abandoned housing block, just after he has been released from prison. As the music begins, the camera pans from a high-angle as the four of them set off towards the busy road, each giving a joyful jump and a kick on the way. Like the young suburban audiences who flocked to the cinema of Fuencarral, their movement here is similarly one from the margins of the city to the centre. The waltz-like tempo of the music shapes the rhythm of the montage sequence which follows, whose exhilarating pace serves to showcase the dexterous ingenuity and skill of the delinquents as they snatch bags, steal motorbikes and force cash from a phone box with a screwdriver.

The Tchaikovsky piece is heard for a second time in a scene in which el Jaro and his friends are riding motorbikes at night, their vehicles following the undulating curves of the road in synchronicity with the three–four beat of the music. The orchestration of their bodies in constant motion is not so much presented as a scourge or a social menace as a series of sensory thrills. Through music and motion, the audience gains an affective attachment to their bodies as well as a complicity in the exhilaration they feel as they commit one criminal act after another without being caught. The scene illustrates the writing of the criminologist Jack Katz, who in accounting for the causes of criminality lays emphasis on the 'lived sensuality' (1988: 312) and 'lived experience of criminality' (1988: 139). Katz highlights the seductive nature of the criminal act and its potential to provide immediate gratification to the criminal, particularly if they are young. Significantly, Katz noted that general descriptions of criminal acts have too often tended to omit the sights, sounds, and tactile and sensory experiences of the offender (1988). In contrast, the fluid orchestration of music and bodies in criminal activity calls our attention to the 'sensual metaphysics' of crime, the hedonistic joy of the delinquents here visibly enjoying what Katz refers to as the 'sneaky thrills' (1988: 52) of the criminal acts in themselves. In alerting us to what he terms the sensual, liberating, creative and 'magical' appeals of crime (1988: 129), Katz's writing resonates with Eloy de la Iglesia's own description of the film as resembling the style of a comic book, which despite being grounded in material facts gives rise to what he calls 'una situación mágica' (a magical situation) (A.S.H. 1980).

The tension between chronicle and comic fantasy is most graphically played out in the film's dramatic climax which depicts the moments leading up to el Jaro's untimely death. The Tchaikovsky piece is played again for the last time, as shots of el Jaro and his gang travelling from their *barrio* to the fateful robbery are cross-cut with those of

3.4 An armed neighbour (Alfred Luchetti) takes aim at el Jaro's (José Luis Manzano) head in the final sequence of *Navajeros* (Eloy de la Iglesia, 1980).

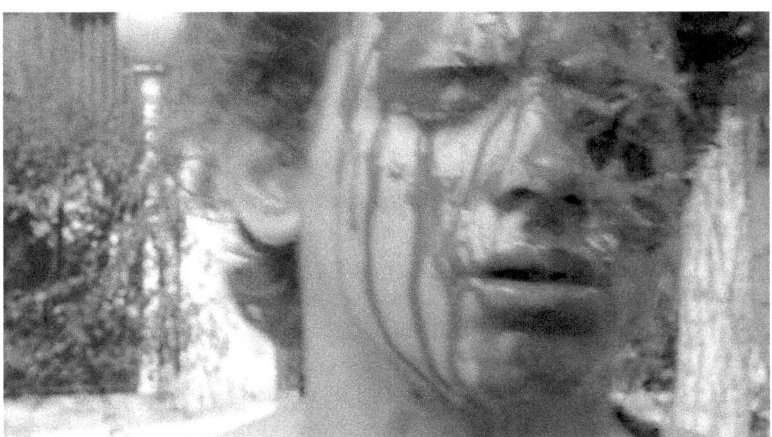

3.5 El Jaro (José Luis Manzano) is shot in the eye in *Navajeros* (Eloy de la Iglesia, 1980).

Irene, her body strapped down on the hospital bed, as she enters into labour with el Jaro's son. As el Jaro prepares to carry out a burglary on a well-heeled street, he is interrupted by a neighbour with a shot gun. As el Jaro approaches him with a knife, the neighbour takes fire at him, shooting him first in the stomach and then in his eye, revealing a gruesome hole where his eye socket should be. Against the absence of dialogue and general ambient sounds, the loudness of the gunshots is felt with particular intensity here, an auditory shock which is followed immediately by the shock cut of the image of a baby's head emerging from the vagina – an editing device which, in graphically matching the wounded eye with the baby, juxtaposes death with birth. Despite insisting on shooting the scene in precisely the same location and street on which the delinquent was killed in real life the year before (Calle Toribio Pollán, now Calle Veracruz), the gory image of el Jaro's bloody eye was the director's own creative embellishment (Fuembuena, 2017: 188). The visceral imagery here provides a deeper and more disturbing iteration of cinematic touch. For Jennifer Barker, cinematic touch is not only enacted haptically, at the surface of the body, but also 'kinaesthetically and muscularly, in the middle dimension of muscles, tendons, and bones that reach toward and through cinematic space', as well as 'viscerally, in the murky recesses of the body, where heart, lungs, pulsing fluids, and firing synapses receive, respond to, and re-enact the rhythms of cinema' (Barker, 2009: 3). The accelerating rhythms created through the combination of music, montage and movement give way to the film's final images: Jaro's dying body, his heart still beating under his tight blood-stained T-shirt, which are cross-cut with the image of his wriggling baby, covered in fluids, its body convulsing as it first enters the air-breathing world. Through its series of juddering pulsations and sensations, the shock aesthetics of the scene dramatically bring together the cinematic body and the human body, the rhythm of the montage and the baby's heart folding into one. The very final shot of the baby is captured in a freeze frame, with his cries continuing to be heard into the closing credits. If, as Maxime Breysse convincingly argues, the editing of the final sequence suggests that the son is condemned to play out the destiny of his father (2011), it also anticipates the narratives of *El pico* and *El pico 2*, which, as we will see, similarly explore the theme of the cycle of paternity through sensationalist aesthetics.

El pico: Heroin and police repression in Euskadi

The motif of skin is felt even more strongly in Eloy de la Iglesia's *El pico*, which centres on the heroin epidemic in Euskadi during the 1980s. The title of the film derives from a play on words: 'pico' is a colloquial word for a syringe, from the verb 'picar', to shoot up, while 'picoleto' is slang for a *guardia civil* (Civil Guard). At the heart of the film is the relationship between the 17-year-old Paco (played by Manzano), who is addicted to heroin, and his strict Civil Guard father Evaristo Torrecuadrada (José Manuel Cervino). The title points to the dialectical forces at play in the film, where the deviant practice of drug taking is pitted against authority and order – a tension further spelled out in its iconoclastic promotional poster in which a bloody needle is sat alongside a *tricornio* (a three-pointed hat worn by the Civil Guards). Originally from Madrid, Torrecuadrada and his family have recently been transferred to Bilbao, a city which, in common with the rest of the autonomous community of Euskadi, was increasingly subject to terrorist attacks, social conflict and police repression during this period. Paco's best friend is Urko (Javier García), the son of a prominent left-wing politician Martín Aramendía (Luis Oriundo). After Urko and Paco shoot the drug-trafficker 'el Cojo' and his wife, the ideologically opposed fathers Torrecuadrada and Aramendía look beyond their political differences and come together to save their sons. The film was a resounding commercial hit: it was the highest-grossing Spanish film at the box office of 1983 (Sánchez Costa, 1984), as well as the most popular film on VHS the following year (Lonzano, 1984). When asked why his film turned out to be so popular, Eloy de la Iglesia explained that a film's commercial success 'siempre obedece fenómenos sociales, no cinematográficos' (always follows social, and not cinematic, phenomena), and attributed its popularity to the general interest of the public in the current themes of hard drugs and the Civil Guards (Sánchez Costa, 1984: n.p.).

As the first of his films to be directed under the new Partido Socialista Obrero Español (PSOE) government, de la Iglesia felt that he was able to explore the theme of police corruption more freely, commenting on its release that he would never have dared make the film had the socialists not been in power (Fernando, 1983: 21). Much of the source material for the film, however, had been in development for at least a couple of years before the elections, and because of the tense and uncertain political climate, had been unable to come to fruition. The inspiration behind the film's final act, for instance, where Paco steals his father's gun and Urko kills the trafficker el Cojo and his wife, was based on a real-life story of a Civil Guard and his son in Madrid (Fernando, 1983: 21). Another source for the film can be found in *Galopa y corta el viento/Gallops and Cuts through the Air*,[8] an unmade screenplay that de la Iglesia co-wrote with Goicoechea, which told the story of a gay romance between a Basque militant and a Civil Guard. Despite finding a production company to fund the film, de la Iglesia and Goicoechea dropped it amid threats that they would be in danger if they pursued the project (Fernando, 1983: 21). Indeed, the screenplay was written the same year that the hostility within the military towards democracy had reached its most violent conclusion, with the failed *coup d'etat* of 23 February 1981, led by lieutenant colonel Antonio Tejero. The Spanish film industry at the time was still reeling from both the censorship and subsequent confiscation of Pilar Miró's controversial film *El crimen de Cuenca/The Cuenca Crime*, which saw the director summoned to a military court in April 1980 for 'injurias a la guardia civil' (slurs against the Civil Guard) (Cerdán et al., 2013: 400–401). After the victory of the socialist government, Pilar Miró was appointed the Director General of Cinematography at the Spanish Ministry of Culture and *El pico* was one of the first Spanish films to receive government subsidies through the *ley Miró* (Miró Law), a series of measures brought in to support Spanish films that were deemed 'de especial calidad' (of special quality).[9]

The unflinchingly authentic portrayal of heroin in the film was no doubt shaped by the experiences of the director, screenwriter and protagonist, who were all addicted to the drug during the production of the film. The agonising extreme close-ups of syringes piercing Manzano's skin were in fact real (though those featuring the actor Javier García, who wasn't an addict, were done by a stunt double) (cited in Melero, 2013: 80). Goicoechea has more recently commented that the film was 'una provocación legalmente' (legally a provocation), as they had to find dealers who could be available during the shoot so that they could provide the actors with drugs (cited in Melero, 2013: 80). The first of de la Iglesia's films to be based in the Basque Country, in the setting of industrial Bilbao, provided a particularly vivid sense of historical immediacy, given that the region had the highest rate of heroin addiction in the whole of Spain at the time, with the price of heroin in Bilbao and San Sebastián the lowest per gram in the country (Miralles, 1983: 27). In an interview at the time of production, the director drew attention to how the toilets in the bars of San Sebastián were full of needles, claiming that the epidemic was so widespread that Basque militants were increasingly swapping their political cause for heroin (P.E., 1983: 107). Indeed, a former member of the Basque separatist group ETA, who had dropped out and had since become a junky, reportedly served as a consultant for the screenplay (P.E., 1983: 107). So grave was the problem that, according to the director, a famous military figure had commented that heroin had now overtaken terrorism as the most serious problem in Spain. If the film is dedicated to reclaiming the experience of ordinary heroin victims, it also shows their agency was frequently mediated and compromised by broader structures of social control. An important exposé published in *Diario 16* in 1983 exposed how police in the Basque country were involved in the drugs mafia, with several frequently 'buying' information on terrorism in exchange for drugs. Police would arrest addicts and, when they were suffering from withdrawal symptoms, offer them heroin and needles in return for information. The villages most severely affected by heroin abuse – Rentería, Bermeo, Ondárrea, Hernani – were also those that were most riven by political tensions (Miralles, 1983: 27). If the pun of the film's title simultaneously points to both drug taking and the police, transgression and social control, it also alerts us to the increasingly blurry and ambiguous reciprocity of these two categories.

Despite the new government, Euskadi nevertheless continued to be marked by terrorist attacks and police repression, a tension which undercut the dominant narrative of civil liberties and progress espoused by the PSOE. The highly fractious political climate in the region, where several political parties simultaneously competed for further regional autonomy, is frequently emphasised through the multitude of different political campaign posters seen on the walls of buildings in the film, often overlaid with graffiti. In an early scene in which Paco and Urko are approached by a teenager looking to buy drugs, Urko replies in Euskara. As they then approach a wall covered in political posters, next to the steps overlooking the docks, Paco asks Urko to stand next to the poster of his politician father Martin Aramendía. Paul Julian Smith has shown how in the film 'the body is marked by the trace of cultural or ethnic difference and its relation to a clearly defined territory', pointing to how Urko is described in the script as having 'rasgos euskaldunes' (unequivocally Basque features) (Smith, 1998: 240). The struggle over territory is articulated not only across ethnic and linguistic lines but explicitly political ones – something that was shored up through the casting strategies of the film. The prominent politician Juan María Bandrés, who belonged to the Basque nationalist party Euzkadiko Ezkerra at the time, was originally offered the role of the politician Martín Aramendía. Despite being generally supportive of the script, Bandrés rejected the role.[10] Bandrés would nevertheless later attend the screening of the film at San Sebastián, accompanied by a journalist from *Diario 16*, who recorded his reactions while watching the film. The politician was struck by the realism of the film, frequently commenting on the accuracy of the most violent scenes, while much of the rest of the audience reportedly turned away from the screen (Gurruchaga, 1983: 31). After watching the scenes of police torture, whose accuracy also further impressed him, he commented to the journalist that the film was going to upset the military (Gurruchaga, 1983: 31). The role of Aramendía was in the end given to the iconic Basque actor and musician Luis Iriondo who was famous for surviving the Nazi bombing of Gernika as a boy.[11] Iriondo also composed the cloyingly sentimental score for the film, whose composition was similarly inflected by regional distinctiveness. A theme played on the *txistu*, for instance, a Basque flute used in traditional folk music, can be heard in the scene where Aramendía presides over a political meeting in Basque.

Despite their differences, Urko's and Paco's close-knit bond is emphasised through the use of framing, where they frequently appear alongside each other in two shots filmed with a medium lens. From sharing joints to spending time in a fairground and fighting, the visual emphasis on the two boys doing things together also serves to partially deflect from the possible homoeroticism between the two of them. In one scene, they have a threesome (without their respective bodies touching) with Betty (Andrea Albini), an Argentinean prostitute who introduces them to heroin. As Paul Julian Smith has argued, the unmade *Galopa y corta el viento* 'recurs in sublimated form in the various relationships between men in *El pico* and in the central theme of heroin addiction presented here as an eroticised spectacle of the male body' (1998: 238). As Urko and Paco inject themselves with heroin, we see fetishising extreme close-ups of their punctured skin, its damaged surface emphasised through harsh frontal lighting. The play of red and white provides a vivid counterpoint to the otherwise muted palette of the film, whose hues of grey and brown atmospherically evoke the rain-drenched and industrial Bilbao of the period. Like those of the tattoo in *Navajeros*, these shots that linger on the surface of the skin compellingly illustrate haptic visuality. As Marks writes, 'haptic looking tends to rest on the surface of its object rather than to plunge into depth not to distinguish form so much as to discern texture' (Marks 2000: 8).

Sound, sensation and syringes

It is during these moments of haptic visuality and listening, which emphasise the texture of damaged skin, that the broader social and political tensions explored by the film are most clearly thrown into relief. Passed back and forth between Urko and Paco, the needle is the quite literal point of contact between the two boys – and by extension the opposing ideologies of their respective fathers. The close-ups subsequently illustrate how, in the words of Caroline Rosenthal and Dirk Vanderbeke, '[o]ur skin is in the most literal sense a contact zone where we encounter other people and our environment for the first time and where various exchanges between the self and other, self and world occur' (2015: 2). It is because of their heroin addiction that the unlikely meeting of Torrecuadrada and Aramendía takes place in the first place. When Urko is called into the police station for questioning, Torrecuadrada holds up Urko's limp arm, whose broken veins are mottled by red needle marks, to Aramendía as evidence of his son's drug addiction. He tells the shocked Aramendía: 'los padres somos los últimos en enterarnos' (us parents are the last to know). At the end of the film, after Urko has died of an overdose, Aramendía tells Torrecuadrada: 'cuantas muertes tenemos en nuestras vidas, comandante' (how many deaths do we have in our lives, captain) – here a reference to the ever-increasing toll of casualties that both heroin and terrorism had claimed at this time. While their meeting does not suggest political reconciliation, it nevertheless illustrates how heroin emerged as a narrative that connected people from disparate sectors of society in Spain in the 1980s.

As Rosenthal and Vanderbeke write, 'skin does not isolate us from our surroundings but rather immerses us in reciprocal relations' (2015: 2). As we have seen, the relationship between law enforcement and junkies during this period in Euskadi was also frequently reciprocal in nature. This is played out in the film by the actions of the drug trafficker el Cojo (Ovidi Montllor) and his wife Pilar (Marta Molins), who are revealed to be informants for the police, and those of the stony-faced Teniente Álcantara (Pedro Nieva Parola) who sadistically bribes detainees with bags of heroin. Frequently caught up in an interwoven web of drug trafficking and terrorism, the junky's body is positioned as a site of transaction – one that was shaped not only by the exchange of opioids and bodily fluids but by the passing back and forth of information. If, as according to Rosenthal and Vanderbeke, 'skin constitutes the permeable border between inside and outside' (2015: 2), this border is seen to be repeatedly violated in the film through the recurring images of needles piercing the flesh of the delinquent bodies. As the object that lends the film its name, the needle not only permeates the external boundaries of the delinquent body but serves to dramatise the complex political and criminological tensions at the heart of the film. The body of the junky in *El pico* is both a physical manifestation and a potent metaphor for the social disorder in the region, whose violation of skin also illuminates the disturbance of the boundaries between centralist authoritarianism and regional autonomy, law enforcement (*el picoleto*) on the one hand, and criminality (*el pico*) on the other.

As with *Miedo a salir de noche,* the film opens with the close-up shot of a television set, showing the investiture speech of Felipe González on 30 November 1982. A reverse shot reveals the protagonist Paco (José Luis Manzano) and his family watching the television over breakfast. Barely able to disguise his contempt, the father Evaristo Torrecuadrada speaks over González's voice, retorting 'A ver cuánto dura' (Let's see how long it lasts). If the Civil Guards are no longer invested with the power they had during the Franco years, Torrecuadrada nevertheless asserts himself as the voice of authority in his home. Embodying the Francoist values of order, hierarchy and honour, Torrecuadrada presides over the home with a patriarchal authoritarianism that runs counter to the new political climate of civil liberties indicated in the speech. As González declares the nation's will for change, underscored by the words 'nuestro pueblo ha querido otras Cámaras, otras leyes, otros contenidos de Gobierno' (our people have demanded another parliament, another set of laws, another government), the father orders his son to come home early before fastidiously donning his hat. The tension established between the overlapping diegetic sounds of background and foreground points to the uneasy coexistence of social and political change with the continuity of the old order. To this effect, de la Iglesia has frequently commented how the Civil Guards were incompatible with the new democracy (Sánchez Costa, 1984: n.p.). Indeed, with his *tricornio* and neatly trimmed moustache, the character recalls the appearance of Antonio Tejero, who as Paul Preston has shown, similarly became radicalised after being stationed in the Basque Country (1995: 178). The family's surname, Torrecuadrada (translated literally as 'square tower') evokes a cloistered fortress away from the outside world, an aspect that is further externalised through the *mise-en-scène* of the apartment, which is crammed with heavy mahogany furniture and chintzy ornaments.

The oppressive nature of the family home is emphasised during Paco's eighteenth birthday party. Depicted in an uninterrupted long take, we hear a cacophony of overlapping sounds, with the blaring television set competing with the voices of his family, and a telephone conversation between his grandmother and his father. Leading his son into the bedroom, Torrecuadrada dresses him up in a police uniform and paints a moustache on his face. Now the mirror image of his father, Paco stands poised within a door frame that is in turn framed by another door. As his father introduces him as 'Comandante Torrecuadrada' to the family and one of his sisters takes his photograph, Paco is vividly captured in a tableau of entrapment in which his initiation into manhood is bound by the Francoist values of patriarchal honour and authority. The tight and restricted framing here contrasts with the more open compositions used when Paco is away from the family unit, such as the scenes in which he is in Mikel's studio (played by Enrique San Francisco), an artist Paco occasionally has sex with in exchange for money. In contrast to his father, Mikel is presented as an empathetic force in Paco's life, whose reparative and nurturing nature is dramatised through his profession as a sculptor. When Mikel asks Paco why he takes heroin, he explains that 'te da la paz' (it gives you peace) – the drug providing him a sense of peace that contrasts with the auditory overload found at home. As Carlos Alberto Gómez Méndez has argued, the consumption of heroin here is presented as a freedom from the restraints imposed by society and the family unit (2015: 317).

As Paco in *El pico* becomes increasingly hooked on heroin, he starts to suffer from dry and excessively itchy skin, one of the first visible signs of heroin addiction. Manzano's fragile skin is emphasised by the use of high-contrast noirish lighting used in Mikel's studio, cross-illuminating Manzano's body so that the smooth contours of his chest and stomach are thrown into relief. Pacing around Mikel's studio, Paco repeatedly scratches his skin; after observing that Mikel looks concerned, he says: 'Oye, que no tengo ladillas ni piojos, ¿eh? … Es

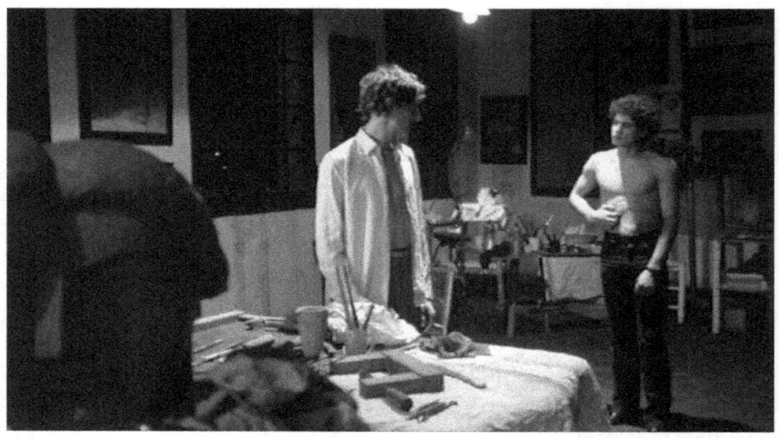

3.6 Paco (José Luis Manzano) scratches his skin, a symptom of heroin addiction, in Mikel's (Enrique San Francisco) apartment in *El pico* (Eloy de la Iglesia, 1983).

que el potro te da picores … Pero es una sensación muy agradable, da mucho gusto rascarse' (Listen, I don't have lice alright? It's just that smack makes you itchy … But it's a great feeling, scratching yourself feels really nice). His performance conflates the visual with the textural: his hands draw our eyes to the shape of his sculptural body, while his fingers and nails alert us to the itchy, flaky texture of his skin. Mikel's studio, filled with sculptures of somewhat dubious quality, further underscores the significance of touch in the film – an aspect which is most vividly dramatised through the presence of a sculpture in the form of a giant hand. As he paces around the room, Paco weaves a path around the sculptures before he places his hand onto a hand-shaped imprint on the sculpture of a female torso. Through his tactile interaction with Paco's art, the *mise-en-scène* draws parallels between the idealised classical beauty conveyed by Mikel's art and Manzano's own eroticised body.

After Paco has run away from home, Mikel offers Paco refuge in his studio, but on the condition that he abandons heroin. Some hours later, Mikel returns to his building to find Paco in the throes of withdrawal symptoms. Paco lies feverishly on his front, dragging himself across the floor before tearing apart a mound of wet clay with his hands. Relayed in a series of dissolves and slow-motion shots, the

3.7 In the throes of withdrawal symptoms from heroin, Paco (José Luis Manzano) tears apart wet clay with his hands in *El pico* (Eloy de la Iglesia, 1983).

distended temporality of these moments emphasise the materiality and texture of the image. Jennifer Barker refers to the editing technique of dissolves as 'a kind of cinematic caress', pointing to how it enables the surface of one image to dissolve into another, 'each one infusing and infecting the other with its heat, its texture, and its meaningfulness' (2009: 60). The complex sound design in this sequence similarly presents us with the dissolving of different sonic textures into one another: the physiological sounds of Paco's sharp gasps and fast breathing overlap with Mikel's reassuring words, their voices distorted in postproduction to create an echo effect, as the discordant synthesiser music commingles with the sound effects of the banging of metal. Mikel attempts to lift Paco's body up from the ground; Paco writhes around in agony, his skin covered in blood and wet clay, as he ejects a stream of vomit into Mikel's face. As Mikel comforts Paco, he strokes his face with his fingers as if sculpting with clay, his reparative touch slowly returning him to a state of clarity. As Bryan S. Turner argues, '[f]luids that flow from the inside to the outside of the bodies are dangerous and contaminating, because fluids on the outside of our body challenge our sense of order and orderliness' (2003: 5). Covered in bodily fluids, Paco's body is similarly presented as a site of disorder in this scene. Yet the violence of his withdrawal symptoms is also externalised onto the entire cinematic body, with the cinematography, editing and sound each working together to convey the visceral and embodied experience of heroin withdrawal.

This is further conveyed in the scene in which Paco and Urko visit the drug trafficker el Cojo and his wife. The soundtrack is dominated by the dissonant sounds of their young baby crying who, because his mother took heroin during the pregnancy, is now also addicted to the drug. Writing on *El pico,* a critic complained that it was the most excruciating film he had ever seen, noting that:

> Las secuencias en las que los chicos se pinchan en vena con sus jerenguillas, el 'mono' de José Luis Manzano y todo lo relatativo a la pareja de traficantes y a su bebé – con la ayuda de un *sonido hiriente* en primer plano – son momentos bestiales de difícil aguante.[12] (Hidalgo 1983: 38, my emphasis)

In registering the sound of the baby at close mike (an effect which was enhanced during the sound mix), its sounds have an 'hiriente' (wounding) effect on the body of the viewer/auditor. As Michel Serres and Lawrence Schehr have observed: '[n]oise and nausea, noise and nautical, noise and navy have the same etymology' (1983: 4). In alerting us to the connection between the two words, Serres and Schehr point to the ways in which our experience of sound is, above all, an embodied experience: like nausea, noise is felt through the body. In traversing and vibrating through us, sound can thus similarly possess the haptic quality which is pivotal to Marks's discussion of 'visual erotics', in so far that it implicates the viewer and demands their response. Like the images that evoke texture and surface, the soundtrack serves to enhance the visceral encounter between the film and the viewer that was so crucial to Eloy de la Iglesia's practice of filmmaking.

El pico 2: Punctured skin and the national body politic

The commercial success of *El pico* swiftly led to a sequel, whose production began in February 1984. De la Iglesia commented that the sequel allowed him to more fully explore the consequences of the themes of the first film (Mauri, 1998: 118–119). Again, agonising close-ups of needles were central to the affective charge in the film, here relayed in even longer takes than in the first film. To this effect, he said in an interview at the time of the release that he expected 'que el espectador se sienta fuertemente impactado' (the spectator feels strongly affected) (Poc, 1984). Opening with a flashback which replays the key events of the first film, *El pico 2* begins as Paco and his father Torrecuadrada (played in the sequel by a different actor, Fernando Guillén) move back to Madrid to live with Torrecuadrada's mother (Gracita Morales), as the father seeks to find detox treatment for his son. After an eyewitness implicates Paco in the murder of el Cojo and his wife, he is sent to prison. In the meantime, Caballero, a journalist, seeks to expose how Paco's crime reveals a broader web of police corruption. In basing much of the narrative in Madrid, *El pico 2* expanded the geographical reach of the drug trafficking and terrorism that had been depicted in Euskadi in the first film to a now national scale. With a narrative even more dense and multifaceted than the first part, the film seeks to uncover the complicity of the Spanish institutions of power within these networks.[13]

Like *El pico*, the shadow of heroin addiction both informed the narrative and hung over the production of the film. Despite attempting methadone treatment, Eloy de la Iglesia and Gónzalo Goicoechea would become increasingly addicted to heroin during this time, with their increased earnings from *El pico* allowing them to comfortably feed their habit daily (Mauri, 1998: 118). Indeed, Goicoechea was so severely affected by drugs at the time that the director brought in a third collaborator on the script, the young theatre writer and director Fermín Cabal (Mauri, 1998: 119). Cabal had a strong interest in marginality and wrote *Caballito del diablo* (1983),[14] a hard-hitting theatrical play about heroin addiction, as well as writing and directing *La reina del mate/The Queen of Maté* (1984), a delinquent-themed film that was also produced by Ópalo Films and which starred José Luis Fernández Eguia 'el Pirri'. Despite his lack of acting experience, Cabal insisted on performing the role of Caballero, a cynical journalist working for the sensationalist press in *El pico 2*, a casting decision that de la Iglesia would later regret (Aguilar, 1996: 159). Manzano similarly continued to take heroin in the months after the film. The popularity of *El pico* had catapulted the actor to fame, with his image now gracing the front covers of newspapers and magazines (Mauri, 1998: 117), including a well-documented appearance on the cover of the Spanish gay soft-porn magazine *Party*.[15] His media exposure even led to his being offered a minor role in the international co-production *The Hit*

(Stephen Frears, 1984), which the actor had to reject as he had recently been called up for military service (Fuembuena, 2017: 355). De la Iglesia had to apply for the actor to be released for twelve weeks in order to carry out the shoot and postproduction sound (Fuembuena, 2017: 359). Fuembuena notes that on his release, the actor's conspicuously pale complexion, circulatory problems and punctures on his arms were plain for all to see (2017: 359). His deteriorated physical appearance can be immediately seen in the film's opening sequence, for instance, where the actor looks directly at the camera, registered in an arresting close-up. With his sunken and dark-ringed eyes, furrowed brow and removed facial expression, Manzano physically embodies the role of Paco as a junky. The camera's proximity to Manzano serves not to glamorise the actor's new-found status as a star but rather to present us with a physical record of his degraded body. Filmed with natural lighting, the materiality of Manzano's damaged skin here possesses an ontological status, one that is further authenticated by the appearance of real-life photographs in the film's penultimate montage sequence where Manzano/Paco can be seen in military uniform kissing the Spanish flag – real-life images that were taken from the actor's period of military service.

3.8 A close-up of Paco (José Luis Manzano) in the opening sequence of *El pico 2* (Eloy de la Iglesia, 1984).

The premiere of *El pico 2* at the Valladolid International Film Festival was beset by scandal. In a further illustration of the affective power of de la Iglesia's filmmaking, the film generated a noisy response from the auditorium. News reports point to how the screening polarised the audience, with his film the recipient of the most boos, whistles, cheers and applause of the entire festival (Viola, 1984a; Viola, 1984b). Eloy de la Iglesia recalls how the audience started kicking against their seats during the scene at the end of the film when the tabloid journalist's photographer is seen taking pictures of the Civil Guard Torrecuadrada's bloody corpse, 'llenando la escena con fogonazos de luz' (filling the scene with flash lights) (Mauri, 1998: 128). The controversy surrounding the film had been exacerbated by the fact that José Luis Fernández Eguia 'el Pirri', one of the main actors of the film, was unable to attend the festival as he had been detained by the police. Manzano had also been denied temporary leave from military service, though in the end was finally allowed to attend. The director was quick to point out their exclusion to the press, declaring that one was being held by the civil authorities and the other by the military (Mauri, 1998: 130). The publicity surrounding their detention situated the struggle of junky delinquents against the broader repressive state apparatus, an irony which only served to further authenticate the narrative of the film. The festival also organised a screening of the film to take place in the prison for the inmates at Valladolid, where it was followed by a conversation on the penal system in Spain and its treatment of drug addicts (Viola, 1984a). Pilar Miró also attended the special screening, and reportedly had to intervene after the debate turned into, in the words of the director, 'un conato de motín' (an attempted mutiny), reportedly steering the questions back to the subject of the film so as to calm the inmates down (Mauri, 1998: 130). The tumultuous reception of the film at Valladolid extended to other cinemas across the country on the film's general release, such as in Barcelona where a gun was reportedly found in the auditorium (Mauri, 1998: 128).

Most of the scenes in which Paco is depicted in prison were shot on location in Carabanchel prison, and the hundred or so extras that appeared in this section were inmates in real life at the time (Poc, 1984).[16] While in the first instalment of *El pico,* heroin is presented as an escape from the repressive family unit, here it is presented as a metaphorical prison from which there is little chance of escape. With only a threadbare mattress to sleep on, Paco is placed in solitary confinement for three days and has his methadone confiscated, a punishment described in the voiceover narration as even worse than losing his freedom. His body is seen to be caught in the grip of violent and involuntary spasms and severe pain, and the sheer physicality of Manzano's performance here calls attention to the visceral effects of heroin withdrawal. De la Iglesia sought to expose how the Spanish penal system was ill-equipped to deal with heroin addicts, commenting at the time of the film that they only administered valium to those suffering cold turkey (Viola, 1984b). Eloy de la Iglesia can be briefly seen in a cameo standing alongside the other prisoners, his beard unkempt and clothes unwashed, an appearance that the director who, as an addict himself, described in the press as a 'gesto de solidaridad' (gesture of solidarity) (Poc, 1984). This solidarity is further spelt out in the film's dedication to the prisoners of Carabanchel and to all those who fight against the enslavement of heroin, which appears just before the end credits. We frequently hear the ambient sounds of the prison, its fortress-like architecture conveyed through the constant noise of metal doors and gates slamming and the echoing sounds of keys in locks. As Paco enters the prison, the song 'Me perdí en las tinieblas' (I became lost in the darkness) by Joaquín Carmona is played non-diegetically, the first of three *rumbas* that can be heard during this section of the film, whose purpose is to articulate the emotional experience of incarceration while addicted to heroin. As chapter 5 discusses, the sound of the *rumba* had become strongly associated with the experience of prisons during this period, its lyrics frequently drawing on an imagery of entrapment, both carceral and symbolic. In a later scene, the song 'Vuela que vuela' (It flies and flies) can be heard as Paco clutches onto the bars of the cell window; a dove flies past the window as his voiceover likens his withdrawal from heroin as being 'hundido en un agujero negro' (sunk in a black hole). The song is then played diegetically in another scene by Joaquín Carmona himself who appears in cameo as a musician prisoner – an appearance which establishes solidarity between heroin addicts and the music industry.

Paco's encounter with the charismatic prison kingpin Lendakari (Jaume Valls), a former ETA member who has been imprisoned for drug trafficking, both resumes and deepens the criminal networks between heroin and terrorism that were established in the first *El pico*. In carrying out research on how these networks operated within the Spanish prison system, de la Iglesia drew on accounts from prisoners from within the prison itself, including three who had been imprisoned for bank robbery and inmates whose sentences had been commuted from the death penalty (Lozano, 1984). Lendakari takes a particular interest in Paco on discovering that he is the son of Torrecuadrada, and invites him to his cell and offers him heroin. As Paco carefully prepares the needle and locates a vein for the injection, Lendakari reveals that el Cojo had been associated with a heroin-smuggling ring, but that he had also grassed on him to the Civil Guards. As he injects himself, we are presented once again with the haptic aesthetic of pierced skin and embodied sound of the sudden intake of breath, sharp and shallow, as the opioids fizz and flood through his body. As the dialogue subsides for a few seconds, the ambient sounds of the prison are amplified in the sound mix, as if presented from the point of audition of Paco, his perceptions suddenly sharpened by the rush of heroin. As in the first *El pico*, the surface of the skin simultaneously reveals the deeper criminal networks at play, whose covert imbrication within Spanish institutions of power have enabled the supply of the drug in the first place.

In his capacity to smuggle heroin and other contraband past the guards, Lendakari is presented as a powerful but slippery figure, able to negotiate and exploit the porous borders of the prison system to his advantage. His nickname 'el Lendakari', which is named after Lehendakari, the official term for the Head of the Basque Government, ironically points to his position in the film as an intermediary between criminal networks on the one hand and structures of power on the other. His liminal status is further dramatised by his cellmate and lover, who is played by a transgender actor who has breasts and a hairy chest, and boasts of still having 'cojones' (balls). After slitting open his own stomach with a machete, Lendakari is rushed from the penitentiary hospital from where he eventually carries out his escape. After Paco's release from prison, Lendakari reveals to Paco that a shadowy organisation has asked him to fight in a 'guerra sucia' (dirty war) against ETA members on the other side of the French border in exchange for the supply of heroin. Lendakari's point of contact with the organisation – a louche character with a moustache and oily slicked-back hair who is seen to be tracking Lendakari's movement, described in the script as simply 'El Enlace' (the contact) – is revealed to be in hock with the Civil Guards. If, following Bryan S. Turner, the disturbed body of the junky in *El pico* was a symptom of a broader body politic of social disorder, *El pico 2* also bears witness to the disturbance of the bodies of powerful institutions whose porous and leaking borders are illustrated though Lendakari's subversive movement. Indeed, the organisation waged in the dirty war here is the very first allusion in Spanish film that was made to the paramilitary group GAL (Grupos Antiterroristas de Liberación/[Anti-terrorist Liberation Groups]), undercover death squads that illegally targeted ETA terrorists, which operated in Spain between the years 1983 and 1987. The newspaper *El Mundo* would later famously link GAL to the heart of power in the PSOE government.

The cross-fertilisation of between criminal bodies and bodies of power is further explored through the use of costume in the film. After Paco and Lendakari are reunited outside prison, they commit robberies with Betti, with whom Lendakari begins to have sex, in order to fund their addiction. Betti threatens two Civil Guards with a needle and steals their uniform after injecting them with sedatives; dressed as police officers, they are then able to rob a security vehicle at gunpoint. It is through the leaking and cross-infiltrations of bodies and organisations that enable the film's dramatic climax to take place. Alcántara leaks information on the hiding place of Lendakari, Paco and Betti to the journalist Caballero, who in turn divulges their whereabouts to Paco's father Torrecuadrada. Torrecuadrada arrives at the secluded house at night and orders his son at gunpoint to accompany him. In retaliation, Paco taunts his father with a loaded pistol, and says 'ya estoy igual que tú: armado' (I'm the same as you: armed), reminding him that he shouldn't be so surprised because he learnt how to hold a gun from watching him as a child. Conveyed through shot-reverse shot editing, their confrontation is further dramatised through the illumination of a naked bulb hanging from the ceiling, swinging back and forth between father and son. Torrecuadrada lowers his gun and eggs Paco on to shoot him; he is suddenly shot, however, by Lendakari instead, who has until now hidden himself in another room of the house. As the father collapses onto the ground, Lendakari hurries towards the window, readying himself to escape. Paco says: '¿Escapar? ¿Pero adónde?' (Escape, but where to?) and shoots him in the back. Alcántara and three other armed police officers storm into the building, followed in turn by journalist Caballero and his photographer. We hear the echoing click of the flashlight as the photographer eagerly takes photographs of the crime scene, the images of the dead bodies relayed through grainy black-and-white still photography. The incorporation of photographic objects into the sequence more broadly illustrates the intermedial nature of *cine quinqui*, where, as we have seen, understandings of delinquency and agencies of control were shaped by their images in the media. Indeed, the journalist's pursuit of Paco's story throughout the film has been portrayed as cynically motivated by shock value rather than any kind of social purpose. Yet if Caballero's news reports primarily appeal to the senses and the emotions, so too does Eloy de la Iglesia's filmmaking. The shock aesthetics of the scene, brought into stark relief through the unflinching glare of the naked bulb and the flashlight, translate the imagery of the sensationalist press into cinematic form.

The final scene, presented as an epilogue, shows Paco in the near future as a powerful drug dealer, married to Betti and with a newly born baby, living in an apartment similar to that of el Cojo in *El pico*. In a clear echo of the earlier film, the piercing cries of the baby can be heard as Paco receives a visit from two teenage boys. Just as Paco and Urko were doing years ago, the boys are collecting the heroin to sell on the streets. Paco then receives a telephone call from Alcántara, his imposing body filmed from a low-angle as he stands in front of a Spanish flag in the police station asking Paco for information on a recent seizure of drugs. The film thus takes us full circle: Paco has now taken on el Cojo's mantle as the local drug baron-cum-informer for the police, a final status that dramatises the endemic cross-fertilisation of the Basque drug trade and the Civil Guards, networks of criminality and agents of social control. A rare moment of tenderness in an otherwise bitter film, the final shot sees Paco comfort the baby, as his crying subsides and he breaks into a smile, as if to suggest that the next generation will break free from the paternal cycle of violence.

Conclusion

After *El pico 2*, José Luis Manzano would make one more film with Eloy de la Iglesia, *La estanquera de Vallecas* (1987). While they initially had lived with each other for two years, their relationship had deteriorated to such an extent that they were barely speaking at this point. For his part, de la Iglesia would not go on to make another film until *Los novios búlgaros/The Bulgarian Lovers* (2003) – despite the well-publicised claim that 'mi adicción a la droga es poca cosa comparada con mi adicción al cine' (my addiction to drugs is little compared to my addiction to cinema) (cited in Melero, 2013: 77). By 1992, the director was living penniless in an apartment without water or electricity (Sherry, 1992). In the same year, Manzano, who had just been released from Carabanchel prison, let himself into de la Iglesia's apartment to say goodbye to him, as he was reportedly leaving for Seville in search of work. De la Iglesia returned three days later to find him dead, with a needle sticking out of his left knee (Parrado, 2017).[17] The scene of his death tragically revealed the damaged surface of his skin for one last time. As this chapter has shown, the directness of de la Iglesia's cinematic aesthetics depended on a mutual imbrication of the skin and the self, the cinematic body and the body of the audience. In particular, this chapter has explored how this relationship was in part established through the soundtrack in the films. Through the physiological sounds of the breath and the body, the films drew attention to the fragility of the delinquent body and the troubled surface of his skin. The porosity of skin, as we have seen, in turn illuminated broader tensions surrounding heroin and police repression, as well as the subsequent damage it wrought to the body politic of Spain during the 1980s.

Notes

1 'This direct contact with the public that my films have is the true basis of their commercial appeal.'

2 Reading the article on a train to Córdoba for a meeting organised by the Partido Comunista de España (Communist Party of Spain), de la Iglesia later commented that the news story would, without him knowing at the time, change the course of his life (Mauri, 1998: 62).

3 See *El Caso Mensual*, 14 April 1979, which was a special monograph issue dedicated to the life and death of el Jaro.

4 See for instance Gurruchaga (1983: 31) and Aguilar (1996) who offer this turn of events.

5 See for instance Marinero (1980).

6 Isela Vega was dubbed by Charo López and Verónica was dubbed by Tina Sáinz, both of whom were regular actresses in Eloy de la Iglesia's films.

7 Bonet Mójica writes : 'Adoptar una postura maniquea, pero a la inversa, donde los buenos son los navajeros y los males son una galería de policías ineficaces y corruptos, supone adentrarse en el terreno de la demagogia' (In adopting a Manichean position, but an inverted one where the knived delinquents are the good guys and the bad guys are a gallery of inefficient and corrupt police, the film verges on the populist) (1980).

8 The title is an allusion to the lyrics 'Mi jaca galopa y corta el viento' from the popular song 'Mi Jaca', which was interpreted by Raphael, Manolo Escobar as well as a host of other popular artists.

9 The law was otherwise known as Decreto Real (Royal Decree) 3304/1983. For a full discussion of the *ley Miró* policies and its impact on the Spanish film industry, see Núria Triana-Toribio (2003: 111–119). Eloy de la Iglesia set up the production company Ópalo Films with the veteran producer Pérez Giner (who had also collaborated on the production of *Perros callejeros*) so as to oversee the production of the film. They received subsidies towards the film's relatively high budget of 47 million pesetas (Martínez Álvarez, 2018: 270) and would similarly receive subsidies for the sequel *El pico 2.*

10 Juan María Bandrés explained that he refused the role because he did not want to appear ridiculous, and that his schedule was too full at the time (C.G., 1983: 38).

11 A key event of the Spanish Civil War, the aerial bombing carried out by Nationalists of the town of Gernika took place on 26 April 1937.

12 'The sequences in which the boys inject themselves in the vein with their syringes, the withdrawal symptoms of José Luis Manzano and everything related to the couple of drug traffickers and their baby – with the help of a wounding sound in close-up – are brutal moments which are hard to bear.'

13 The camerawork and lighting are notably more polished than in *El pico,* no doubt due to the input of the prominent cinematographer Javier Aguirresarobe. Aguirresarobe also worked on *La muerte de Mikel/The Death of Mikel* (Imanol Uribe 1984), a Basque film that was another commercial hit of that year which also addressed the theme of ETA, and *27 horas* (Montxo Armendáriz, 1987) which dealt with heroin abuse in San Sebastián. For an excellent overview of Javier Aguirresarobe's work, see Ann Davies (2016: 111–137).

14 *Caballito del diablo* is 'dragonfly' in English. The word 'caballo' (horse), however, also means heroin in Spanish slang.

15 See *Party*, no. 247, September 1984.

16 Eduardo Fuembuena writes that the scenes that take place in Lenda's and Paco's prison cells were filmed in Cinearte studios, Madrid (2017: 271). This accounts for the more dramatic lighting scheme used in these scenes.

17 José Luis Fernández Eguia 'el Pirri' also died of an overdose in May 1988, and was similarly discovered with a needle in his arm on a piece of wasteland in Vilcávaro. See García Santa Cecilia (1988), for instance, for a report of his death.

4

Listening to the delinquent voice

One of the defining features of *cine quinqui* was the sound of the delinquent voice. In both its distinctive use of slang and its timbre, the voice was central to the affective charge of the films. This was particularly borne out in the case of *Deprisa, deprisa* (Carlos Saura, 1981) and *Yo, 'el Vaquilla'* (José Antonio de la Loma, 1985), where the vocal delivery and the distinctive sonorities of the delinquent voice were shaped by the use of location shooting and direct sound. The close relationship between geography and sound technology, space and microphone in these films firmly grounded the delinquent body within its spatial context. As the delinquent actors recount or re-enact their experiences of criminality and the Spanish penitentiary system, we hear the voices of the delinquents in the locations they frequented in real life: the stolen vehicles, discotheques, prison cells and the streets of the marginal suburbs of Madrid and Barcelona. As this chapter aims to show, the embeddedness of their voices in space also had an important testimonial function. As well as a vehicle for self-expression, their voices served to bear first-hand witness to the material conditions of life on the margins of Spanish urban centres, as well as to the systemic torture and abuse encountered in Spain's penitentiary system in the late 1970s and 1980s.

Through a close analysis of *Deprisa, deprisa* and *Yo, 'el Vaquilla'*, this chapter explores how, through their blurring of the boundaries between fiction and real-life, the vocal performances of the delinquents undermined conventional notions of film acting. The chapter traces the development the delinquent slang found in the films within its urban context, exploring the ways in which their language was defined by its spatially transgressive and covert nature. It not only attends to their use of language but the sound of the *quinquis*, exploring the political resonance of the grain of their voices, an aspect which was emphasised through the use of direct sound. In doing so, this chapter extends the discussion of voice to encompass a broader range of symbolic and political meanings attached to vocality. If, in the chapter that follows, the discussion of voices slides easily from its material vocal expression to its more symbolic associations, this is because, as Jacob Smith reminds us, 'the voice's ability to operate on so many levels is an important part of its fascination as a vehicle of performance' (2008: 3). Indeed, the chapter ultimately aims to show how through sound design and vocal performance, *Deprisa, deprisa* and *Yo, 'el Vaquilla'* quite literally 'gave voice' to a social group that had been deprived of one, providing them with textual authority and political agency. As such, their voices came to symbolise the broader struggle of all delinquents and social prisoners in Spain during the transition to democracy.

Locating the delinquent voice during the transition to democracy

One of the key ways in which *cine quinqui* broke new ground in the history of Spanish film was in its attempt to depict what marginal people actually sounded like. Much in the same way that American audiences were exposed to the Chicago delinquent slang of the time through the Warner Brothers gangster cycle in the 1930s, whose films were produced shortly after the invention of synchronised sound, *cine quinqui* presented audiences with the kinds of marginal diction and slang that had rarely been heard on Spanish screens. The novelty of the delinquent voice subsequently elicited strong reactions in the Spanish media. Writing in the magazine *Gaceta Ilustrada*, the essayist and philosopher Julián Marías (father of novelist Javier) expressed dismay on listening to the dialogue of *Deprisa, deprisa*, which he dismissed saying 'apenas es una lengua' (it's barely a language), writing that:

> Su pobreza es increíble; su vocabulario es mínimo, comparable con el de algunos pueblos primitivos; su sintaxis es literalmente inexistente, porque no hay elocución coherente, sino muñones de frases, 'completadas' por interjecciones, principalmente tacos.[1] (Marías, 1981)

Marías further likens their language to 'una regresión hacia el hotentote, el bosquimano o tal vez el hombre de Cro-Magnon' (regression into hottentot, bushman speak or maybe Cro-Magnon man) (1981). Marías's hyperbolic reaction to what he perceived to be a deformation of standard Spanish is perhaps not that surprising, given that he was a prominent member of the Real Academia Española, the official royal institution which oversees the linguistic standardisation and unity of the Spanish language. Yet his comments also illustrate the extent to which the delinquent argot was impenetrable to much of the population. This is borne out by the several glossaries appearing in the press which explained their slang terms to the general public, such as one from *Interviú* in 1979, 'Así hablan los marginados' (This is how marginal people speak) (Sánchez, 1979). Providing over 500 terms along with their definitions, the glossary describes their language as a heady mix of *caló* (gypsy dialect), slang, Romani and English, claiming that 'Los marginados, a pesar de ser muchos, no pretenden que les sea reconocida su lengua como oficial' (despite there being many of them, marginalised people don't want their language to be officially recognised) (Sánchez, 1979: 61).

In its hybridity and exclusion to outsiders, their marginal speech has much in common with what sociolinguist M. A. K. Halliday has termed an 'anti-language'. As Halliday explains, an anti-language is 'a language relexicalised', in that it tends to use 'new words for old' (1976: 571). In its process of relexicalisation, an anti-language creates different vocabulary in particular areas, 'typically those that are central to the activities of the subculture and that set it off most sharply from the established society' (1976: 571). Correspondingly, the slang spoken by delinquents during this period is particularly rich when it comes to criminal activities (in particular, stealing and dealing in and consuming drugs) and the law (police, cells, prisons and prison officers), as well as for describing money. Halliday explains that the language is not only relexicalised in these particular areas but is in fact *over*lexicalised, where we find several words that are practically synonymous with one another (1976: 571). In the glossary provided in *Interviú,* for instance, there are six words which denote the meaning of steal (afanar, lañar, mangar, mariscar, picar, salvar), seven for thief (bailador, bailaón, bajamano, choro, mangurrillos, tegui, topero), nine for prison or prison cell (cangri, chirona, catre, chabolo, chupano, maco, talego, trena, trullo), and eleven for money (cala, cangrejo, guitar, lata, libra, lechuga, lechugón, manteca, nipos, tejo, tela) (Sánchez, 1979: 61–63). While the proliferation of these words is often interchangeable, a good deal of vocabulary is used to distinguish between sub-categories of the same thing. For instance, while the glossary provides a total of five slang words for the police which appear to be used synonymously (bofia, guri, guripa, pasma, pestañí), other words denote particular types of police: 'espeta' for a police officer working in the drugs squad; 'mono' for an armed police officer; 'picoletos', 'Pies Planos' and 'sapos verdes' for Civil Guards; and 'señores' for plain-clothes policemen.

Taken together as a whole, these overlexicalised fields of vocabulary, explicitly in the *quinqui* slang areas of criminal activity and surveillance, form the expression of the alternative social structure which Halliday terms an 'anti-society' (Halliday, 1976: 570). An anti-society is set up within established society yet is also a conscious alternative to it, a subcommunity which establishes its own construction of reality. Within an anti-language, overlexicalisation has two consequences: firstly, it enhances the possibility of verbal play and display within the anti-society, both heightening and maintaining a sense of solidarity; secondly, it makes the anti-language especially impenetrable to outsiders, and as such, the illicit dealings of the speakers can 'remain semi-confidential, even when conducted in relatively public spaces such as the club, bar or street' (Montgomery, 2008: 115). As an anti-language, the *quinqui* argot is similarly marked by its covert nature. This is not surprising, given both their social and geographical marginalisation in Spain, as well as their antagonistic history with the authorities. As Jesús de las Heras and Juan Villarín have shown, the first wave of *quinquis,* whose movement within Spain was nomadic, developed a secret way of speaking which they referred to as '*caliente*' ('hot' or 'warm') so that their language would not be understood (1974: 253). To this effect Heras and Villarín also describe how their slang was forced to rapidly evolve so as to ensure that the authorities would not recognise it (1974: 252). In constantly shape-shifting and adapting to its surroundings, the protean flexibility of *quinqui* slang ensured it would remain impregnable to an outsider's ear. As such, the distinction between language and anti-language, standard Spanish and *quinqui* slang, cannot be neatly mapped onto corresponding geographies of belonging and exclusion. As criminologists Keith Hayward and Jock Young have argued, while spatial segregation and division inevitably occur in urban life, deviant action can be more productively understood as a 'thinly veiled nether world that bubbles up just under the surface of appearances', something that happens in the 'underlife' of the city and its institutions (2004: 265). In its description of marginal argot, *Interviú* evokes a strikingly similar description of the urban underlife whose delinquent slang is spoken, they show, with a similar set of spatial coordinates. They write that marginal language is spoken 'debajo, al lado, dentro, fuera de nuestra sociedad' (underneath, beside, within and outside our society) (Sánchez, 1979: 61).

Delinquent speech therefore possessed its own fluid geography that imperceptibly moved over and between the cracks of power, a complex spatiality that was difficult to pin down. Defining the precise localisation of their speech became particularly complex in the late 1970s and 1980s, where certain elements of their argot began to be incorporated into Spanish youth slang more generally. Quite regardless of their social class or background, the speech of many young people in Spain, and especially those living in Madrid, dramatically evolved during this period. Young people began to appropriate some of their words and expressions as well as to speak with speech patterns and intonations which appeared to mirror the *quinqui* slang. Fernando Lázaro Carreter was the first linguist to provide a scholarly study of this emerging youth slang, which he termed *cheli* in his 1980 book *Estudios de Linguística* (1980: 244). *Cheli* slang had become so prevalent in Spain that Lázaro Carreter also published an article in the newspaper *ABC* on the subject.[2] The general changes in youth slang are not only arguably attributed to the increasing dissemination of delinquent slang during these years but to the physical movement of second generation rural-to-urban migrants living on the peripheries of cities. This was observed by the anthropologist Esperanza Molina Roy, in her landmark 1984 book *Los otros madrileños*, a study of life in El Pozo del Tío Raimundo, in the Puente de Vallecas district of Madrid (1984: 110). Drawing on fieldwork and her own first-hand experience of living among shanty-town communities for several years, Molina noted how differently the children of migrants spoke from their parents, who had originally settled in the *barrio* in the late 1950s and early 1960s (1984: 110). Their language, she observed, was neither like that of their parents nor like those who lived in the centre of the city (Molina, 1984: 110). She shows that quite unlike their parents, who rarely moved beyond the confines of their own *barrio*, these younger residents of El Pozo spent considerable time in the city for both work and leisure, and that their slang was in turn influencing the phonetics of the way other people spoke in Madrid (1984: 110).

While like most slangs, *quinqui* and *cheli* argots were mainly found in the spoken language, they also increasingly found their way into the written form in the 1980s. Countercultural fanzines associated with the Movida Madrileña, such as *La Luna de Madrid*, *Gratis* and *Star* further popularised the slang among its young readers. Yet it was Francisco Umbral, the prominent essayist and writer, who most notably brought *cheli* to the establishment in 'El Spleen de Madrid', a column he wrote for the newspaper *El País* which documented youth culture in Madrid. Significantly, his fascination with youth slang lay not just in its inventive and ever-evolving range of vocabulary but in its distinctive tone of voice. Umbral writes that 'El núcleo del cheli, como el de un dialecto griego o una lengua imperial, es la *guturalidad*, lo que en un poeta llamaríamos la voz personal, el estilo inconfundible, el son, que "hace la cancion"' (1983: 3).[3] In highlighting the gutturalness of youth slang, Umbral here alerts us not only to the language that they used but the distinctive sound or timbre of their voices when speaking. Francisco Umbral's description therefore brings to mind Roland Barthes's writing on the grain of the voice, which refers to the physical trace of the body in the voice, or 'the body in the voice as it sings' as he has famously written (1977: 185) – a description that resonates with Umbral's description of *cheli* as that which 'hace la canción' (sings). In emphasising the link between body and voice, the use of direct sound in *Deprisa, deprisa* and *Yo, 'el Vaquilla'* vividly captured the grain of the delinquent voice. As we will see, the spontaneity and naturalism of their performances alert us to the broader political significance of the grain of the voice, one which emerges in the films as a vehicle for self-expression and agency.

Deprisa, deprisa: Voice, realism and agency

Produced during 1980 and released in Spain in May 1981, *Deprisa, deprisa* signalled both a rupture from Carlos Saura's filmmaking of the 1960s and 1970s, which was known for its metaphorical critiques of the Franco regime, as well as a return to the theme of delinquency of his cinematic debut *Los golfos* (1960). The film was a co-production between his regular producer Elías Querejeta Producciones and the French production company Films Molière (with the latter also having co-production credits on his more recent films *Los ojos vendados/ Blindfolded Eyes* (1976) and *Mamá cumple cien años/Mama Turns 100* (1978)). Saura began writing a script that was based on a file of newspaper clippings about juvenile delinquency that he had been collecting over the years, particularly about robberies (D'Lugo, 1991: 163). In the press notes for the film, Saura notes that after scouting for locations on the periphery of Madrid and speaking to its residents, he was surprised to find how little he knew of the city and its changes in recent years. He noted in particular that 'incluso el lenguaje era diferente; se hablaba de distinta manera, con otros giros, en los barrios de la periferia (even the language was different; people spoke in a different way, with other expressions, in the *barrios* on the outskirts) (Saura, 1981). In light of his findings, the director began work on a new script which contained several new scenes and pieces of dialogue (D'Lugo, 1991: 164). For the cast, he wanted to find teenagers who came from the same neighbourhood, who were already friends, if possible, and who spoke in the same way (D'Lugo, 1991: 164). Carlos Saura had originally cast a teenage boy named Matías, a blue-eyed local delinquent from the district of Villaverde, Madrid, for the role of the protagonist, Pablo.[4] Shortly before the beginning of the shoot, however, Matías was killed by the police and José Antonio Valdelomar González (whose nickname was 'el Mini') was subsequently brought in as a last-minute replacement. Valdelomar was reportedly paid 300,000 pesetas for the role (approximately 1,800 euros).[5] Jesús Arias Aranzueque ('el Susi') and José María Hervás Roldán played the roles of Meca and Sebas, two members of Pablo's gang, and Berta Socuéllamos the role of Ángela, who becomes Pablo's girlfriend.

The pre-production stages of the film were arduous and complicated, leading Saura to convince Elías Querejeta to allow them to spend more time on the project (Galán, 1981). The rehearsals with the non-professional actors were particularly rigorous, with Saura initially filming them with a video camera so as to get the actors accustomed to acting in front of a film crew. Ensuring that the dialogue was as naturalistic as possible, Saura incorporated the delinquents' suggestions for changes into the script and continued to work on it as the rehearsals progressed (Galán, 1981). The actual shoot of the film took place over a period of nine weeks and its overall budget was 36 million pesetas (Fernández Santos, 1992). Its premiere was held at the Berlin Film Festival in February 1981, two months before its general Spanish release in April that year. Despite receiving a divided reception amongst the public, the film unexpectedly won the Golden Bear, with boos reportedly heard in the auditorium as the prize was announced (Anon, 1981a). The film's surprise success was quickly overshadowed by the arrest of Valdelomar one month later, whose dramatic events were widely reported in the Spanish media. In an anti-mimetic twist of fate that had now become typical of *cine quinqui*, Valdelomar was arrested after carrying out an armed robbery at a branch of the Banco de Vizcaya on Calle Ríos Rosas in Madrid – a real-life crime that mirrored the bank robbery that Pablo and his gang carry out in the film. Indeed, his robbery and subsequent arrest were the very stuff of cinema. Valdelomar and his accomplice stole 167,000 pesetas and got away in a taxi (a SEAT 131) which they apprehended after threatening the driver at gunpoint (Anon, 1981c).[6] They were followed in an unmarked car by Juan Antonio González Pacheco (known as Billy 'el Niño') (Llopis, 1981: 101), one of the most prolific and infamous torturers of political dissidents during the regime – and who controversially remains unpunished for his crimes to this day. At the moment of his arrest, the delinquent was reportedly carrying a copy of his contract for the film (Llopis, 1981: 101).

With just days until the Spanish premiere, the story of the arrest in the Spanish media no doubt generated hype around the forthcoming film. Elías Querejeta, whose production office received dozens of phone calls from journalists, staunchly defended Valdelomar's behaviour during the shoot (Llopis, 1981: 101). During a press conference in Barcelona, moreover, Querejeta strongly denied accusations from journalists that Valdelomar's arrest had been used as a ploy to promote the film (Esteban, 1981: 181). To add to the controversy, the press also drew on police records that showed that Valdelomar had been taking heroin during the shoot (Anon, 1981b). The right-wing newspaper *ABC* went as far as accusing Carlos Saura of supplying the teenagers with drugs throughout the duration of the shoot, an allegation that was roundly denied by both director and producer. Saura explained that the journalist (who, according to the director, had previously been a member of the police force) saw the film as a defence of delinquency and had a personal vendetta against him (Sánchez Vidal, 1988: 147).[7] *Deprisa, deprisa* was still showing in cinemas in Madrid in August that year when news broke about a second arrest.[8] Jesús Arias Aranzueque ('el Susi') had similarly been

AÑO 6 nº 260 **interviu** 1981 7-13 Mayo

El protagonista de «Deprisa, deprisa», en Carabanchel

UN PRESO DE PELICULA

Por JOSE F. HEREDIA

Ocupó la cabecera de las carteleras cinematográficas. Era actualidad. Acaparaba premios y el reconocimiento público de su labor. Luego, siguió acaparando las páginas de los periódicos. Su nombre, **José Antonio Valdelomar**, *ya no aparecía en las páginas de espectáculos, sino en las de sucesos. Había protagonizado en la vida real lo mismo que habían captado las cámaras en el terreno de la ficción. Había atracado un banco. A partir de entonces,* **José Antonio** *era carne de presidio, carne de Carabanchel, lugar al que ha acudido* **INTERVIU** *para entrevistarle.*

4.1 The recent imprisonment of José Antonio Valdelomar, the leading actor of *Deprisa, deprisa* (Carlos Saura, 1981), reported in the news magazine *Interviú*, no. 260, 7–13 May, 1981, 82–83.

involved in an armed robbery of a bank, where he fled with 950,000 pesetas and like Valdelomar escaped in a SEAT 131. *El Caso* described the scene of the robbery as 'igual a la filmada de Saura' (the same as the one filmed by Saura) (C.A., 1981: 7). Like Valdelomar, Arias Aranzueque's motivation for the crime was to fund his heroin addiction, on which he was reportedly spending 15,000 pesetas a day, and his addiction had led to an alarming loss of weight (C.A., 1981: 7). Aranzueque would join Valdelomar in Carabanchel prison in Madrid, where they would reportedly watch a screening of *Deprisa, deprisa* together in the projection room of the prison (García, J. 1981).

Evidence of their addiction can be found in Valdelomar's and Aranzueque's performances during the film. Their raspy voices and slurred speech, slack-jawed expressions and glazed-over eyes reveal the anaesthetising effects of heroin on their bodies. In their presentation of drug taking and other criminal activities, their performances therefore possessed an evidential status of actuality. Even one of the guns used in the film (most likely the one used when Pablo and Ángela practise their shooting range on discarded tin cans) allegedly contained real bullets (Baeta 1981: 19). Through the frequent use of long takes and long depth of field, their criminal acts are presented with a matter-of-fact realism that ran counter to the salacious depiction of *quinquis* in the media. Carlos Saura's refusal to cast a moral judgement on the characters was criticised in the right-wing press and the film industry alike. The Catholic newspaper *Ya*, for instance, attacked the film for depicting delinquency in an attractive and aesthetically pleasing way, concluding that it was inciting crime (Blanco Vila, 1981). The report of the Spanish classification board, moreover, stated that *Deprisa, deprisa* posed a danger to young audiences, who might feel attracted to the behaviour of the delinquents who were, in the words of the official, presented as 'héroes del asfalto' (heroes of the asphalt) (Hernández Les, 1986: 186). In France, the Commission de Contrôle Cinématographique was equally as damning. Limiting its release to 70 copies in France and providing it with an 18 certificate, their report stated that its portrayal of crime was too seductive and presented a serious risk to younger viewers (Laborde, 1981).

Although Carlos Saura did not seek to moralise the criminal behaviour of the delinquents, he was equally keen not to portray them as victims of their surroundings either. To this effect, the film withholds the motivations behind their criminal acts. As Saura has commented: 'No sé por qué hay esa obsesión de buscar la causa-efecto, de buscar las razones' (I don't know why there has to be an obsession with the search for cause and effect, with searching for reasons) (Comas, 1981). Indeed, in frequently appearing in a state of absorption, the characters appear closer to the anti-psychological characters of the modern art film, which András Bálint Kovács terms the 'abstract individual' (2007: 65). Meca stands transfixed and speechless by the sight of burning vehicles, for instance, while Ángela is frequently seen watching the actions of the gang, the camera lingering on her introspective and quizzical gaze. Presented without direction or orientation, the actions of the teenagers are not always causally linked to the progression of the film's narrative. When they are not committing robberies, their movement is loose and episodic, as they drift hazily between discoteques, the hinterlands between Madrid and Getafe and the sea. If, for much of the narrative in the film, the actors appear to be passively adrift, the question of their agency – or rather lack thereof – was similarly brought into focus at the press conference at the Berlin International Film Festival, where José Antonio Valdelomar and Berta Socuéllamos were interviewed alongside the director Carlos Saura. A German critic reportedly accused Saura of treating his actors like objects. For his part, Valdelomar appeared perplexed and defensive during the questions, and took off his headphones and mouthpiece and abruptly left the press conference before it ended (Comas, 1981). Valdelomar's handling of the questions, which was described by Comas as unpolished and inarticulate, betrayed an absence of media awarenesss that professional actors, who most frequently serve as ambassadors for their films, take all too easily for granted. His inability to adapt to the discourse of the press conference pointed to the broader inability of non-professional actors to be able to distinguish between what James Naremore famously terms 'performance frames' (1988: 9). Naremore uses the notion of the performance frame to mark out a distinction between theatrical acting and aleatory acting (or in other words, the way we act in everyday life). As inexperienced non-actors, filmed on location in areas they lived in or frequented, the nuanced distinctions between the different possible performance frames were inevitably blurred. *El Caso*, for instance, wrote of how Jesús Arias Aranzueque's performance in *Deprisa, deprisa* 'no hacía más que repetir lo que diariamente hacía' (not doing anything other than repeating what he did everyday) (C.A., 1981, 7). Significantly, it is Valdelomar's vocal expression, marked by a speech and diction markedly distinct from the audience of critics and the film crew, which revealed his failure to negotiate the 'performance frame' of a press conference. Like several of the *quinqui* actors in this book, the continuity of his spontaneous self – from everyday life to his performance in the film and his subsequent media appearances – found its most vivid expression through his voice. Valdelomar demonstrated the extent to which *quinqui* actors, simply put, spoke as themselves.

Vocal performance and geography

Deprisa, deprisa begins *in media res* with a tracking shot of a row of cars parked in front of a respectable apartment block in suburban Madrid. The camera closes in on a silver-coloured SEAT to partially reveal Pablo and Meca, sat in the passenger and driver's seat respectively, furtively attempting to hot-wire the vehicle. As Marvin D'Lugo has observed, the windscreen shields the delinquents from the full view of the audience, with the reflection of the modern apartment block on the glass obscuring the full view of the delinquents (1991: 167). The reflected image of the buildings, captured at an oblique angle, locates us within a space that first appears immaterial and fleeting: an establishing shot founded on absence rather than presence. Typical of the scores of suburban apartments constructed during Spain's miracle years, their intangible reflection suggests an urban geography that remains out of the reach of the delinquents. Yet if both the camera and the car serve to frame Pablo and Meca at a distance, their vocal performance that follows nevertheless establishes a closer relationship with the audience. The following shot, this time with the camera positioned from within the car, pans the surrounding buildings from Pablo's eye-line. As Meca attempts to start the engine of the stolen car, Pablo asks: 'Qué te pasa, ¿se te olvida cómo se hace o qué? (What's wrong, have you forgotten how it's done or what?). Their dialogue is conveyed in auditory close-up, even during shots when the camera is positioned from outside of the car. The sound of their vocal performances stands in pointed contrast with that of the owners of the vehicle, a smartly dressed middle-aged man and woman, who, with their daughter and her nanny in tow, are introduced in a long shot as they are walking out of their apartment block. On seeing Pablo and Meca in his car, the man abruptly breaks off their conversation

4.2 Pablo (José Antonio Valdelomar, 1981) speaking from within a stolen car in *Deprisa, deprisa* (Carlos Saura, 1981).

about their daughter's birthday and shouts '¡Martita, me están robando el coche!' (Martita, they're stealing my car!). While Pablo's and Meca's dialogue is captured in direct sound, the voices of the married couple are quite conspicuously dubbed. Recorded entirely during postproduction, their vocal delivery appears both heightened yet removed from geographical space.

In both its sound and diction, their vocal performances establish a disruptive contrast with that of the delinquents. Unlike Pablo and his friends, who tend to drop their consonants and elide words, their words are marked by their crystal-clear and exaggerated enunciation. The actors here draw on a range of expansive gesticulations and facial expressions which border on the hyperkinetic. We see the man charge decisively towards his car, banging his clenched fists against the window. He then dives into the road, his arms flailing about frantically in the air, as he attempts to enlist the help of a passing vehicle. Meanwhile his wife, stood petrified at a distance away from the action, tightly grips and wrings her scarf in distress, calling out '¡ladrones! ¡ladrones!' (thieves, thieves!). In common with her husband's dialogue, her cries for help, physically conveyed through her heavily painted lips atremble and her mouth aghast, are very loosely synched in this scene. In both voice and gesture, their acting here exhibits a far greater degree of

4.3 The victim of the car robbery angrily confronts Pablo in *Deprisa, deprisa* (Carlos Saura, 1981).

'ostensiveness' (to borrow James Naremore's term [1988: 17]), which stands in pointed contrast with the delinquents whose register of performance is far more contained than it is exhibited. Even when angry, José Antonio Valdelomar's vocal delivery is cool and laconic, casually dragging out each consonant in a way typical of delinquent slang of this period. The spatial division inside and outside here is reinforced through the coexistence of two vocal performances: the 'authentic' anti-language of the delinquents against the artificial sound of carefully enunciated and correct Spanish. The sound design quite literally gives voice to the delinquents, at once providing them with agency and visibility. From the outset, then, we are immersed within the sonorous world of the delinquents, while bourgeois society is placed on the sidelines.

The contrasting vocal performances here not only owe themselves to the way in which the actors speak but to the technical conditions in which they were recorded, thereby illustrating Pamela Robertson Wojcik's observation that 'screen acting is constructed as much by sound design as by labour' (2006: 73). Indeed, the vocal performances of the married couple are shaped by the way in which they speak directly into the microphone, as well as the space of the anechoic chamber in which they voices are recorded. Carlos Saura is known for his frequent attacks on the use of dubbing, a practice that he has described as 'el mayor error cometido por el cine español' (the worst error committed by Spanish cinema) (Anon, 2009). To this effect, he argues in relation to post-synch sound that: 'Porque si el tono es falso, el gesto es falso también' (Because if the tone of voice is false, gestures are false too) (cited in Brasó, 1973: 289).[9] Yet in the opening sequence of *Deprisa, deprisa*, the vocal delivery of the married couple is demonstrative of precisely the kind of 'false tone' that Saura was usually keen to avoid in his actors. In contrast, the performances of the delinquents – in both this opening scene and throughout the rest of the film – is freer and more naturalistic. As has been observed elsewhere, Carlos Saura was an early adopter of direct sound in Spanish film, and his 1970 film *El jardín de las delicias/The Garden of Delights* was the first to use this technology in Spain (D'Lugo, 1991: 104; Gubern and Vernon, 2013: 382). The use of direct sound in the film places the dialogue of the actors in a rich acoustic landscape, where spatial depth is produced as much through sound as it was through the image. The sound technician, Bernardo Menz, who also provided the direct sound for *Maravillas* (Manuel Gutiérrez Aragón, 1981), vividly captures the ambient sounds, echoes and resonances of geographical space. In theorising the relationship between voice and space, Jacob Smith has coined the term 'sonotope'. Smith's 'sonotope' here takes inspiration from Bakhtin's 'chronotope', which refers to the 'intrinsic connectedness' between temporal and spatial relationships in literature (2008: 245). Applying Bakhtin's concept to the context of sound, he shows how the sonotope can similarly 'describe the "intrinsic connectedness" of sound and space as it draws attention to the way the nexus of sound and space helps to shape performance' (2008: 245). In recording the *quinqui* voice in its geographical milieu, the performances of *Deprisa, deprisa* were strongly defined by an 'intrinsic connectedness' of sound and space. The sonotope of the delinquent voice not only brought a naturalism to film performance that had rarely been witnessed in Spanish film but vividly captured the acoustic experience of marginal youth.

The film's opening sequence differs from the one provided by the script, where the narrative begins with a television news bulletin on the final bank heist and the shooting of Sebas – the dramatic turn of events which, in the final version of the film, brings the narrative towards its conclusion. The original script subsequently relays the rest of the plot in flashback, an alternative structure that suggests a more deterministic view of juvenile delinquency. According to the script, the end of the news bulletin is followed by an inter-title which reads 'Madrid 1980', a detail that was dropped in the final version. In contrast, in the final cut of the film, the news bulletin is broadcast on the television set in Pablo's and Ángela's dimly lit bedroom, as the latter nurses the dying Pablo, who is writhing in pain from a bullet wound after being shot escaping from a bank robbery. Ángela watches as the broadcast cuts to an interview with the security guard of the bank, filmed at the crime scene. Fastidiously fastening his tie for the camera, he gives a description of the teenagers, describing their disguises in detail, before adding that they seemed young by the sound of their voices. In common with the two other heists that take place in the film, the delinquents are dressed in disguise during this sequence, with Ángela wearing a fake moustache. Yet despite their attempts at a disguise, their true identities are revealed by their voices, bringing to mind Mladen Dolar's assertion that the 'voice is like a fingerprint, instantly recognisable and identifiable' (2006: 22). As in the car robbery scene, the voices of the witnesses have been dubbed, an effect that tends to sit awkwardly with the ostensible spontaneity of television footage. The sonotope of the disembodied voice of the security guard is contrasted with that of Pablo, whose agonising gasps uncomfortably reveal the grain in the voice. As it becomes increasingly more pronounced, his laboured breathing here alerts us to the body – or rather the failure of the body – in the voice as he approaches his death.

Elsewhere in the film delinquent voice is presented as both out of sync and out of place with the politics of Spanish national identity. In one sequence, the group of teenagers are filmed visiting El Cerro de los Ángeles, a hill that marks the geographical centre of Spain. Raised above the flatlands of Getafe just south of Madrid, the site houses the Sagrado Corazón de Jesús (The Sacred Heart of Jesus), a dramatically imposing statue which welcomes onlookers with open arms. The original statue was in part destroyed by the Republicans, and Franco, in an act of defiance, oversaw the construction of the replica, which can be seen towering in the background of the scene. A reverse tracking shot films the teenagers walking in a row towards the camera as they joke and reminisce about the first time they were detained by the police. In turn, Sebas responds by telling the group how he was first arrested at 12. The recent personal memories of petty criminality of the teenagers are set in counterpoint against the historical memory of the Sagrado Corazón. As Marvin D'Lugo has observed, the historical significance of the site eludes Pablo and his friends, who are 'bereft of any form of historical consciousness, they cannot identify with any of the cultural or historical forces that have given a center of coherence to old Spain' (1991: 169–170). Framing and vocal performance further emphasise the tension between background and foreground, stasis and movement, the commemorative weight of the past with the contemporaneity of the present moment. Most significantly, the frontality of actors within the *mise-en-scène* serves to visually underline the presence of their voice. This is emphasised through the sonotope of their voices, which is registered in auditory close-up even when their bodies are held in an extreme long-establishing shot at the beginning of the sequence. As the group finally reach the opposite side of the site, they stumble towards the remains of the original statue, riddled with bullet holes from the Spanish Civil War. A new shot shows a couple of elderly ladies as they inspect the desecrated Sagrado Corazón and complain about its state of crumbling disrepair. Meca asks them what happened to the stone; one of the ladies, dressed impeccably with a pearl necklace and coiffured hair, responds that the monument was destroyed by the 'rojos' (reds) during the war. Turning to his friends, Sebas jokes '¿De qué guerra habla esta tía?' (What war is this woman talking about?). As in the opening scene, their voices establish a confrontation between different generations and social classes, a tension which is further marked out through the visual presentation of vocal performance. Unlike the teenagers, the voices of the elderly ladies – speaking in an enunciated, correct Spanish – are not visually privileged through the staging and *mise-en-scène,* as they are introduced with their backs to the camera.

Moments later, two police officers arrive on the scene, dressed in beige uniforms, the new colour of the democratic national police force. [10] Ordered to stand against the wall, the teenagers put their hands in the air as the officers begin to frisk them heavy-handedly. As Pablo cheekily asks what kind of democracy they are supposed to be living in, the officers order him to be quiet. Despite the recent democratic constitution, the delinquents continue to be subjected to the authoritarianism that was associated with the Franco regime. If here the assertion of civil order also becomes a policing of sound, the scene also illustrates how, according to Carlos Saura, the delinquents were oppressed by a 'fría máquina burocráta' (cold and bureaucratic machine) which he describes as:

> llena de sirenas apabullantes y misteriosas llamadas de radio, de tácticas, alarmas y metralletas que se disparan al menor roce del dedo, para la tranquilidad del ciudadano bienpensante.[11] (cited in Anon, 1981a)

In describing the overwhelming sounds of sirens, alarms and police radio calls, Saura calls attention to the auditory dimension of social control and surveillance to which marginal delinquents were frequently subjected during these years. As we have seen, these kinds of ambient sounds are captured realistically through the direct sound recording of Bernando Menz in the film. If, as we have seen, the film establishes a close relationship between geography and the voice, it also demonstrates the extent to which the soundscape of social order constantly threatened to overwhelm and silence marginal delinquents like Pablo and his friends.

Yo, 'el Vaquilla' and the carceral voice

If the sound design in *Deprisa, deprisa* placed the delinquent voice within the marginal hinterlands of southern Madrid, in *Yo, 'el Vaquilla'* the voice was recorded within the confines of Ocaña prison. Part melodrama part documentary, the film presents a dramatised version of Juan José Moreno Cuenca 'el Vaquilla's' childhood which is introduced and narrated by the delinquent himself, who is filmed speaking from within prison. Moreno Cuenca's narration of events accompanies a re-enactment of scenes from his childhood, where he is played by the child actor Raúl García Losada. Produced in 1985, five years after the end of José Antonio de la Loma's *Perros callejeros* cycle of films, *Yo, 'el Vaquilla'* also therefore marked a return to the original inspiration behind *Perros callejeros,* which was initially based on some of the elements of el Vaquilla's life. As we have seen, Moreno Cuenca was unable to appear in the original film because he was pursued by the police, and was replaced by Ángel Fernandez Franco 'el Torete' instead. While Fernández Franco, much to Moreno Cuenca's envy, would go on to find fame in the late 1970s, Moreno Cuenca would have to wait until *Yo, 'el Vaquilla'* for his cinematic debut, and his appearance in the film was eagerly anticipated by the Spanish press. The film was co-directed by José Antonio de la Loma and his son José Antonio de la Loma Jr, and produced by Golden Sun, Jet Films and In Cine. The shoot took place over eight weeks, and was filmed on location in La Mina, Barcelona, El Rosellón and, most significantly, within the cells and galleries of Ocaña prison. The film was widely exhibited within Spain, being shown initially in forty cinemas (EFE, 1985).

While de la Loma paid less attention to the soundtracks of his films than Carlos Saura, *Yo, 'el Vaquilla'* marked a departure from his earlier Spanish films, which had relied on post-synchronised sound. Critics in the Catalan press praised the film for its authenticity, something that owed itself to the close relationship established between vocal performance and geographical context in the film. *El Periódico* noted how the film uses direct sound 'para captar con el máximo realismo los ambientes y los característicos personajes que se reflejan' (so as to capture with the greatest realism the environments and the distinctive characters reflected by them) (Anon, 1985a), something that was similarly observed by *El Correo Catalán,* which praised the role of direct sound in its ability to capture the habitual expressions and idioms of the gypsy actors who appeared in the film (Anon, 1985b).

The emphasis in *Yo, 'el Vaquilla'* on vocal authenticity was in no small part shaped by the original source material on which the screenplay was based. As was widely publicised at the time, the film was closely based on the memoirs of Moreno Cuenca's childhood, which he had written by hand while serving time in several different prisons. Completed and self-published under the name *Le llamaban 'el Vaquilla'* (*They Called Him 'el Vaquilla'*) in 1983, de la Loma helped the delinquent edit a reworked version for its official publication with Barcelona-based publisher Seix Barral, by whom it was finally published two years later 1985. While little of its content was altered (a photocopy of the original handwritten document can be consulted in the Biblioteca Nacional, Madrid), its title was changed to *Yo, 'el Vaquilla'* (I, el Vaquilla) (Moreno Cuenca, 1985). In this respect, the film adaptation remains faithful to the autobiographical book, whose writing is similarly peppered throughout with the 'anti-language' which he and his family spoke. [12] Completing the film script in just three days, José Antonio de la Loma commented that he was able to write it so fast because he knew Juan José Moreno Cuenca's life story to perfection (Sánchez Costa, 1985a).

In its shift from third person to first, the title of the book and subsequent film initially did little to dispel the persona of 'el Vaquilla' that Moreno Cuenca wanted to leave behind. In press interviews at the time of the release, he was quick to assert that his greatest enemy was 'el Vaquilla' (Anon, 1985c): that from now on he wished to be known by his real name Juan José Moreno Cuenca and to leave his criminal alter ego behind. He explains how from the age of 13, his alias became inextricably bound up with his notoriety as a criminal:

> Las celdas de castigo tenían mi nombre escrito en las paredes. Los jóvenes internos de los reformatorios necesitaban un héroe al que admirar en sus fantasías de pequeños delincuentes. La policía tenía otro nombre con el que podía hacer méritos para su historia de servicio. 'He cogido al Vaquilla', 'He herido al Vaquilla' … La prensa se hizo eco de mis acciones y esta publicidad me llevaría de una cárcel a otra.[13] (Moreno Cuenca, 1984: 12)

Here, we see how deviant subcultures, agencies of control and the media each appropriated the meaning of the name 'el Vaquilla' to different ends. His name – and, by extension, identity – are caught up in a complex interplay between the experience and the representation of crime, an echo chamber where the self and its mediation, substitute and surrogate are constantly blurred. Indeed, in an interview for the television programme *La tarde* for Televisión Española in January 1985, Moreno Cuenca tellingly refers to el Vaquilla as his 'doble' (double).[14]

Like *Deprisa, deprisa*, *Yo, 'el Vaquilla'* uses sound to interrogate the agency of the delinquent voice. Yet in its focus on Spain's most infamous and mediatised delinquent, Juan José Moreno Cuenca 'el Vaquilla', the performance of his voice was situated within a series of even more complex 'performance frames'. His constant escapes from reformatories and prisons, as well as his leading role in a number of prison riots and mutinies, had already been extensively reported within the Spanish media by the time of the film. This was further complicated through the initial quasi-re-enactment of his teenage years through the character 'el Torete' in *Perros callejeros,* and the subsequent feedback loop of media coverage that followed in its wake. Yet in personally relating his life story in the first person to the camera, *Yo, 'el Vaquilla'* provided Moreno Cuenca with an entirely new and unprecedented performance frame, an opportunity that enabled him to finally reclaim his textual agency and set his story straight. The voice subsequently serves as a testimonial function in the film, a crucial presence that bears witness not just to Moreno Cuenca's own narrative of criminality but to the physical mistreatment of many social prisoners and delinquents during this period in Spain. To this effect, the director commented that both the book and the film will serve as a 'testimonio histórico' (historical testimony) to the issue of juvenile delinquency in Barcelona, but also to the police brutality which occurred in the final years of Franco and the transition, and Spain's youth justice and penitentiary system (Anon, 1985a).

As in the beginning of *Deprisa, deprisa*, *Yo, 'el Vaquilla'* opens with the sonotope of the delinquent voice. Its pre-title sequence begins within the confines of Ocaña prison, in the province of Toledo, where Moreno Cuenca was at that moment being interned. A long shot reveals a prison ward with a row of cells on each side. Moreno Cuenca is filmed leaving his cell and walking steadily towards the camera. With a furrowed brow, he looks defiantly towards the camera and says: 'Yo soy Juan José Moreno Cuenca, aunque todos me llaman

4.4 Juan José Moreno Cuenca narrates his life story from behind bars in *Yo, 'el Vaquilla'* (José Antonio de la Loma, 1985).

'"el Vaca" o "el Vaquilla"' (My name is Juan José Moreno Cuenca, although everyone calls me Vaca or Vaquilla). The camera pulls back to reframe the image from behind a large cell door, its heavy metal bars now dominating the foreground of the image. His face now framed and partly obscured by the bars, Moreno Cuenca continues: 'Ya lo ven, nací aquí a este otro lado de la sociedad y nunca pude o nunca supe pasar al otro' (As you can see, I was born on this other side of society and I never could or knew how to pass over onto the other side).

In breaking the fourth wall and addressing the camera directly, Moreno Cuenca's vocal performance seeks to establish a closeness and connection with a public that has too often misunderstood him. Indeed, de la Loma commented in an interview that he wanted *Yo, 'el Vaquilla'* to be 'una película más intimista' (a more intimate film), one that provided more of a focus on the development of character, and had therefore excluded the scenes of car chases and violence which were in the *Perros callejeros* cycle (F.F., 1985). If the direct address of Moreno Cuenca's voice seeks to establish an intimate relationship with the audience, it also serves to 'authenticate' the narrative that we are about to see as the real turn of events, rather than that which has been too often portrayed in the media. In recounting the vicissitudes of his life story, he is also ostensibly reclaiming his narrative as his own for the first time. Through focalising the film through a quasi-first person narrator, the opening sequence bears witness to the testimonial and autobiographical powers of the human voice – a voice which, from the outset, vividly brings into motion the first person subject of the film's title, *Yo, 'el Vaquilla'*. The 'Yo' or 'I' announces the voice as a speaking subject of textual authority.

Despite his intimate plea to the audience, the prison gate physically separates him from the camera, its metal frame shielding parts of his face and body. Quite literally framed by the bars, the *mise-en-scène* vividly reinforces his speaking position as one from 'the other side of society'. As in *Deprisa, deprisa*, the sonotope of vocal performance serves to immerse the delinquent within his physical environment right from the outset. His voice here figures as just one component within a broader soundscape of the prison, with its sounds of clanging metal, slamming of heavy doors, and weighty keys turning in locks. These background sounds do not appear to have been 'cleaned up' or modified during postproduction. As such, the sonorous materiality of the prison space, evoked through the echoes that bounce off its hard and metallic surfaces, commingles and competes with the sound of his voice. The unvarnished presentation of vocal performance here therefore more strongly resembles that of the raw 'liveness' of news footage and documentary than it does fiction film. Yet its sonotope, inflected and shaped as it is by carceral space, also strongly points to a life that has been lived mostly behind bars – even when he was a baby. As several sources have shown, Moreno Cuenca's mother gave birth to him when she was in prison.[15] With the exception of a period of two years, the 23-year-old Moreno Cuenca at the time of the film had been confined in reformatories and prisons since the age of 13. As Susana Dasca from *Diario 16* commented, 'la cárcel se ha convertido en hogar' (prison has become his home) (Dasca, 1984: 33).

Although Moreno Cuenca speaks with fluency and ease in front of the camera, the vast majority of his time in Ocaña prison was spent in imposed silence. As a prisoner of the highest possible category,

Moreno Cuenca was only allocated one hour per day in the prison yard, and during the remaining 23 hours he was required to remain in solitary confinement in his cell (Anon, 1985c). The opening shot of the prison ward, which shows rows of individual prison cells that are presented in plunging perspective, reveals an architecture of physical isolation where the prisoners are estranged from society but also from one another. Brandon LaBelle points to how criminal bodies, from the nineteenth century onwards, have been controlled through the role of disciplinary silence (2010: 66–72). The surveillance of the criminal body is thus not just enacted through vision but also sound. Yet, as witnessed in the opening sequence, even in the wards of solitary confinement where voices are less frequently heard, the acoustic space of the prison is far from silent. Richard Wener observes that, despite the imposed silence, what visitors first notice about prisons is their noise (cited in Hemsworth, 2015: 20). The cacophonous soundscape of the prison has a negative and dehumanising effect on the embodied experience of its prisoners (Hemsworth, 2015: 20). The acoustic architecture of the prison overwhelms the individual as much as its physical architecture, serving to decentre both the voice and agency of the criminal body.

The tension between voice and silence is similarly conveyed in a passage of his autobiographical book *Yo, 'el Vaquilla'* (Moreno Cuenca, 1985) where, after escaping from reformatories twice, the 16-year-old Moreno Cuenca is sent to the same adult prison where his brother, Julián, is also being detained. Considered a dangerous influence to the other prisoners, Julián has been kept in solitary confinement and Moreno Cuenca is surprised at the sudden transformation of his appearance, a change which he perceives through the monotonous sound of his voice (Moreno Cuenca, 1985: 297). He then writes of the seemingly interminable days of his own solitary confinement, during which the silence became unbearable: 'El silencio era intenso; profundo; solo se oía el clok clok de los pasos, del que ocupa la celda contingua' (The silence was intense; profound; I could only hear the 'clip clop' of footsteps of the person in the cell next to me) (Moreno Cuenca, 1985: 299). The imposition of silence here encourages an intense mode of listening, where Moreno Cuenca becomes finely attuned to the soundscape of the prison. The brutalising nature of silence is potentially relieved through speaking. Wondering who is in the adjacent cell, he asks himself: '¿Quién será? Si al menos pudiera oír su voz, escaparía esa sensación que estoy muerto' (Who could that be? If at least I could hear his voice, I would escape that feeling that I am dead) (Moreno Cuenca, 1985: 299).

Re-vindicating the prisoner's voice

While the transition to democracy saw the long-awaited re-vindication of the voice of political prisoners, the struggle of non-political prisoners such as Moreno Cuenca, who were frequently from the most marginal sectors of society, rarely appeared to be a priority for the state. Yet during this period, much of the Spanish public became increasingly aware of the sordid conditions of Spanish prisons, whose institutionalised violence and overcrowded and inadequate facilities were frequently reported in more liberal news magazines such as *Triunfo* and *Diario 16*. The authoritarian penitentiary system inherited from the Franco regime had become associated far more explicitly with brutality and corruption than with re-education. While the Spanish Constitution of 1978 declared the purpose of custody to be primarily one of rehabilitation, as well as ushering in a series of other crucial reforms such as the abolition of torture and capital punishment, the penal code that was inherited from the regime still nevertheless remained in force during these years.

Despite the remarkably slow overhauling of Spain's penal law, a number of significant penitentiary reforms were introduced during the transition to democracy. Their implementation, however, would all too often turn out to exacerbate rather than ameliorate the conditions of many prisoners. The prime minister Adolfo Súarez approved the long-awaited liberation of political prisoners through the amnesty laws of 1976 and 1977. Yet as Aranda Ocaña and Rivera Beiras have observed, while political prisoners during the regime were being systematically released, conditions for social prisoners largely remained the same (2013: 248). They observe how the Minister for Penitentiary Institutions at the time, Manuel García Valdés, even admitted how the amnesty granted to those sentenced for political crimes implied a form of discrimination against other types of prisoners, such as delinquents and petty criminals like Moreno Cuenca (Aranda Ocaña and Rivera Beiras, 2013: 248). The general unrest swiftly led to a series of high-profile prison riots, with significant outbreaks occurring in Modelo, Barcelona and Carabanchel, Madrid (see also chapter 1).

Some prisoners attempted to escape, while others participated in hunger strikes and collective suicide attempts, carried out through increasingly desperate means, with prisoners cutting their veins and swallowing objects such as razors, keys, stones – and even taps (Galván García, 2007: 129). The deteriorating conditions of the prisoners led to the mobilisation of COPEL (Coordinara de Presos en Lucha [Coordinating Body of Prisoners in Struggle]), a grass-roots activist group that demanded that non-political prisoners (whom they termed 'presos sociales' [social prisoners]) be given the same rights as their political counterparts. While COPEL was initially established by relatives of the inmates and ex-prisoners, their fight was brought more clearly into the public domain at a conference at Madrid Complutense University, where lawyers and public intellectuals such as Fernando Savater co-signed a document in support of their cause (Galván García, 2007: 129). The Penitentiary Law of 1979[16] did little to stem the unrest in Spanish prisons. With its explicit repudiation of authoritarian violence and its emphasis on rehabilitation of prisoners, the law reflected the reformist values of the new democratic era. Yet Ramón Draper Miralles writes that despite its progressive outlook, the government had insufficient economic means to carry out the new reforms of the law (1984: 255).[17] Moreover, despite the release of political prisoners, the overall prison population grew substantially during these years. By the end of 1980, the prison population had increased by 93% compared to 1976, with many of the new inmates incarcerated on charges of terrorism (Draper Miralles, 1984: 247). While riots continued to break out with frequency well into the 1980s, the suicide rate within prisons increased at an alarming rate: while there was one suicide in 1976 and seven in 1977, by the years 1981 and 1982 there were 23 and 21 reported respectively (Draper Miralles, 1984: 245). At the same time the law was passed, a letter was co-written by high-profile artists and intellectuals, including Carlos Saura and Elías Querejeta, denouncing the unreformed state of Spanish prisons since the regime (Draper Miralles, 1984: 256).

By the time of the release of *Yo, 'el Vaquilla'*, Moreno Cuenca's maltreatment at the hands of Spain's penitentiary system had been already well documented. Most publicised was his incarceration in Lérida-2 prison, from which he escaped with five other inmates on 11 December 1984. Seventeen hours later, TV-3 managed to film the precise moment of Moreno Cuenca's dramatic arrest by armed police in Barcelona, after a lengthy car chase during which several shots were fired. Moreno Cuenca lies spread-eagled on the road, as a Civil Guard holds him down with a foot and pulls his hair. A cacophony of police sirens can be heard as a dense crowd of onlookers gathers in the background. A shaky close-up captures Moreno Cuenca's facial expression, contorted with anger and desperation. His voice almost inaudible under the police sirens, he shouts in front of the camera: 'Si me he fugado, ha sido porque me maltrataban' (If I have escaped it's because I was mistreated).[18] Even during the spontaneous 'liveness' of a dangerous armed arrest, Moreno Cuenca is all too desperately aware of the performance frame here. The raw actuality of the moment, unscripted and unrehearsed, is nevertheless also framed by the camera crew and crowd of onlookers who, standing in the background, have been cordoned off from the action. Photographs taken from the film footage, depicting his face in grainy close up against the ground, mouth open in a desperate mid-shout, circulated in newspapers following his arrest and subsequently became well known. Intriguingly, a very similar image some months later would be used for the promotional material of *Yo, 'el Vaquilla'*, where the child actor Rául García Losada is depicted splayed out on the ground, mouth open as a policeman's gun is pointed towards his head. The image is taken from the very final scene of the film where the 13-year-old Moreno Cuenca has been arrested, a moment which marks the beginning of an adolescence which will be spent in almost perpetual incarceration. Much like the famous final shot of the young Jean Pierre-Léaud in *Les quatre cents coups/The 400 Blows* (François Truffaut, 1959), the final image of the film is presented in a freeze frame, pausing the narrative *in media res* at its most dramatic juncture. The final credits run over the frozen image, as the song 'Yo el Vaquilla' by Los Chichos (see chapter 5) is played. As in Truffaut's film, the immobile frame here is one of entrapment, both spatial and temporal. Not only does the frame brutally serve to incarcerate the actor's child body but it also points to how Moreno Cuenca will, over the years, be repeatedly condemned to play out the same pattern of escape and arrest well into his adulthood. If the fictional image of his past arrest and actual image of his present echo and reinforce the other's meaning, they are also both connected in the image of an inaudible cry for help.

Moreno Cuenca was also held responsible for leading a mutiny in La Modelo, a maximum security prison in Barcelona that was already

4.5 The child actor Raúl García Losada plays the young Juan José Moreno Cuenca, threatened at gunpoint by the police in *Yo, 'el Vaquilla'* (José Antonio de la Loma, 1985).

infamous as the location of a huge-scale prison break in 1978, when 45 inmates managed to escape its grounds. Moreno Cuenca and other inmates held four prison officers hostage in a cell before requesting to speak to officials. Led by Moreno Cuenca, the inmates had written a list of their grievances about the conditions inside the prison, and wanted to communicate them via a radio transmitter (Anon, 1984b). As scores of journalists and television cameras hastily assembled at the scene, Moreno Cuenca took to the prison gallery and demanded an end to the physical torture of prisoners, as well as seeking assurance that drug addicts be sent to the infirmary for treatment.[19] The mutiny turned into a live press conference of sorts, with Moreno Cuenca leading the Director General of Penitentiary Services and television crew around to inspect the poor conditions within the prison gallery and cells (Moreno Cuenca, 2001: 171). In both the mutiny and its prompt media coverage, Moreno Cuenca's voice possessed a crucial testimonial charge, one that bore witness to the injustices of the

4.6 Juan José Moreno Cuenca in dialogue with the journalist Xavier Vinader in *Yo, 'el Vaquilla'* (José Antonio de la Loma, 1985).

Spanish penal system as well as entreating others to witness them too. In speaking through the radio transmitter and to the journalists, he emerges as the literal voice of the mutiny. Speaking on behalf of his fellow inmates, his voice came to symbolise the broader struggle of all social prisoners in Spain during these years. Yet, much like the moment of his arrest, his voice is mediated and framed by both technology (the camera and the radio transmitter which he reportedly demanded) and the audience.[20]

The testimonial charge of Moreno Cuenca's voice is similarly emphasised throughout *Yo, 'el Vaquilla'*, and is in particular brought to the service of four scenes where he recounts his life story to the journalist Xavier Vinader, a prominent investigative journalist during Spain's transition to democracy. Prisoner and journalist are filmed in discussion together in various locations within the prison grounds, with each of the scenes leading to a dramatised re-enactment of the events being described. The last one of these sequences, which provides a segue to the conclusion of the film, is filmed within his prison cell,

4.7 The journalist Xavier Vinader in dialogue with Juan José Moreno Cuenca in *Yo, 'el Vaquilla'* (José Antonio de la Loma, 1985).

as Vinader asks Moreno Cuenca to recount the best and worst memories of his childhood. Both journalist and criminal are presented as relaxed in each other's presence, sat together on Moreno Cuenca's narrow bed. In their use of unpolished direct sound, these sequences also formally resemble the kinds of interviews associated with news reports. Widely viewed as an iconic symbol for the freedom of speech, Vinader was best known for publishing several reports in *Interviú* uncovering the far right's dirty war against Basque nationalists in 1981. This caused him to be sentenced for reckless endangerment, leading to a period of exile in France and eventual incarceration in Carabanchel prison in 1984, though the sentence was suspended three months later amid much public outcry. Released from prison just one year before the production of *Yo, 'el Vaquilla'*, his controversial sentence served to cement him in the public imagination as a tireless, truth-seeking voice against corruption, an aspect which further lends a reportage-like credibility to Moreno Cuenca's story. Significantly, Vinader was chosen for the role because he was also the first journalist to interview Moreno Cuenca when he was a teenager living in La Mina. In his autobiography, he notes that during the shoot Vinader was joined by Paco Elvira, an award-winning photographer who had taken his pictures during the same earlier interview. Like Vinader, Elvira's work also appeared in *Interviú* and his hard-hitting photo journalism covered the university protests against Franco, ETA and other controversial subjects. Moreno Cuenca recalls how, during the shoot, he told Vinader the names of the prison officers who had abused him, in the hope that the latter would write an investigative report about them. One particularly violent guard, whom he referred to as 'Pistolas', frequently attempted to obstruct the production of the film during the shoot, though de la Loma reportedly managed to put him in his place (Moreno Cuenca, 2001: 283).

Xavier Vinader's and Paco Elvira's association with *Interviú* provided a further dimension to the complex intermediality of the film, in that the magazine had the exclusive rights to the first publishing excerpts from Moreno Cuenca's handwritten diary on which the final film script was based. The first of these articles, published shortly after his famous arrest after escaping from Lérida prison, is entitled 'Así me convertí en delincuente' (this is how I became a criminal) (Moreno Cuenca, 1984: 12). Written in the first person, it also prefigures the title of the autobiography and the book. As well as publishing his accounts of the systematic abuse he received in the juvenile court, the article seeks to authenticate his testimonial through also providing photographs of the actual pages from his diary, amongst which is included the front cover, which Moreno Cuenca has entitled 'El otro lado de la sociedad' (the other side of society) – words which, as we have seen, are incorporated into the opening monologue of the film.[21] At the end of each of the interviews, Moreno Cuenca's voice in the film serves as a sound bridge which carries over to the following sequence, where his (now invisible) voice serves to further contextualise the images. During these brief moments, Moreno Cuenca's disembodied voice therefore takes on the role of voiceover. The sonotope of his voice, along with his use of delinquent slang, provides a clear departure from the usual voice-of-God narrator found in Spanish film, spoken in a neutral, often theatricalised register.

In his first voiceover, Moreno Cuenca introduces the viewer to his family background and earliest childhood memories, referring to his mother and his father 'de raza gitana' (of gypsy race) whom he had never met. His words accompany an establishing shot of Torre Baró, the poor *barrio* where he lived as a young child, located on the outer reaches of Barcelona. In a panoramic shot so commonly found in the *quinqui* film, the camera slowly surveys the hinterlands between landscape and cityscape, with agricultural land and vegetation criss-crossed by electric pylons and a busy motorway. Described in his autobiography as 'un trozo de mundo olvidado donde los seres crecen al amparo del instinto de sobrevivencia' (a forgotten piece of the world where beings grow up under the protection of the survival instinct) (Moreno Cuenca, 1985: 13), the *mise-en-scène* provides a striking geographical reflection on his marginal upbringing. The camera hones in on his stepfather, Antonio Moreno, and two of his associates, who are heard speaking in criminal slang about a robbery they plan that evening, one of the latter asking '¿es un tío legal?' (is the guy *legal*?). In his *Diccionario cheli*, Francisco Umbral explains that the slang use of the word *legal* signifies precisely the opposite, writing that 'La marginalidad invierte los valores convencionales burgueses' (marginality inverts conventional bourgeois values) (Umbral, 1983: 125). Rather than meaning law-abiding, 'legal' denoted someone who was brave and who could be relied upon within criminal communities. Crucially, the measure of their loyalty was expressed in their efficient adherence to criminal codes of behaviour, thereby reinforcing their social position as outsiders. As we have seen, M. A. K Halliday shows how anti-language is a product of an 'anti-society', an alternative society which provides a mode of resistance to normal society. Halliday writes that 'an anti-language is not only parallel to an anti-society; it is in fact generated by it' (Halliday, 1976: 570, 583). The anti-society into which Moreno Cuenca is born is established with great economy in this sequence. Through voice, language and space, the film immerses the viewer within the 'other side of society', an alternate social structure that is both radically distinct from Spain's capitalist economy yet also an integral product of it.

Although the narrator says that Antonio Moreno was not his biological father, he explains that he was like a father to him and he therefore took his name 'Moreno'. He adds that Antonio would later die of a heart attack after being pursued by the police for several hours. Introduced as the protagonist's sole father figure and moral authority, Antonio Moreno not only passes on his name to the young Moreno Cuenca but his criminal norms and values. In both the film and autobiography, his early years are presented as an inverted *Bildungsroman*, in which criminal acts are marked out as crucial rites of passage to manhood. Early in his autobiography he writes that 'Robar era una palabra que en mi familia siempre significó heroísmo y superioridad … "Ya es un hombre", se decía cuando alguno se convertía en delincuente' (Moreno Cuenca, 1985: 29).[22] Prestige was conferred on hypermasculine acts of bravery and resistance in his *barrio* rather than on more legitimate markers of success such as academic attainment. While early on in the film Moreno Cuenca shows academic promise in primary school, telling his mother Rosita (played by Teresa Giménez) that he wishes to study hard to become a lawyer so as to enable her release from prison, he soon enough instinctively succumbs to petty crime. After class, he sneaks into the classroom with two friends, where they steal handfuls of pencils and rubbers from the teacher's stationery drawer. In exchanging them for cigarettes at the tobacconist's kiosk, the boys take rapid drags as they strut across the road, imitating the macho behaviour of the men in their *barrio*.

As the narrative progresses, the child actor García Losa adopts an increasingly performative hypermasculinity in his role as Moreno Cuenca, an aspect that is emphasised through his use of voice in later scenes. In the scenes set in Campo de la Bota, when he has reached his early teens, his voice is projected more loudly and confidently, while his speech patterns, in which he appears to spit out his words, are notably more confident and assertive. The shift in his vocal performance is a reflection of his growing ascendancy and autonomy within the hierarchy of the criminal anti-society, an aspect which becomes increasingly played out in his persistent resistance to the authorities. As well as a more explicit outward manifestation of hegemonic masculinity, his vocal performance here also conforms to the characteristics of the delinquent voice, closely resembling the coarse gutturalness which Francisco Umbral writes is typical of juvenile slang. His performance therefore reveals the extent to which the grain of the voice in *cine quinqui* was not only an index of realism but a symbol of belonging and enfranchisement 'en el otro lado de sociedad' (on the other side of society).

Conclusion

Like several films studied in this book, *Deprisa, deprisa* and *Yo, 'el Vaquilla'* placed much importance on the way that delinquent youth spoke. In their ability to capture the distinctive grain of the delinquent voice, recorded in the real-life geographical environment of the actors, the vocal performances in the films possessed a naturalism and indexicality that had been rarely heard in Spanish film. In its ability to powerfully dramatise questions around agency and self-expression, the voice also had a political resonance whose implications far exceeded the contours of the films. Indeed, through their realistic use of vocal performances, the films reclaimed and re-vindicated the marginal voice that had been symbolically silenced by the residual authoritarianism of the Spanish police force and penal system. The films therefore demonstrate the transformative potential of performance – something which was most clearly played out in the case of Juan José Moreno Cuenca who was remembered as the public voice for penal reform. His voice therefore illustrated Shoshana Felman's and Dori Laub's assertion that the 'testimony is a "speech act" that occasions beneficial change' (1992: 204).

Notes

1 '[The] poverty [of their language] is unbelievable, comparable to that of some primitive people; their syntax is literally inexistent, because there is no coherent elocution, just stumps of phrases, 'completed' with interjections, which are principally swear words.'

2 As well as explaining some of its most common words to the readers (such as 'tronco' for 'friend' and various terms associated with drug taking, like 'costo' and 'chocolate' for cannabis, for instance), Lázaro Carreter stressed that *cheli* is more strongly associated with people of a particular age than with social class (1979: 6–7).

3 'The nucleus of *cheli*, like that of Greek dialect or an imperial language, is the *gutturalness*, which in a poet we would call a personal voice, the unmistakable style, the sound that 'sings'.'

4 Carlos Saura reported that Matías, whose audition was filmed on videotape, was killed by the police on a piece of wasteland (M.R.E., 1981). Valdelomar's wife Genoveva López similarly mentions how Valdelomar was brought in hurriedly just before the shoot was about to commence as Matías's replacement after his death. López sold her story to the

gossip magazine *Semana*, after Valdelomar had been in prison for six months. See Anon (1981d: 6).

5 See Beata (1981: 9). Valdelomar reportedly invested the money in a record store which soon went bust (Sánchez, 1983).

6 His accomplice was the delinquent Manuel Sola Téllez.

7 The director also commented that 'estos chaveles no tienen necesidad de que les des tú la droga, porque se buscan ellos solitos' (these youngsters don't need you to give them drugs because they can get it themselves) (Sánchez Vidal, 1988: 147).

8 The film was exhibited for 28 weeks in Madrid in 1981 (Cineinforme, 1982: 18–38).

9 Carlos Saura continues: 'Es algo que tengo comprobado. Mi obsesión siempre en el cine español son dos cosas: una, eliminar el gesto inútil, y otra, conseguir el tono correcto de los actores' (This is something I've demonstrated. I have two obsessions in Spanish cinema: one is to eliminate useless gestures, and the other to achieve the correct tone of voice in the actors). Saura further says that direct sound brings a particular kind of tension to the shoot which cannot be created with post-synch sound, adding that 'es un clima un poco especial. Y para mí es totalmente necesario' (it's a particular kind of atmosphere. And for me, it's totally necessary). Cited in Brasó (1973: 289–290).

10 As John Hopewell shows, the Policía Armada, whose grey uniforms and submachine guns were symbols of repression during the regime, were renamed Policía Nacional in 1978 and kitted out in khaki and beige instead (1995: 212).

11 'full of overwhelming sirens and mysterious radio calls, of tactics, alarms and submachine guns that are triggered off with the slightest touch of the finger in order to keep the peace for self-righteous citizens.'

12 This register is even more explicitly encountered in its sequel, *Hasta la libertad* (Moreno Cuenca, 2001), which at the very beginning contains a three-page glossary of all the argot used throughout the book.

13 'All the police cells had my name [el Vaquilla] written on the wall. Youngsters held in the reformatories needed a hero to look up to in their little delinquent fantasies. The police had another name they could score brownie points with for their police record: "I've caught el Vaquilla", "I've injured el Vaquilla" … My actions were echoed in the media and this publicity would carry me from one jail to another.'

14 *La tarde*, TVE1, 1 January 1986.

15 See for instance Otero (1988: 117).

16 Known in Spanish as Ley Orgánica, de 26 de septiembre, General Penitenciaria.

17 See Draper Miralles (1984: 255).

18 See Dasca (1984: 32) for a description of his appearance.

19 See Juan José Moreno Cuenca's description of this in the sequel to his biography, *Hasta la libertad* (2001: 158). *El País* reported that the inmates demanded heroin; see Anon (1984b).

20 Just days before the release of *Yo, 'el Vaquilla'*, Juan José Moreno Cuenca was held responsible for leading another mutiny, this time in Ciudad Real prison where he had recently been transferred from Ocaña. Holding the guards hostage with knives and metalwork tools, he demanded to speak to the wife of his lawyer, as well as de la Loma's wife, whom he called 'Mami'. The director, yet again, subsequently came to his defence, claiming that he was being exploited by other inmates. See García (1985: 37).

21 See Moreno Cuenca (1984: 12).

22 'Thieving is a word that in my family has always meant heroism and superiority' … "Now he's a man", it was said when someone became a criminal.'

5

The place of the *rumba* in *cine quinqui*

Much of the enduring popularity of *cine quinqui* can be attributed to the role that popular music played in the films. In particular, the *rumbas* of gypsy groups such as Los Chichos and Los Chunguitos occupied an integral part of the *quinqui* soundtrack. Originating from the similar kinds of marginal spaces that were depicted in the films, the music of these groups vividly resonated with the criminal experiences of the delinquents, as well as contributing towards the commercial success of the films. The cross-promotion of the two media was found most noticeably in the release of the album soundtracks of *Perros callejeros 2, Deprisa, deprisa* and *Yo, 'el Vaquilla'*. As K. J. Donnelly has argued, soundtrack albums of music extend the reach of individual films beyond their physical bounds and screen time (2013: 369). Indeed, as this chapter shows, music in *quinqui* film was far more than an accompaniment to the image. Through the recent invention of the radio cassette, the *rumbas* were integrated into the everyday lives of marginal urban populations. At the same time, through their live appearances in prisons where delinquents such as Juan José Moreno Cuenca 'el Vaquilla' were being held, the songs created an important sense of acoustic community and solidarity amongst marginal people. In spite of the significant role that groups like Los Chichos and Los Chunguitos played in marginal youth subcultures of the transition, their music has been largely dismissed by flamencologists and overlooked by scholars of popular music more generally.

In exploring the significance of the *rumba* to *Perros callejeros 2*, *Deprisa, deprisa* and *Yo, 'el Vaquilla'*, this chapter explores how the films dramatise the relationship between marginality, location and mobility. In particular, it shows how through mobility – in both the movement of recent migration routes, and the consumption of the songs as mobile objects through the prominent use of car stereos in the films – the delinquents were able to actively produce space of their own, both inside and outside the film text. According to Tariq Jazeel, 'sounds evade fixity and easy definition', and as such 'they are difficult to draw boundaries around' (2005: 236). It is precisely the fluid dimension of sound that enabled *quinquis* to negotiate their oppressive material surroundings, allowing them to transcend geographical segregation that had been established through the urbanism of the Franco years. Finally, the chapter explores how this relationship between space and sound has been re-articulated through contemporary Spanish rap, through examining the music videos and promotional paraphernalia of the artist el Coleta (otherwise known as Ramsés Gallego). Through developing a genre he has termed 'rap quinqui', I explore the ways in which el Coleta's playful re-appropriation of the music and visual iconography of *cine quinqui* illuminates the intermedial relationship between the two media.

The *rumba vallecana*: Movement and the sound of marginality

While musical genres are never static, and are always subject to constant transformation and flux, this is most strikingly the case when music follows the routes of migration. This is clearly borne out in the development of the *rumba*, whose sound was shaped by the cultural movement of people. The style of *rumba* heard in the *quinqui* films differed from the original genre of *rumba*, however, which originated in Cuba and had African roots. The incorporation of the *rumba* into Spanish flamenco music dates back to the early twentieth century, where it became known as an example of '*cantes de ida y vuelta*' (literally 'roundtrip songs'), one of several hybrid musical forms that 'travelled back' to Spain from its former colonies of Cuba and Latin America (Gómez Gufi, 2014). If the *rumba* has been dismissed by flamencologists as a minor or 'light' style of flamenco (Gómez Gufi, 2014), this likely owes itself to the increasing commercial popularity of the genre from the late 1950s and 1960s. During this period, the genre became increasingly associated with Catalan gypsies living in Barcelona, where the enormously popular artists Peret and Antonio González Batista 'el Pescailla' pioneered a style that became known as the *rumba catalana.* As José Manuel Gómez Gufi shows, Catalan gypsies developed a new way of playing flamenco guitar which became known as 'ventilador' (fan), where the player claps their hand against the guitar case (2014). Eclectic in form, the *rumba catalana* combined the upbeat rhythms created by the 'ventilador' with elements of Caribbean music and rock 'n' roll. As the musician Gato Pérez stated, 'La Rumba nace en la calle, hija de Cuba y de un gitanillo' (the *rumba* is born in the street, daughter of Cuba and a gypsy' (Brown, 2012: 11). The streets to which Pérez refers, Brown writes, were in the clearly demarcated gypsy areas of inner-city Barcelona such as Gràcia (Brown, 2012: 11–12). If this *rumba* was shaped by its geography, its development was equally shaped during these years by rapid technological change, with its popularity coinciding with the ever-increasing accessibility of vinyl records in Spain in the 1960s (Brown, 2012: 11).

By the end of Spain's miracle years in 1973, and its subsequent economic recession, new styles of commercially minded *rumbas* emerged from Madrid that were markedly less joyous and upbeat than their Barcelona counterparts. One of these styles became known as 'caño roto', named after Caño Roto, the impoverished *barrio* situated in the district of Carabanchel. Drawing on elements of American funk, psychedelic rock and soul, it emerged as a distinctly hard-edged sound whose relationship to urban space – and, in particular, marginal urban space – was far more explicit than the *rumba catalana*. Pivotal to the development of this style was the composer, singer and in-house producer for CBS Records International, José Luis de Carlos. De Carlos's trademark sound during this period was known for drawing heavily on the use of the electric bass and guitar, pedal effects, the Hammond organ and keyboards, instrumentation that was innovative for Spanish popular music at the time. He was initially significant for his collaborations with female duo Las Grecas, whose debut album *Gipsy Rock* (1974) exemplified this style. Following the success of Las Grecas, Carlos was the creative force behind the gypsy band Los Chorbos, whose only album *El Sonido Caño Roto/The Caño Roto Sound* (1975) became hugely influential. In the same way that the geography of the postindustrial ghetto was the focus of American funk, the lived experience of Madrid's outer *barrios* became a means of promoting *caño roto*. In the sleeve of their second single, 'Tendrás una nueva ilusión' (You Will Have a New Dream), CBS describes the band as follows: 'Los Chorbos son un ejemplo claro de nueva raza gitana de origen urbano, concretamente del barrio de Caño Roto de Madrid'

(Los Chorbos are a clear example of the new gypsy race of urban origins, specifically from the *barrio* of Caño Roto in Madrid) (1973). The emphasis here on the clumsily worded and essentialising 'nueva raza gitana' places Los Chorbos in crude distinction with the 'established' gypsies like Peret who popularised the Catalan sound, many of whom Brown notes were integrated into the city and spoke Catalan (Brown, 2012: 12). Unlike the inner-city gypsy areas of Barcelona such as La Gràcia, this new sound spoke to marginal *barrios* and workers' colonies on the outer suburbs of the city, areas that were struggling to keep up with the influx of rural-to-urban migration from Extremadura, Castile-La Mancha and Andalucia.[1]

More significantly, another style of *rumba* emerged that became known as *rumba vallecana* (also sometimes referred to as *rumba suburbiana*, *rumba urbana* or *rumba calorra*), a sound that was closely related to the Puente de Vallecas, another deprived district in the southern outlying area of Madrid. The gypsy trio Los Chichos, who signed to Phillips Records in 1973 and released their first album *Ni más, ni menos/No More No Less* shortly after, was the earliest and most influential group associated with this sound. In the early years, Los Chichos were often associated with the *caño roto* sound, and the lead singer-songwriter Juan Antonio Jímenez Muñóz (known more simply as 'Jero' or 'Jeros') initially wrote songs for Los Chorbos and Las Grecas. While Los Chichos' sound was similarly hard-edged, the production of their music was in reality quite different, notably without the soulful and psychedelic influences of *caño roto*. The producer José Torregrosa helped to create the Los Chichos 'sound', marked by a slow tempo and prominent bassline. The electric guitar was frequently accompanied by a horn section and Cuban-style piano arrangements (which, later on, were replaced by synthesisers) and female backing singers. Like thousands of other inhabitants in Vallecas, the trio were gypsy migrants: Jero was from Valladolid, while the two other members, the brothers Emilio and Julio González, were from Ciudad Real. Their *barrio* of Pozo del Tío Raimundo, found in the south of the district, was mostly made up of houses that had been illegally constructed of mud and tin by the migrants who arrived in the 1950s and 1960s. The subject of the documentary film, *Flores de luna/Moonflowers* (Juan Vicente Córdoba, 2008), the houses were nicknamed 'moonflowers' by its residents, named thus because they were hastily erected during the hours of darkness so that the authorities could not see them. The *barrio*'s association with criminality was so notorious that the national police did not dare enter until 1969, and the last of its shanty towns was not removed until as late as 1986 (Fresneda, 1986).

Jero's lyrics explicitly broached subjects such as prostitution and domestic violence that were still taboo in Spain at the time, subsequently earning them controversy with the board of censors. To this effect, the group was made to change the lyrics of the 1974 single 'La Historia de Juan Castillo' (The Story of Juan Castillo), whose original title was 'La Historia del sargento Barriga/The Story of the Pot-Bellied Sargeant', a reference to a policeman who allegedly killed relatives of the *quinqui* delinquent el Lute (Anon, 2008: 63). They were also made to alter the lyrics of 'La Cachimba' (The Hookah), a song from the same year, as the censors believed that it was promoting drug use (Peña and Valderrama, 2004: 118). They were also marginalised by the musical establishment, with the highly popular radio station Los 40 Principales (which is owned by the PRISA group, and is now known as 'Los 40') refusing to play their song, in spite of sales of their records reaching 22 million (Viana, 2018). Frequently described as 'una voz para la calle' (the voice of the street) (Queipo, 2016: 106) and 'la voz del pueblo oprimido' (the voice of the oppressed) (Brown, 2012: 180), the lyrics of Los Chichos vividly chronicled their lived experience of place. In a recent interview, 'Junior', son of Emilio González García and the singer who subsequently replaced Jero after he left the band, commented: 'Estábamos cantando a la situación que tenía el país; todo era jolgorio, toros y flamenco … Pero no era así' (we were singing about the situation the country was in; everything was fun, bulls and flamenco … But it wasn't like that). Julio González García added that 'Lo nuestro eran canciones reales' (real songs were our thing) (Vázquez, 2018).

Los Chunguitos were another gypsy group closely associated with the Vallecas sound, composed of the brothers Juan, José, Manuel and Enrique Salazar. Released in 1977, their debut album *Los chunguitos* signalled a similarly eclectic sound, drawing on elements of rock and funk, albeit with less polished production values than those of Los Chichos. The Salazars were originally from Badajoz and were known for their musical background, and their uncle was the noteworthy flamenco *cantaor* José Salazar Molina 'Porrina de Badajoz'. Like the Chichos, their background was similarly shaped by internal migration:

their family moved to the Puente de Vallecas in search of a better life when they were children, and the brothers grew up in the Madriles area of the district, close to where the M-30 motorway would be constructed. With album titles such as *Callejón sin salida/Dead End Street* and *Contra la pared/Up Against the Wall* and song titles 'Me paso la vida encerrado' (I Spend My Life Locked Up) and 'La chabola' (The Shanty Town), their music drew on a vivid imagery of social exclusion and confinement that was as spatial as it was psychological, with a fatalistic impulse which frequently surpassed that of Los Chichos. Yet if their music emphasised the theme of confinement, it also equally drew attention to movement – and, in particular, movement marked by its itinerant and transgressive nature ('Vagando por ahí' [Roaming Around] and, of course, 'Perros callejeros'). In a later interview in which the brothers Juan and José reflected on their childhood growing up in Vallecas, they spoke of the empty wastelands they played in as well as the police station where they were sometimes locked up for 'travesuras de nada' (mischief that wasn't serious) (Iñiguez, 2001). In illuminating both confinement and movement, their anecdote here foreshadows the tension that would subsequently inform the themes of their songs as well as those of the *rumba vallecana* more broadly. Los Chichos' first single 'Quiero ser libre' (I Want to Be Free), for instance, a song which expresses the desire to escape the metaphorical prison of a loveless relationship, has taken on a more literal meaning over the years, with Spanish prisoners considering the song to be a hymn (Peña and Valderrama, 2004: 15).

The transience of Puente de Vallecas, as Alberto Urrutia Valenzuela shows, is evoked through the name of the district: the toponym 'puente' (bridge) points to a site of transit, a crossing to another side (2007: 90). Both the isolation of Puente de Vallecas and its subsequent lack of resources were a material legacy of Francoist urban planning. Inbal Ofer shows how the oppressive social and ideological outlook of the regime explicitly informed its conception of urban space (2017). While the centre was where 'administrative, leisure, consumption and residential spaces of the higher and middle classes congregated', the periphery was 'where heavy industry and the bare residential necessities of the working classes and the newly arrived migrants were met' (Ofer, 2017: 9–10). Moreover, she writes how the working-class neighbourhoods and workers' colonies on the periphery were designed 'almost exclusively as dormitory suburbs, devoid of spaces of leisure, consumption or social interaction as part of the regime's strive to crush the existing social networks of the Spanish working classes' (Ofer, 2017: 10). It is striking that the vagrant movement of Los Chunguitos, so often underscored in their lyrics, similarly represented a movement enacted from the peripheries to the centre (Román, 2014). As young men, they began their musical career busking, playing their own versions of the *rumbas* of Peret and Bambino, around the centre of Madrid (Román, 2014). The specific areas in which they performed – Sol, Callao, Plaza (Román, 2014) – are illustrative of the spaces of leisure and social interaction to which Ofer refers, concentrated sites of consumption that the Puente de Vallecas conversely lacked. Their interaction with the crowds of Madrid can thus be seen as sonic encounters, where their street performances enabled the margins and the centre to meet and interact with each other. Most significantly, these street performances would lead to their being discovered by the music industry. The producer and musician Argusa Alcón, who was also a member of Dúo Dinámico, first heard the brothers as they were busking outside the Corte Inglés department store in Callao (Calvo, 1988: 36), an encounter which soon led to their signing with EMI.

While the *rumba vallecana* of Los Chunguitos and Los Chichos was shaped by the cultural movement of people, it was transmitted and circulated by another structure of mobility: the relatively new invention of the radio cassette, which as a moving sonic object significantly transformed the ways in which music was consumed. Several compilation cassettes of their *rumbas* were sold in Spanish petrol stations at bargain prices, and, as Peña and Valderrama have noted, Los Chichos' music can be described as 'música de viaje' (driving music) (2004: 95). Frequently heard in moving vehicles, the consumption of the *rumba* thus dramatises the fluid dimension of popular music – a fluidity which, as John Connell and Chris Gibson show, not only relates to its ever-changing transformation as a cultural form but also 'quite literally, as sound waves moving through air' (2003: 9). For younger generations of fans, memories of listening to their radio cassettes as children has established a nostalgic relationship to the *rumba*. In a recent interview with Los Chichos, accompanied in turn by a photograph of the trio posing in front of a vintage car with old leather suitcases tied to its roof, Junior comments that when fans attend their concerts they also return to the past, to the time when they would to listen to the songs with their parents in the car (Vázquez,

2018). Indeed, the enormously popular *rumba* group Estopa, who emerged in the late 1990s and whose fusion of rock and *rumba* was greatly influenced by Los Chichos, have commented that they grew up listening to Los Chichos in their father's car (Gayo, 2004: 48). While the *rumba* mapped out a vivid relationship between music and space, the mobile context in which it was heard articulated a desire to transcend the fixity of their physical surroundings, to overcome their geographical exclusion through movement. In both its production and the patterns of consumption, the *rumba* held in ambivalent tension both locatedness and dislocation, the periphery and centre. Travelling between the Andalusian and the Anglo-American (via the sounds, as we have seen, of Barcelona and its attendant Afro-Cuban influences) the mobile routes of the *rumba vallecana* eloquently articulated ontological insecurity and transience. As the following parts of this chapter will show, this movement was frequently defined by its transgressive and deviant nature. While Los Chichos have sold millions of copies of their albums over their career, for instance, their music has also succumbed to one of the worst rates of piracy in Spain (Peña and Valderrama, 2004: 91). The act of listening to the *rumba*, frequently with pirated copies of cassettes, could therefore be seen as an act of transgression in itself.

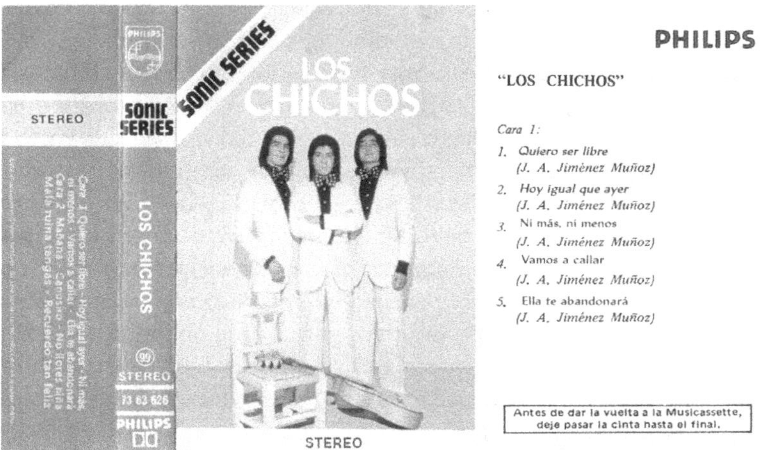

5.1 Cassette album cover of *Los Chichos* by *rumba* group Los Chichos.

Setting the scene: Sound and space

Los Chunguitos' first collaboration with Spanish film was on *Perros callejeros II* (1979), which featured their songs 'Ven por favor' (Please Come), 'Como yegua brava' (Like an Untamed Mare) and 'Para que no me olvides' (So You Don't Forget Me), as well as the eponymous 'Perros callejeros'. The film coincided with the release of the soundtrack album, released by EMI in the same year, which as well as containing these tracks also featured the sentimental incidental music by Armando Trovajoli, an Italian composer who also wrote the score for the first *Perros callejeros* of the cycle.[2] The cross-promotion between the record industry and delinquent film proved to be a lucrative strategy, and Los Chunguitos' collaboration on the soundtrack albums for *Perros Callejeros II* and the slightly later *Deprisa, deprisa* went on to increase the sales of their future records (Anon, 2018). The image of the actor Ángel Fernández Franco lying on the pavement with his fists clenched in pain featured on both the promotional poster of the film and the album cover – a strategy that emphasises the synergy between the two media. Taken from the film's final scene, the image depicts el Torete as he is dying, having been knocked over by a car that swerved into him only moments after his release from prison. As he falls unconscious the camera pulls back in a long shot to show a stray dog approaching his body. Captured in a freeze frame, the final shot is accompanied by the titular song 'Perros callejeros' as the closing credits roll over the image of both the delinquent and the dog.

In a clear illustration of the cross-fertilisation of the film and music industries, the director José Antonio de la Loma himself contributed to the lyrics of 'Perros callejeros', and was credited as one of its writers alongside the Salazar brothers. With its heavy bass and slow tempo, the song contrasts with the frenetic pace of the film that we have just seen. The lyrics to the opening chorus present el Torete's solitary and vagrant movement as a product of broader social forces: 'Soy un perro callejero/y yo digo que más da/vivo solo y como puedo/que me dio la sociedad.'[3] In comparing the figure of the delinquent to that of a stray dog, moreover, the song offers a bitter indictment of how Spanish society dehumanised its teenage delinquents. David Sibley has written that gypsies and other minorities have been historically excluded through their relegation to nature, where their representation as '"naturally" wild, savage, uncivilised, is also expressed in the

5.2 Album cover of the soundtrack for *Perros callejeros 2,* featuring songs by the *rumba* group Los Chunguitos.

representation of people as animals, either as animals generically distinct from humans or as particular species which are associated with residues or the borders of existence' (1995: 27). The street here is similarly depicted as a site of residual waste and exclusion. Bringing together both the delinquent and the dog, the street illustrates Sibley's 'borders of existence' between humans and animals. Yet the street, as we have seen, is also where Los Chunguitos began their career, a site of sonic encounter that brought together the centre and the margins of the city. The vagrant and roaming movement of the stray dog therefore bears parallels with the spatial trajectory of the Los Chunguitos in their early years – a movement that is further dramatised by the title of their song 'Vagando por ahí' (Roaming Around).

The use of the songs in the film is markedly distinct to that of the other incidental non-diegetic music, such as the pieces composed by the composer Armando Trovajoli. In demonstrating how pop music has a different effect in film from traditional non-diegetic music, K. J. Donnelly draws attention to Philip Tagg who points out that pop music is 'still mainly confined to usage in sequences that require a clear, geographical, social and historical denotation of environment and mood, being seldom utilised consistently as codes for illustrating changes in affective message throughout an entire film' (cited in Donnelly, 2002: 2). After an initial car chase between Ángel and the police on the Paseo de Gràcia, the following sequence shows the protagonist arriving by taxi to the *barrio* in search of a place to hide. While the frenetic car scene is accompanied by an upbeat funk-inflected score, Ángel's arrival at the *barrio* is indicated by Los Chunguitos' song 'Una tarde de verano' (One Summer Afternoon). Signalling his movement from the centre to the margins of the city, the song can be heard in the background as he encounters María de las Basuras, an elderly gypsy woman with a walking stick and a large sack over her shoulder, who tells him she is going off to rummage through the garbage. María is established as being dependent on the residues of the city, while the neighbourhood in which she lives is introduced as a residual space whose spontaneously built shanty dwellings rest precariously on unpaved streets made of mud. As well as lending a degree of authenticity to the social practices of the gypsies from marginal spaces of Barcelona, the sound of the *rumba* here further embeds the characters within their specific geographical context.

In a later scene where we hear the *rumba* 'Como yegua brava' , the song has a different function and effect. Heard during a scene in which Ángel shares a joint and has sex with Verónica (played by Verónica Miriel), the song becomes the prominent element of the soundtrack, drowning out all other ambient sounds, as well as mostly replacing the role of dialogue. The explicit depiction of sex and drugs here is extraneous to the plot in the way that was typical of the popular cinema of the *destape* (see introduction), their presence freezing the flow of the otherwise fluid narrative. The use of three-point lighting flatteringly illuminates the contours of their bodies, while the actor's digital watch and various items of flashy gold jewellery underline the spectacle of conspicuous consumption. Claudia Gorbman argues that songs – both diegetic and non-diegetic – can similarly contribute towards the creation of spectacle in films. In reference to the songs played over *Rancho Notorious* (Fritz Lang, 1952), she writes that 'rather than participating in the action, these theme songs behave somewhat like a Greek chorus, commenting on a narrative temporarily frozen into spectacle' (Gorbman, 1987: 19). The music in this scene from *Perros callejeros 2* fulfils a similar function: the sexual and misogynistic lyrics of the song ('eres como yegua brava que pide rienda' [you're like an untamed mare that needs a firm hand]) not only comments on but competes with the ostentatious visual display of male virility. The song is abruptly cut midway through as two armed policemen force themselves into the room to take Ángel away for questioning. In a final defiance of his virility, Ángel continues to have sex until he orgasms before answering back to one of the police officers, who then hits him with his gun. In coinciding with the eruption of police brutality, the suddenness to the cut of the song – a crude sound editing technique which has been used instead of fading the music out more gradually – points to the violently enforced silencing of the delinquent. In both its presence and then blunt removal, the use of the song here configures the transgression of the delinquent as an 'excess' that needs to be contained by both the agents of law and order as well as the logic of the narrative.

Sonic routes

Los Chunguitos' contribution to the soundtrack of *Deprisa, deprisa* was even more significant, given the prominent role that music plays within the film. The soundtrack album for the film was similarly released by EMI and featured music by Los Chunguitos as well as by the Andalusian-based flamenco acts Lole y Manuel and Los Marismeños, and the Badajoz-based flamenco singer La Marelu. The two tracks provided by Los Chunguitos, '¡Ay! Qué dolor' (Oh What Pain) (1978) and 'Me quedo contigo' (I'll Stay With You) (1980),[4] had been previously released as singles. The involvement of the group in the film's soundtrack marked a pivotal point in their career. As Juan Salazar recalls, the film brought their music to a broader audience and vastly increased the sales of their records, commenting that 'rockeros' (rock fans) and other types of people started to come to their concerts after its release (Iñiguez, 2001). The recontextualisation of Los Chunguitos' music within the film by Carlos Saura, Spain's foremost director of art cinema at the time, heard alongside avant-garde acts such as Lole y Manuel who were associated with Nuevo Flamenco, arguably conferred on them a new-found degree of cultural capital. Their subsequent appearances in the live music venue La Sala Rock Ola and on the music television programme, *La edad de oro,* both iconic institutions that were associated with the Movida Madrileña, brought them further kudos. While *Deprisa, deprisa* led to a critical revaluation of Los Chunguitos, it also signalled the beginnings of a broader re-vindication of flamenco music in Carlos Saura's filmmaking, demonstrated most famously in his flamenco dance trilogy *Bodas de sangre/Blood Wedding* (1981), *Carmen* (1983) and *El amor brujo/Love the Magician* (1986) – films that were choreographed by Antonio Gades – and the later *Taxi* (1996), whose soundtrack contains music of the *rumba* group The Gipsy Kings.

Carlos Saura is known for being a particularly musical director. Music, for Saura, does not just inform the postproduction stages of editing and sound mixing but is fully integrated into the consideration of every stage of the filmmaking process from development and pre-production onwards. Saura has said that 'when I write or when I'm shooting, I see the scenes with music. The music almost always comes first. It's previous music' (Castro, 2003: 132). Music is even played, as Linda Willem shows, when he shoots his scenes so as to 'establish the mood for the actors portraying the roles' (Willem, 2003: xiv). Far from being relegated to the background of the soundtrack, the use of music in his films frequently calls attention to its presence, carving out its own space within the film. To this effect, Saura has commented that music 'functions not only as the catalyst for something, but it can turn into the protagonist. And it's not the usual American music of accompaniment, but rather something very specific' (Castro, 2003: 133). This is especially the case when it comes to using pre-existing songs, whose own internal rhythms both contribute to as well as cut against the temporal shape of Saura's films.

In the case of *Deprisa, deprisa*, Saura's choice of songs was informed by what he found the teenage actors were listening to at the time, an aspect of the production of the film which further enhanced its documentary-style actuality. He comments that the teenagers carried around an enormous radio-cassette player wherever they went, whether in Villaverde, Getafe or on the metro, with the volume blaring out. He took the cassettes of their music, which included those of Los

Chunguitos, Los Chichos and El Fari and from the 200–300 songs that he heard, he chose the three or four that he liked (cited in Sánchez Vidal, 1988: 147). Several of the scenes of the film are correspondingly structured around the act of listening. The teenagers are frequently depicted listening to music in *discotecas*, bars – and most significantly – cars. As in real life, the way in which the teenagers consume music emphasises a particularly mobile structure of listening, emphasised through the diegetic source of the portable radio-cassette which is seen in several scenes.

The title sequence begins with Los Chunguitos' *rumba* 'Ay qué dolor' played non-diegetically, as the protagonists Pablo and Meca are filmed carjacking a vehicle in a middle-class suburb of Madrid. The music fades out so that we hear the confrontation between the teenagers and the unsuspecting owner of the car (see also chapter 4); as they drive away in haste, we hear the grinding noise of the ignition and screeching of tyres as they ram the vehicle into bins and haphazardly hit the curb. A close-up shot shows Meca putting a cassette in the cassette deck and turning up the volume. The sound of the engine crossfades into the song again, which, in contrast with the first time, is now heard diegetically. In driving from a well-heeled suburb to their *barrio* in Villaverde, their stolen vehicle marks a passage from the centre to the peripheries – the spatial trajectory that, we have seen, was similarly shared by Los Chunguitos in their formative years. An extreme long shot follows the car as it passes onto the M-30 orbital motorway, whose imposing presence bisects the *mise-en-scène*. Flanked on both sides by high-rise buildings, the M-30 is not only depicted as a passage but as a border, a frontier that both spatially and symbolically separates the poorer districts of Vallecas and Villaverde from central Madrid and its suburbs. Parking their car outside a bar, the music stops abruptly, giving way to the diegetic sounds of birdsong, a peaceful contrast to the frenetic soundscape of the motorway, described in the script as 'una calle ensordecida por el tráfico' (a street deafened by traffic).

As a mobile sonic object, the car in the opening sequence establishes a clear link between the sound of *rumba* and movement. This is visually dramatised through the *mise-en-scène* of Pablo's bedroom, in which a portable cassette player next to the bed can be seen against the walls that are adorned with posters of motorbikes and racing cars. Yet heard within a stolen vehicle, this mobility is foregrounded as

5.3 Meca (Jesús Arias Aranzueque) puts on a cassette of Los Chunguitos in a stolen vehicle in *Deprisa, deprisa* (Carlos Saura, 1981).

explicitly transgressive in nature, a dynamic that is further dramatised through their reckless driving. We soon learn that 'Ay qué dolor' is Meca's favourite song, and he plays it after they drive away from two further heists – each within different stolen vehicles – as well as when they dance to celebrate after sharing out the booty in Pablo's and Ángela's new apartment. Through its frequent repetition, the song serves as a *leitmotif* that brings together the teenagers in an act of collective listening, demonstrating how, in the words of Brandon LaBelle 'sound brings bodies together' in 'connective moments' (2010: xxiv). In framing the actors together as a group as they listen to the music, the camera underlines the relational quality of sound. Their shared experience of music therefore provides a compelling example of how sound serves 'to operate as an emergent community' (LaBelle, 2012), one that, he says, 'weaves individuals into a larger social fabric' (LaBelle 2010: xxi). The relational nature of sound is most clearly illuminated in the film in moments when it serves as a form of social bonding. In two scenes that take place in the discotheque, the camera again holds back to frame the actors together as they sit back next to the dance floor stoned and motionless, and tracks laterally to register their individual faces in passive contemplation as they collectively experience the resonance and rhythms of the music.[5] As they dance to the *rumba* in the apartment, moreover, Sebas tells Ángela, Pablo and Meca that they will always be together.

In creating an 'emergent community', the auditory experience of the *rumba* provides the teenagers with a social structure which is at odds with the hostility of their physical environment. Brutalist housing projects populate the horizon in the film, their heavy and monolithic architecture presented in establishing shots like a shield or exclusionary border. For instance, in a scene in which the teenagers gather beside a polluted lake, Saura describes the recently constructed buildings in the distance in the script as a kind of medieval wall. The treatment of architecture in the film underscores the great distance of the delinquents – one that is both geographical and symbolic – from the centre of the city whose host of opportunities and wealth lie beyond their grasp. In an early scene during sunrise, Saura describes the city in the script as appearing 'misteriosa entre la bruma' (mysterious in the mist), its enigmatic remoteness emphasised through an evocative description of its soundscape in which he describes the faraway sounds of cars and lorries, and the distant whistle of a passing train.[6] As they move further into the city, their movement becomes increasingly trammelled and subject to surveillance – a dynamic which is articulated primarily through performance and framing. As the teenagers loiter outside a bank before the bank robbery, their bodies are partly obscured by stationary cars as they insinuate themselves between background and foreground as if passing through the cracks of the city. Even when Pablo and Ángela have stolen enough money to afford a more spacious apartment, the camera pans around to emphasise the geometric repetition and alienating quality of the buildings.

Acoustic territories

Through their shared consumption of music, the delinquents of *Deprisa, deprisa* are able to carve out a space of their own within this oppressive geography. LaBelle refers to the process of creating acoustic space as 'acoustic territorialisation', whereby 'the divergent, associative networking of sound comes to provide not only points of contact and appropriation but also meaningful challenge; it also allows for participation … of the excluded' (2010: xxiv). If the acoustic territories of the delinquents challenge these geographies of exclusion, this becomes especially meaningful when these territories are shaped by movement – and, in particular, through the act of listening in cars. The mobile soundscape of the car exemplifies LaBelle's assertion that 'the temporal and evanescent nature of sound imparts great flexibility, and uncertainty, to the stability of space' (LaBelle, 2010: xi). The sonic routes of the *rumba* are evanescent and fleeting, and able to travel distances, moving in, across and *through* the physical spaces of the fortress-like city. It is precisely this fluid dimension of sound that resonates so effectively with the geographical trajectory of the *quinquis*. This fluidity provided a means of survival within a geography of oppression, enabling the teenagers to negotiate the fixity of their immediate environment. Through its centrifugal and centripetal movement between the periphery and the city, the musical routes of the delinquents cannot be controlled: they are able to penetrate forbidden spaces, passing through the material and social boundaries of the city that contain and exclude them.

The sonic routes of the delinquents are contrasted with the other routes of transport that appear throughout the film. A commuter train can be seen repeatedly from Pablo's and Ángela's new apartment, its whistle marking out an official passage of mobility that evades the delinquents. In one scene, the friends sit on the top of a towering hill in Getafe, a town just beyond the outskirts of Madrid, looking down at the city from a distance as if stretched out like a map below them. An aerial shot reveals its extended networks of busy roads and train lines. Meca says in reference to the drivers in the cars below: 'van como locos …' (they are going like crazy …). Unlike the cars below, the movement of the delinquents is errant and ambulatory, unfolding at a rhythm at odds with the daily bustle of the city. Pablo spontaneously suggests that they should go to the sea, an element of the plot that mirrored the practices of the actors in real life. As Carlos Saura said in an interview, the delinquents 'practicaban un cierto nomadismo' (practised a certain nomadism), commenting that they would drive off to the sea in Galicia or the Levant, half drugged or asleep (Sánchez Vidal, 1988: 150). Los Chunguitos' contemplative ballad 'Me quedo contigo' can be heard in the following scene as Pablo, Meca and Ángela drive at night to a beach in Almería. Arriving at the coastline during the early morning, the depiction of the sea shore, with the sun gently illuminating the contours of the waves, suggests an idyllic counterpoint to the oppressive city in the previous sequence. An earlier sequence shows the friends riding on horseback in the semi-rural hinterlands of Madrid. As they cross the Carretera de Toledo, one of the busiest arterial routes into the city, the steady trotting of the horses is set in contrast with the speed of the cars. The significance of cars and other vehicles here is an illustration of how Spain had truly become established as a 'mobile nation' at this time, a term that Tatjana Pavlović has used to show how automobility and consumerism were pivotal to Spain's entry into modernity during the *desarrollismo* (development years) (Pavlović, 2011). The movement of the delinquents here pulls against and resists this mobility yet at the same time finds itself driven in search of the acquisition of material wealth that consumer capitalism brings – albeit obtained through illegitimate means. As Marvin D'Lugo writes, 'Saura continually stresses the paradoxical ways in which these youths embody the rejection of middle-class norms and yet are caught up in the acquisitive activities that middle-class culture promotes' (1991: 66). It is not without irony therefore that the robbery of a cement factory enables them to put down the deposit for a new apartment. Ostensibly serving the demand for the construction of apartment blocks like Pablo's and Ángela's which have proliferated during the urban expansion of Madrid since the 'miracle years', the factory is presented as a monolithic complex of grey buildings on the horizon whose striking presence looms behind rows of olive trees that populate the foreground.

The *mise-en-scène* here evocatively points to the fragile coexistence of the city and the countryside, industry and agriculture, a tension which informs much of the treatment of landscape in the film. When not committing robberies, the teenagers roam around the wastelands on the fringes of the city, occupying landscape where the urban and the rural bleed into each other. The wastelands in the film are similar to those in which Los Chunguitos, as we have seen, used to roam as children, and occupied much of the undeveloped land of the outer stretches of the city at this time. This is a space that I have described elsewhere as a 'no-man's land' (Whittaker, 2008). Farley and Roberts call these unkempt and overlooked spaces 'edgelands', territories that they define as 'a complex landscape, a debatable zone, constantly reinventing themselves as economic and social tides come in and out' (2011: 6). The edgelands of Madrid in the film are similarly registered as a landscape in flux whose margins register Spain's recently accelerated transition from an agricultural nation to an urbanised consumerist economy. In one stretch of wasteland strewn with abandoned agricultural machinery, Pablo teaches Ángela how to use a gun by using rusty tin cans as targets. Images of decay and detritus like these frequently populate the film as the delinquents interact with waste that has been expelled from both its urban and rural economies. In another scene, the friends gather beside a lake which is clogged with effluence and rubbish. As they observe the pollution, Meca says that he used to bathe there and go fishing as a child, and that there was once a house at the bottom of the lake. Once an area of childhood play and unfettered imagination, the lake has become a dumping ground into which the city's waste has been expelled. Litter and waste have even encroached upon the Segovian village of Maderuelo, located in the heart of rural Castile, where Pablo takes Ángela to meet his grandmother. Much like the debris they frequently encounter, the teenagers are discarded from the city and the countryside, cast adrift in the neglected edgelands.

Drawing on the work of the geographer Tim Edensor, Farley and Roberts write that edgelands 'often exist in a hiatus between the end of one industrial era and potential future redevelopment' (2011: 151). As spatial as it is temporal, the hiatus to which they here refer is similarly articulated in the setting of the film, whose landscape captures both the youths and Spain in a moment of transition. The materiality of this landscape is felt even more vividly when viewed from a contemporary perspective, with several of the wastelands now transformed into residential areas and the knowledge that the *quinqui* actors – with the exception of Berta Socuéllamos whose whereabouts are unknown – have died tragically young. Their liminal state between childhood and adulthood is further underscored in the film through a series of ironic juxtapositions of adult and child codes of behaviour. The sound of a police siren fades out at the end of one scene as the police chase the delinquents after they practise shooting, and is mirrored by the sound of a Space Invaders arcade game which opens the following sequence. In their local bar Pablo drinks beer whilst Meca has some cold milk. In their apartment, Ángela can be seen watering plants and undertaking housework while Pablo reads the comic *Mortadelo y Filemón*. His gun and ammunition are kept inside their bedroom, the walls of which are covered in teenage posters. With the exception of Pablo's grandmother, the families of the teenagers are neither seen nor spoken of during the film. Left to fend for themselves, the delinquents are alone within an adult's world. Urrutia Valenzuela shows that for gypsy youths from Vallecas, music was a crucial means of subsistence and survival, something that was borne out, we have seen, through Los Chunguitos' busking in the early 1970s (2007: 93). While the delinquents in *Deprisa, deprisa* are consumers rather than producers of music, their creation of acoustic territories enables them to give meaning to and reclaim these adult spaces as their own. In providing an 'emergent community' in the film, the shared experience of music helps to form a kinship that the teenagers otherwise lack through their absence of familial relations.

While the music emphasises the 'bringing together of bodies', a glue that binds the social structure of the group of friends, Ángela is left as a solitary figure after the deaths of Meca, Sebas and Pablo at the end of the film. As D'Lugo has pointed out, she is first introduced to the viewer through the flamenco song that Pablo plays on the jukebox, 'Érase una vez una mariposa' (There Was Once a Butterfly) by Lole y Manuel, 'as if invoking the fictional story that will transform what might otherwise have been simply a documentary into a Saurian meditation on the status of individuality' (1991: 172). Yet while their

5.4 Ángela (Berta Socuéllamos) leaves the *barrio* behind in *Deprisa, deprisa* (Carlos Saura, 1981).

lyrics speak melancholically of a beautiful butterfly that is captured by a collector only to be preserved and mounted in his collection, Ángela at the end of the film is the only one to have achieved freedom, albeit through tragic circumstances. An extreme long shot depicts Ángela at dusk, as she walks away from the apartment where Pablo has just died, carrying the stolen money. With her back to the camera, she walks away from the apartment blocks that have served as a border, ostensibly making her way into the city that has until now eluded her. The music of Los Chunguitos can be heard for the last time, with their ballad 'Me quedo contigo' played non-diegetically. This time, however, the song fades into the ambient sounds of the neighbourhood as the music gives way to the voices of children playing outside. The silencing of the *rumba* here signals both the end of the 'emergent community' to which she belonged as well as the acoustic territories it mapped out. Unlike the errant and wandering movement of the delinquents during much of the film, Ángela here walks with a clear sense of direction, forging a linear route into the city.

Carceral music

Some twelve years after their first album in 1985, Los Chichos were approached to create the soundtrack of *Yo, 'el Vaquilla'*. They were the favourite group of Juan José Moreno Cuenca, who had reportedly been a fan of their music since he was a child. For Moreno Cuenca, the trio were part of his world because the social significance of their music resonated with his own experiences of oppression (Peña and Valderrama, 2004: 100). Long before the production of the film, the music of Los Chichos had been an integral part of the soundtrack to Moreno Cuenca's life, and he recalls, in particular, hearing the group during the moments when he committed crimes. In his autobiography, he speaks of how when he carried out a bank robbery in La Caixa de Barcelona, he could hear Los Chichos being played from a jukebox in a nearby bar (Peña and Valderrama, 2004: 100). Some years later, when he escaped from the prison Lleida-1 dressed as a guard, he stole a car close to the prison building; on opening the glove box, he discovered several Los Chichos cassettes along with a lump of cannabis (Peña and Valderrama, 2004: 100). So important was the music of Los Chichos that when Moreno Cuenca's gang of delinquents stole cars, they would reject those that did not have a cassette player as they would not be able to listen to their songs (Peña and Valderrama, 2004: 101). After reading the script of the film, Emilio, Julio and Jero requested to interview Moreno Cuenca directly, and from the stories he told them the group composed a total of thirty songs in just two weeks, with just a few finally selected for the soundtrack (Peña and Valderrama, 2004: 101). Having grown up in similar kinds of neighbourhoods, the trio readily empathised with Moreno Cuenca's plight. Jero, in particular, who had committed crimes as a youth and had spent time in prison, reached an 'entendimiento espiritual' (spiritual understanding) with Moreno Cuenca and the two remained in contact for several years after their meeting (Peña and Valderrama, 2004: 102).[7]

Like *Perros callejeros 2* and *Deprisa, deprisa*, the songs informed the overall shape of the film. When the director de la Loma first heard the recorded version of their songs, he decided to make changes in the script so that the songs had more presence in the film (Peña and Valderrama, 2004: 103). This is most prominent when songs are played non-diegetically over entire montage sequences in which no other sounds can be heard on the soundtrack. Here, the relationship between sound and image has much in common with the structure of the music video, a medium which rose to prominence in Spain in the 1980s. According to Carol Vernallis, the audiovisual relationship in the music video is distinct from that of the film. She argues that while in films the image may adopt a denotative function and the music a connotative one, in the music video the situation is reversed: 'in order to showcase the music, the image connotes, providing the gloss on the music' (2004: 194–195). A similar dynamic, to an extent, is borne out in the *quinqui* films discussed in this chapter: the films can be seen as music with pictures rather than as the more classical mode of pictures with the accompaniment of music. If it is these moments in the films that more clearly alert us to the synergy between *cine quinqui* and the *rumba vallecana*, they also provide us with an exploration of space.

In several of the musical montage sequences, for instance, setting is not merely treated as a backdrop to the narrative but as a point of inquiry in itself. The song 'Campo de la Bota', for instance, is played over a montage of scenes of life in the eponymous *barrio*. The filming of groups of gypsy non-actors engaged in a series of everyday activities provides the sequence with a documentary-style quality. The camera frames them in long and extreme-long shots so as to emphasise their interaction with their material surroundings. Like the scenes that take place in the prison, the emphasis on individuals situated within their geographical context brings an evidential and urgent quality to the film, one that frames Moreno Cuenca's struggle as belonging to a broader group rather than an individual. The lyrics 'cada persona es su mundo, y cada uno vive como puede' (each person is in their own world, each one lives the best they can) accompany the image of toddlers hosing themselves down with water outside, an indication that the houses do not have running water. As with *Perros callejeros 2* and *Deprisa, deprisa*, the gypsies are depicted among the other debris that have been expelled from the city. The camera reveals rows of informal housing that have been constructed rapidly on the side of rusty train tracks, their roofs covered in discarded toys and other detritus. The sequence reveals the materiality and transience of the shanty town, whose physical environment is figured here in the literal process of construction. One shot shows a group of men, one of whom is carrying a wheelbarrow, building one of the houses. Like *Deprisa, deprisa*, the film provides a vivid archive of urban space in the process of transformation and flux, captured here at a time shortly before the neighbourhood was cleared away. Here, the open-ended depiction of space – illustrated through the images of the inhabitants' physical interaction with self-constructed houses in informal settlements – brings to mind Doreen Massey's assertion that the political dimension of space resides in its opennenss. The politicality of space, she writes, lies in the fact that it is 'always in the process of being made. It is never finished; never closed' (2005: 9). This continual openness and contingency of space here echoes Brandon LaBelle's writing on the ontology of sound. Drawing on the work of Stephen Connor, who shows the ways in which sound acts to 'disintegrate and reconfigure space', he argues that '[t]he temporal and evanescent nature of sound imparts great flexibility, and uncertainty to the stability of space' (Brandon LaBelle, 2012: xi). In its dynamic energy and potential for participation, the disintegration and configuration of space 'becomes a political process' (2012: xxiv).

Location is similarly important in the scene in which 'el Vaquilla' is played the most explicitly biographical song of the film, which begins by narrating both his childhood and his criminal education: 'El nació, por amor un día libre/libre como el viento, libre/como las

5.5 One of the images of daily life in the shanty towns of Campo de la Bota in *Perros callejeros 2: Busca y captura* (José Antonio de la Loma, 1979).

estrellas, libre/como el pensamiento.'[8] Yet the accompanying images of the seaside resort of Castell de Mar, however, present an economic context that appears to be worlds apart from life in Campo de la Bota. The montage sequence opens with a shot of a luxurious yacht gliding through the water, a type of mobility that is far beyond the reach of el Vaquilla and his family. Presented in a postcard-like palette of vivid orange, blues and greens, the resort is a direct legacy of Spain's miracle years, when under the ministry of Manuel Fraga, tourism was positioned as one of the key engines of its transition into a consumerist economy. A colourful site of visual spectacle and consumption, with images of tourists sunbathing and buying souvenirs and clothes, the *mise-en-scène* of Castell de Mar is in marked contrast with the earthy palettes of brown, copper and grey of Campo de la Bota. Like that of the delinquents of *Deprisa, deprisa*, when they enter the city, el Vaquilla's movement within this setting is emphasised by its deviant and errant nature. A series of aerial shots shows the young el Vaquilla nimbly moving his way through the crowds of tourists, stealing jewellery and snatching bags, as the song continues with the lyrics: 'es feliz aunque vive errante, vive como un fugitivo siempre' (he's happy despite his wandering life, always living like a fugitive). As the montage sequence suggests, his criminal education arose from straying from his *barrio* into spaces of capitalist accumulation, as played out by his errant movement here in Castell de Mar. Through emphasising that his robberies are motivated by altruism rather than greed, the song expresses his outlaw status in almost heroic and mythical dimensions: 'alegre bandolero/porque lo que ganas repartes el dinero' (happy bandit/ because you share out the money that you make). In the following sequence, he gives his mother a present bought with money exchanged for stolen goods, informing her that he will always provide for her.

Along with the other songs of the soundtrack, Los Chichos performed 'Campo de la Bota' and 'el Vaquilla' in a free concert that they gave to the prisoners at Ocaña, where Juan José Moreno Cuenca was an inmate at the time. Attended also by several journalists and music executives, the well-publicised concert also served to simultaneously launch the release of the album as well as the premiere of the film, which was screened immediately after the concert. Los Chichos reportedly performed in the outside central patio of the prison, as almost the entire population of the prison – two hundred and fifty or so inmates, one journalist noted (Calvo, 1985: 37) – sat to listen to the performance. One row was reserved for visitors to the prison (who before reaching their seats had to pass through a metal detector and a total of five security doors), another was for second-grade prisoners, while the front row, where Moreno Cuenca sat, was for first-grade prisoners (Sánchez Costa, 1985b: 51). 'Cartas de arrepentimiento/Letters of Repentance' and 'Campo de la Bota' were the songs that received the most applause, and the inmates reportedly broke out in applause during the verse of the song which was critical of 'chivatos' (grasses) (Calvo, 1985: 37). Julio shouted to the audience that: 'El Vaca es de los nuestros y vamos a hacer conciertos en todas las cárceles que nos dejen cantar' (El Vaca is one of us and we are going to do concerts in all the prisons which let us sing), a quotation that was also circulated widely in national press.[9] When at the end of the concert, the prisoners demanded an encore, the group shouted to the audience '¿Qué queréis?' (What do you want?) to which they in turn responded 'Co-ca-í-na' (Co-caine). The unusual setting of the patio for their performance – a space that Moreno Cuenca was otherwise only able to enter for just one hour a day (Calvo, 1985: 37) – further illustrates the kinds of unexpected spaces in which, for Brandon LaBelle, acoustic spatiality becomes pertinent. If the sound of the *rumba* served to carve out an 'emergent community' (as borne out by Julio's comment that 'el Vaca es de los nuestros', as well as by the shared complicity of drug taking), the setting of the prison is an example of how 'acoustic spatiality opens up for unique forms of inhabitation, of gathering'. Brandon LaBelle writes that 'acoustic spatiality provides special conditions of *dwelling* by unfixing conventional notions of the "public"' (2012).

Again, here the *rumba* reconfigures questions of space through sound, redrawing the boundaries between public and private space, echoing the ways in which the *rumba* is used in the films. Los Chichos' performance within the physical space of the prison can be seen as a microcosm for the broader structures of carceral geographies in the films, in which sound is used to negotiate the static imagery of borders, walls and other sites of exclusion and surveillance. The well-publicised concert brought into clear focus the tension between motion and containment – or rather, in this case, motion *within* containment – which lay at the very heart of the *rumba*: their songs offered the potential for collective resistance and agency, albeit fleeting and temporary, to the panoptic structures of space. After the concert, Los Chichos fulfilled a promise they made to Moreno Cuenca and undertook a tour of twenty or so further prisons, including those of Carabanchel and Modelo. Reflecting on their tour years, Junior later commented that 'se les está dando una vía de escape a su monotonía, y eso les da alegría', but also that 'Pero también te digo que es muy difícil, porque tú te vas, pero no puedes olvidar que ellos se quedan allí' (Vázquez, 2018).[10] Indeed, after giving their concert to Moreno Cuenca, a journalist notes that Los Chichos drove away in a white luxury BMW sports car (Gómez, 1985) – a conspicuous symbol of mobility and consumerism, the likes of which their audience that day could only have dreamt of. The journalist also noted that while the prisoner continues his hobby of painting seagulls in flight, in solitary confinement, Los Chichos have achieved a new gold-selling album (Gómez, 1985).

Quinquis remixed: El Coleta and *rap quinqui*

The blurring between popular music and *cine quinqui* has more recently provided inspiration for a generation of contemporary Spanish rap artists. Ramsés Gallego, who is more widely known through his rap moniker el Coleta, has released several songs that self-conciously draw on the visual and sonic iconography of *rumba vallecana* and *cine quinqui*. Self-described as the 'macarra de Moratalaz' (thug from Moratalaz), a working-class district on the south-eastern outskirts of Madrid, his music is similarly shaped by his experience of urban space. Like Vallecas, the district of Moratalaz straddles the M-30 ring road, and the area fell victim to poorly constructed housing projects in the 1960s and 1970s. Just as American hip hop and rap music has used the city – and, in particular, the ghetto – as its thematic focus, el Coleta's so-called 'rap quinqui' similarly draws on Moratalaz as a site of authenticity. Like Los Chichos and Los Chunguitos before him, el Coleta has emerged within the socioeconomic context of a sustained recession, triggered by the banking crisis of 2007–2008 from which Spain still has not recovered. Like the *rumba vallecana* too, his music is intimately embedded in the experience of place, providing a candid reflection of life growing up in a marginal *barrio* in Spain – an aspect to his music that enabled him to maintain a faithful following of young people from similar backgrounds. He says that 'Siempre estoy reivindicando mi barrio, pero podría ser cualquier otro … todos los barrios obreros de España son Moratalaz' (Andrés, 2017).[11] As one journalist has noted, his concerts are more likely to be attended by everyday 'chavales de barrio' (kids from working-class neighbourhoods) than rap fans, who see their lives reflected back at them in his lyrics (Queipo, 2015). If rap has been a crucial platform for the articulation of his struggle within geographical space, it has also enabled him to transcend the lack of confines of his *barrio* and its attendant lack of opportunities. To this effect, he refers to himself as 'quinqui reformado' (a reformed *quinqui*) (Mariño, 2016) – a transformation that has been occasioned through music, but also, like the original *quinqui* actors who have inspired him, through his cathartic performance of delinquent *alter egos* in the music videos that he produces and stars in. Indeed, acting and directing are equally important to his artistic vision as music is: he has commented that he sees himself as an actor, and elsewhere that he has always dreamt of becoming a film director. He taught himself how to create music videos through using just a computer, YouTube and pirated software as his tools (Ollero, 2016). His most obvious homage to *cine quinqui* is his album *Yo, el Coleta* – an evident reference to *Yo, 'el Vaquilla'* – which contains the tracks 'Deprisa, deprisa', 'Nanai nanaina' and 'Perro callejero'.

Like much of his work, the video content associated with this album self-consciously draws on the synaesthetic relationship between music and image in the *quinqui* film, an aspect that is most clearly played out through the representation of space. In common with other videos, the urban cityscape of Moratalaz features heavily in the video of 'Deprisa, deprisa'. While the cinematography of the video, which has been shot with a lightweight digital camera, is obviously less polished than that of Carlos Saura's film, the treatment of urban space in the video has nevertheless been influenced by the *mise-en-scène* of the original film. In a direct echo of the opening sequence to Saura's film, the video opens with aerial shots of the M-30 ring road. In the images that ensue, el Coleta raps in a semi-rural landscape that has been turned into wasteland, covered with the kinds of debris and rubbish that populated the film, alongside the remains of a house that has been reduced rubble. While in Saura's film Spain is symbolised by the location of El Cerro de los Ángeles, the geographical centre of the country, the music video alerts us to the rather more literal Spanish flag, whose presence can be made out amongst the rubble. His lyrics are replete with references to famous delinquents of the 1980s: 'Masticando el chicle como el Pedja/Trompeando como el Trompetilla/con el chandal de Santi Corella/Una leyenda como el Vaquilla.'[12] The chorus 'Deprisa, deprisa, deprisa, deprisa/con bigote y pasamontañas' (Deprisa, deprisa, deprisa, deprisa/with a moustache and balaclava) is mimed by a girl dressed as Ángela from the film, disguised with the fake moustache that she wears in the scene where she holds up the factory office at gunpoint. The video cross-cuts repeatedly between the girl's performance and a shot of the traffic at night, an image of mobility that as well as underscoring the rhythm provides a thematic contrast to the images of the wasteland.

The music video to 'Nanai nanaina', a song from the same album, is even more explicitly presented as a pastiche of a *quinqui* film. A pre-credit title sequence contains footage from the opening sequence of *Perros callejeros*, which, as we have seen in chapter 1, features key images of the city as the voiceover announces: 'Esto es lo que suele llamarse una gran ciudad, tiene sus anchas avenidas, sus casas señoriales ...' (This is what they call a big city, it has its wide boulevards, its stately buildings ...). After a dramatic pause, the voiceover continues '... y sus problemas' (and its problems), as the documentary footage cuts to images of tower blocks. The words 'y sus problemas' are then repeated various times, as if it is heard on a broken record, while the images of the buildings are now seen on a rapidly moving celluloid strip. The narrator's words blend into the opening refrain of the song in which a sampled fragment of Las Grecas' song 'Te estoy amando locamente' (I'm Loving You Like Crazy), taken from the chorus when they sing 'Nainai nanaina', can be heard over a stuttering and syncopated bassline. This sample becomes a hook that is played repeatedly on a loop over the entire track, providing the track with its rhythm. It then cuts to the video's 'opening credits', which are similarly meant to resemble those of *Perros callejeros*, where Ramsés Gallego has front billing as the director, while the leading actor is billed as his rap pseudonym 'el Coleta'. Drawing on the work of Michel de Certeau, who writes that 'everyday life invents itself by *poaching* in countless ways on the property of others' (de Certeau 1984: xii, emphasis in original), Gina Arnold et al. suggest that the medium of 'music video also poaches on foreign terrain, borrowing from its visual language and … its actual significance from a number of different disciplinary territories' (2017: 6). In its appropriation and subsequent reassembling of sonic and audiovisual fragments from the recent past, the construction of the music video keenly dramatises this kind of textual poaching – an aspect that is mirrored through the rather more literal 'poaching on the property of others' that follows in the video, which sees 'el Coleta' and friends depicted as a group of *quinqui* delinquents, dressed in double denim, attempting to carjack a vehicle.

If Ramsés Gallego is positioned as the auteur of his film in the credits (presented in a similar font to that in which Carlos Saura is announced in the title sequence of *Deprisa, deprisa*), his claim to authorship is also an ironic 'in joke' – a knowing wink to fans who are savvy and committed enough to understand the collage of intertextual references. While the practice of sampling originated in New York's Bronx in the late 1970s, the lyrics emphasise a distinctly Spanish negotiation of the genre: 'Delincuencia y drogadicción/Petando 'Las Grecas' y cortando jamón' (Delinquency and drug addiction/pumping out 'Las Grecas' and cutting up ham). Here, allusions to Spain's recent uneven development are mentioned in the same breath as ham, a food that is particularly symbolic of Spanish national identity. The lyrics therefore draw on the well-worn trope of economic underdevelopment being a characteristic intrinsic to the Spanish national character

– a dimension to the music that has led to it being classified by journalists as 'hip hop cañí' (traditionally Spanish or folkloric hip hop) (Lenore, 2014).

In playfully drawing our attention to an archaeology of *quinqui*'s sounds and styles, el Coleta illustrates music critic Simon Reynolds's notion of 'retromania', a term he uses to describe how current pop and rock music exhibits an increasing obsession with its recent past (2011). Our access to these styles, he argues, has been greatly facilitated by technological advances such as YouTube that offer up immediate access to dizzyingly vast quantity of audiovisual materials. 'Audio recordings and other types of documentation (photographic, video) not only provide retro with its raw materials', Reynolds argues, 'but they also create the sensibility, based as it is on obsessive repeat-play of particular artefacts and focussed listening that zooms in on minute stylistic details' (2011: xxxv). The repeated sample of the words 'Nanai nanaina' similarly directs our detailed focus on the serrated timbre of the voices of Las Grecas and the funky *caño roto* bass of the song. Minute stylistic details are similarly reinforced in the visual merchandising of his music. Take, for instance, the vintage sports cars gracing the covers of his album 'Iberikan Stafford' and single 'Siempre', or the image of a purple chiffon ruffed collar of a man's shirt, unbuttoned so as to reveal a medallion with the word 'Yonki' – a visual reference to the shirts that Jero from Los Chichos famously wore in the 1970s – which is used to promote the recent single of the same name. For the album cover of 'Más cornás da el hambre/Hunger is worse than gorings', Gallego appears in what appears to be a mock-up of the front cover page of the crime weekly *El Caso*, which, as we have seen, was especially well known for its reporting on delinquents in the 1960s and 1970s. In a recreation of the well-publicised image of el Lute's arrest, Gallego is represented in a black-and-white photograph escorted in handcuffs by two Civil Guards, while his rap moniker el Coleta appears at the top of the page, in the style of the iconic red-and-white masthead *El Caso* used. This cross-fertilisation of aesthetic styles and textures can also be found in his music video for 'el Piko 3', where he appears in collaboration with Jarfaiter, another *quinqui* rapper. A reimagined sequel to Eloy de la Iglesia's *El Pico 2,* the video centres on Jarfaiter and Gallego who appear to reprise the roles of Paco (who, as we have seen in chapter 3, is played by José

5.6 The rap artists Jarfaiter (here as el 'Jarfa') and 'el Coleta' in the music video for the song 'el Piko 3'.

Luis Manzano) and el Pirri (played by himself) in the film. A number of scenes, such as that of the fight in the prison patio and of Paco and el Pirri injecting heroin together in the prison cell, are recreated in the video. Yet the homage combines specific images from *El Pico 2* with the broader iconographical images of *cine quinqui*. For instance, a poster in their prison cell imitates the design of the original poster for *Perros callejeros*, but this one features the words 'Naina nainana' instead as its title.

If, as we have seen, el Coleta's work has been made possible by the proliferation of digital audiovisual media, his 'retro' style also displays a fascination with the materiality of older and near-obsolete technologies. As well as appearing on YouTube and Spotify, the album *Yo, el Coleta* was pressed onto a series of limited-edition vinyl records, whose sleeves contained photographs of el Coleta driving a red vintage sport car and photographs of tower blocks. The cover to the album contains a photograph that has been glued to a grey brick wall, where Gallego sits behind a tape cassette player in the centre, flanked by a group of friends who are engaged in various transgressive acts (one is heating heroin on a spoon, while another appears to be loading a weapon). Across the poster are emblazoned the words 'Yo, el Coleta', which have been sprayed with a graffiti can. As with the free concert that Los Chichos gave during the release of *Yo, 'el Vaquilla'* the album cover

5.7 Image of the cover of el Coleta's album *Yo, el Coleta* (2015).

artwork holds in tension both mobility and stasis: the visual centrality of the mobile object of the cassette player, a large clunky model from the 1980s, contrasts with the concrete bricks of the wall behind the image. As well as signalling the name of the album, the graffiti visibly marks out an acoustic territory – one that, in common with the films explored in this chapter, points to the artistic reimagining and re-appropriation of urban space through a collective act of listening.

Conclusion

Like el Coleta, contemporary fans of *cine quinqui* have, over the last decade or so, created their own video homages of delinquent stars on YouTube, posting their favourite songs by Los Chichos and Los Chunguitos over montages of scenes or images from different *quinqui* films. In common with the films explored in this chapter, it is the music that drives the rhythm of the images in these homages rather than the other way round. The *rumba* continues to find new audiences through the appearance of Los Chunguitos in the television show Gran Hermano VIP (the Spanish version of Celebrity Big Brother) in 2015 and the singer-songwriter Rosalía singing her own version of Los Chunguitos' 'Me quedo contigo' at the Goya Awards ceremony in February 2019, to huge critical acclaim. In exploring the place of the *rumba* in *cine quinqui*, this chapter has explored the ways in which spatial mobility is crucial to understanding not only the migratory patterns that shaped Spanish delinquency but the experience of marginal urban life during these years. The circulation of these songs, both within the films and beyond them, through the soundtrack albums and live concerts, testifies to the mutually reinforcing relationship between *cine quinqui* and the *rumba vallecana*. As this chapter has shown, both the music and the films not only mirrored the material conditions of marginal young people but in turn shaped them, providing a crucial acoustic community and means of negotiating a hostile urban space that excluded them.

Notes

1 Caño Roto, in particular, had become a byword for experimental urban planning and poor-quality housing projects that were hastily built in an attempt to eradicate the burgeoning shanty towns in these areas. Located in the southern district of Carabanchel, Caño Roto was one of the regime's first *poblados dirigidos* (literally 'directed settlements') that had been commissioned after the 1956 Ley de Suelo (Land and Urban Planning Act). As David Cohn shows, the most unusual feature of *poblados dirigidos* like Caño Roto was its guiding concept of 'auto-construction', where tenants who were unable to contribute towards the cost of the dwelling were asked to contribute their share in the cost of labour, working every Sunday on the construction of the settlement (Cohn, 1992).

2 Trovajoli's music would later be discovered by Quentin Tarantino and it featured in *Kill Bill: Volume I* (2003).

3 'I'm a street dog/And I say who cares?/Living my life alone the best I can/The life that society gave me.'

4 The song '¡Ay! Qué dolor' featured on the 1978 album *Vive gitano*, and 'Me quedo contigo' on the 1980 album *Pa ti, pa tu primo*.

5 They are listening to the disco track 'Hell Dance With Me' by Cappuccino.

6 According to the script: 'Se escucha el tráfico lejano, el pitido de un tren lejano, el claxon casi animelsco de un camión pesado' (The traffic can be heard from afar, the whistle of a distant train, the almost animal-like horn of a heavy lorry).

7 In a newspaper article at the time of the film's release, Jero said that he was proud to have been in prison (Gómez, 1985).

8 'He was born one day, out of love, free/free like the wind, free/like the stars, free/like thought.'

9 See also Pedro Calvo (1985: 37).

10 'You giving them a means of escaping their monotony, and that gives them happiness'... 'But it's also very difficult, because you leave, but you can't forget that they remain there.'

11 'I'm always defending my *barrio*, but it could also be any other... All the working-class *barrios* in Spain are Moratalaz.'

12 'Chewing gum like el Pedja/Fighting like El Trompetilla/with Santi Corella's tracksuit/A legend like el Vaquilla.' Santi (Santiago) Corella, alias 'el Nani,' was a delinquent who went missing in mysterious circumstances in 1983 and whose life was depicted in the film *Matar al Nani/Kill Nani* (Robert Bodegas, 1988).

Conclusion

Cine quinqui continues to exert a fascination on younger generations of filmmakers and audiences alike in Spain. Filmed on the outskirts of Alicante, *Criando ratas/Raising Rats* (Carlos Salado, 2016) featured a cast of non-professional actors who were delinquents, or who had at least lived amongst delinquents. Salado proudly dubbed the film 'neokinki' on its release, commenting it was explicitly influenced by the cinema of José Antonio de la Loma and Eloy de la Iglesia. Echoing the fate of several *quinqui* actors in this film, the filming was aborted because the lead Ramón Guerrero (who plays 'el Cristo') was sent to prison for nine months. Produced on a miniscule budget of 5000 euros, the film was shot in continuity with stark, unvarnished DV footage – something which produces an effect closer to the reactive testimonial documentary or news report than to narrative film. In the same way that *cine quinqui* was shaped by the recession of the 1970s, the human impact of Spain's current economic crisis looms large in the background in *Criando ratas*: during the film's production in 2013, the youth unemployment rate had just reached a staggering high of 56%, a rate second only to Greece.

The social conditions of the 1970s and 1980s in Spain have more recently been re-evaluated in the documentary *Quinqui Stars,* which was directed by Juan Vicente Córdoba in 2018. Significantly, in its collaboration with the rap artist el Coleta, the documentary interrogates *cine quinqui* and the historical period in which it was produced through sound. Presented and narrated by el Coleta himself, the documentary combines original scenes from *quinqui* films with contemporary interviews with surviving actors such as Enrique San Francisco and Bernard Seray. In cross-cutting between the scenes of the original films and documentary images taken of present-day *barrios,* such as Moratalaz where el Coleta lives, the film establishes a continuity between the economic, social and material conditions of the transition with those of today. El Coleta performs a rap song within La Modelo prison, its grounds lying empty since the closure of its facilities in 2017. As we have seen, La Modelo was the site of a huge-scale prison break led by Moreno Cuenca, where he would become the voice of prisoners who were subject to mistreatment and torture. Some years later, Los Chichos performed a concert to prisoners in the patio of the same prison, one of a series of performances which began with the well-publicised concert that was held in honour of Moreno Cuenca in Ocaña prison. As well as explicitly placing contemporary rap music in dialogue with the music of the *quinquis*, el Coleta's performance here draws attention to the acoustic history of marginality, one where sound has been repeatedly mobilised in the social and political struggle of delinquents. As Brandon LaBelle writes, 'sound works to unsettle and exceed arenas of visibility by relating us to the unseen, the non-represented or the not-yet-apparent' (2018: 2). If in La Modelo the sounds of protest unsettled and disrupted the carceral regime of silence, the concerts underlined the relational and affective potential of sound, its capacity to strengthen bonds and community. A sonic archaeology of the prison demonstrates how sound has the capability to both transgress and to bring together, to mark out dislocation and a sense of place.

As the films explored in this book show, this tension also informed the acoustic experience of juvenile delinquency more broadly during these years. Through the prominent noises of car engines, police sirens, delinquent slang and *rumbas*, their soundtracks powerfully captured the experience of delinquency and social control. Yet if, as we have seen, *cine quinqui* all too frequently blurred the contours between fiction and reality, the soundtracks of the films extended from the noisy auditoria and spilled into everyday life, shaping the argot that teenagers spoke and the types of music they listened to in their cars and in the street. *Cine quinqui* was therefore a truly popular cinema, one whose close and often visceral relationship between film and audiences, delinquent actors and their fans, was frequently established through sound. As I have shown, the films demanded a response that was not just physical but political. Through their often unprecedented depictions of police brutality and the youth criminal justice system, the films exposed how the most marginal in Spanish society in the early years of democracy were also the most vulnerable to the residual authoritarianism of the regime. The films not only resonated with audiences but with the wider public and media, triggering and shaping a series of debates, from housing and heroin abuse to penal reform and the age of criminal responsibility. This book has thus shown not only what *cine quinqui* meant but what it *did*. In its resonance and its capacity to affect the world around it, the *quinqui* film shows how, in the words of Brandon LaBelle, 'sound is a powerful force … that extends from the depths of bodies and into the energetics of social formations and their politics' (2018: 7).

References

Aguilar, C. (1996), *Conocer a Eloy de la Iglesia*, San Sebastián: Filmoteca Vasca-Euskadiko Filmategia.

Aguilar, P. (2001), *Memory and Amnesia: The Role of the Spanish Civil War in the Transition to Democracy*, Oxford: Berghahn Inve.

Aguilar, P. & I. Sánchez-Cuenca (2009), 'Terrorist violence and popular mobilization: The case of the Spanish transition to democracy', *Politics & Society*, 37(3), 428–453.

Aguilera, C. (1979), 'Año nacional del niño delincuente. La oleada de crímenes infantiles comenzó en Barcelona, pero ahora alcanza su máxima intensidad en Madrid'. *El Caso*, 31 March.

Andrés, J. (2017), 'El Coleta: "Ser macarra es una actitud"', *El Diario Vasco*, 15 September, https://www.diariovasco.com/planes/macarra-actitud-20170915004334-ntvo.html.

Anon (1977a), 'Los "Perros callejeros" ladran', *Fotogramas*, 4 November 1977, no. 1516, 13–14, 41.

Anon (1977b), 'Perros callejeros', *Informaciones,* 25 October.

Anon (1979a), 'Cine: "Perros callejeros 2": Delincuentes actores', *Cambio 16*, no. 413, 4 November, 119.

Anon (1979b) 'Hubo una anterior fuga en junio de 1978', *El País*, 19 December.

Anon (1980a), 'Navajero'(sic), *El Periódico,* 17 October.

Anon (1980b), 'De la Iglesia muestra los "Navajeros" tal como son', *El Periódico* (Barcelona), 14 October.

Anon (1981a), 'El protagonista de la última película de Saura, capturado "Deprisa, deprisa"', *Diario 16*, 12 March.

Anon (1981b), 'Valdelomar se drogaba con heroína de Deprisa, deprisa', *El País*, 15 March, n.p.

Anon (1981c), 'Delincuente de película. José Antonio Valdelomar, El Mini, protagonizó el film "Deprisa, deprisa", y poco después fue detenido por cometer un atraco', *El Caso*, 21 March.

Anon (1981d), 'Confesiones de Genoveva López: Creo que mi marido cometió el atraco influido por Saura', *Semana*, 897, 7.

Anon (1984a), 'Mañana le robarán a usted. En las ciudades españolas crece el pavor ante la ola de delincuencia impune', *Cambio 16*, 20 February, no. 638, 20–26.

Anon (1984b), 'Un motín en directo', *El País,* 16 December.

Anon (1985a), 'Rodaje de la primera película sobre la de El Vaquilla', *El Periódico*, 23 June.

Anon (1985b), 'Próximo estreno de Yo, El Vaquilla', *El Correo Catalán*, 17 August.

Anon (1985c), 'Moreno Cuenca asegura, en su celda del penal de Ocaña, que su principal enemigo es "El Vaquilla"', *La Vanguardia*, 1 November.

Anon (2008), 'El Vaquilla no robaba un coche si había un casete de los Chichos, *El Periódico de Catalunya*, 7 December, 62–64.

Anon (2009), 'Carlos Saura carga contra el doblaje de películas', *Público*, 16 December.

Anon (2018), 'Los Chunguitos', *Elepé*, http://www.elepe.com/los-chunguitos/.

Aranda Ocaña, M. & I. Rivera Beiras (2013), 'The Spanish Penal and Penitentiary System: From the Re-Socialising Objective to the Internal Governance of Prison' in (eds.) V. Ruggiero & M. Ryan, *Punishment in Europe: A Critical Anatomy of Penal Systems*, Basingstoke and New York, 245–262.

Arango, E. R. (1995), *Spain: Democracy Regained*, Boulder; Oxford: Westview Press.

Arasa, Daniel (2014), 'El Vaquilla', *La Vanguardia*, 11 November.

Arnold, G., D. Cookney, K. Fairclough & M. Goddard (2017), 'Introduction: The Persistence of Music Video Form from MTV to Twenty-First Century Social Media' in (eds) G. Arnold, D. Cookney, K. Fairclough & M. Goddard, *Music/Video: Histories, Aesthetics, Media*, New York: Bloomsbury Academic, 1–14.

A.S.H. (1980), 'Eloy de la Iglesia: "'Navajeros' es una película entre la crónica y el comic"', *El País*, 5 October.

Attali, J. (1985), *Noise: The Political Economy of Music*, Minneapolis: University of Minnesota Press.

Back, L. (2007), *The Art of Listening*, Oxford: Berg.

Baeta, F. (1981), '*Deprisa, deprisa* ... a la cárcel, a la cárcel', *Diario 16*, 4 August, 18–19.

Bálint Kovács, A. (2007), *Screening Modernism: European Art Cinema, 1950–1980*, Chicago: University of Chicago.

Barker, Jennifer (2009), *The Tactile Eye: Touch and the Cinematic Experience*, University of California Press.

Barthes, R. (1977), 'The Grain of the Voice' in R. Barthes, *Image Music Text*, London: Fontana Press, 179–190.

Biddle, I. (2017), 'Romance Cartographies: Flamenco Articulations of Queer Spaces in Urban Andalusia', *Radical Musicology*, 7.

Biddle, I. (2019), 'Madrid's Great Sonic Transformation: Sound, Noise, and the Auditory Commons of the City in the Nineteenth Century', *Journal of Spanish Cultural Studies*, 20 (30), 227–240.

Blanco Vila, L. (1981), 'Deprisa, deprisa. Demasiado patético para ser hermoso', *Ya*, 3 April

Blunt, A. & R. M. Dowling (2006), *Home*, London: Routledge.

Bonet Mójica, L. (1980), 'Navajeros', *La Vanguardia*, 15 October.

Brasó, E. (1973), *Carlos Saura*, Madrid: Taller de Ediciones Josefina Betancor.

Breysse, M. (2011), *Le Cinéma 'quinqui' selon Eloy de la Iglesia*, Paris: Éditions Publibook.

Brown, T. (2012), *Achilibook: biografía gráfica de la rumba en España, 1961–1995*, Lleida: Milenio.

Bull, M. & L. Back (2003), 'Introduction: Into Sound' (eds) Bull and Back, *The Auditory Culture Reader*, Oxford: Berg, 1–24.

C. A. (1981), 'Igual que en la película. Los protagonistas de "Deprisa, deprisa" van cayendo uno a uno', *El Caso*, 8 August, 7.

Calvo, P. (1985), 'Los Chichos presentaron su disco dedicado a "El Vaquilla" ante los reclusos de Ocaña', *Diario 16*, 1 November 85, 37.

Calvo, P. (1988), 'Los Chunguitos: "Nuestras canciones tienen la verdad de lo que pasa"', *Diario 16*, 25 February, 36.

Cañellas, C., R. Torán, O. Junqueras, J. F. Marín, G. Garriga & i Josep Solé i Sabaté (2000), *Història de la presó Model de Barcelona*, Lleida: Pagès Editors.

Capilla, R. (1985), 'Yo, El Vaquilla', *Marca*, 30 November 1985, n.p.

Castro, A. (2003), 'Interview: Carlos Saura' in (ed.) L. M. Willem, *Carlos Saura: Interviews*, Jackson: University Press of Mississippi, 115–143.

Cerdán, J., R. Gubern, J. Labanyi, S. Marsh, T. Pavlović & N. Triana-Toribio (2013), 'Censorship, Film Studios, and Production Companies' in (eds.) J. Labanyi and T. Pavlović, *A Companion to Spanish Cinema*, Chichester: Wiley Blackwell, 391–433.

C.G. (1983), 'Bandrés: "No hice de diputado en la película por miedo al ridículo"', *Diario 16*, 16 September, 38.

Chion, M. (1994), *Audio-Vision: Sound on Screen*, New York; Chichester: Columbia University Press.

Cineinforme (1982), 'Un año en los cines de estreno en Madrid', *Cineinforme: Revista Cinematográfica Española*, May 1982, no. 831, 18–38.

CIS (Centro de Investigaciones Sociológicas (1978)), 'Informe Sobre la Encuesta de Victimización', *Revista Española de Investigaciones Sociológicas*, 223–278.

Cohen, S. (2011), *Folk Devils and Moral Panics: The Creation of the Mods and Rockers*, Abingdon, Oxon: Routledge.

Cohen, L. E., Felson M. & K. C. Land (1980), 'Property Crime Rates in the United States: A Macrodynamic Analysis, 1947–1977; With Ex Ante Forecasts for the Mid-1980s', *American Journal of Sociology*, vol. 86, no. 1, 90–118.

Cohn, D. (1992), 'The Directed Settlement of Caño Roto, Madrid', *Deutsche Bauzeitung*, June, 95–100, http://www.dncohn.es/directed_settlements.htm.

Collectiu de Ciencies Socials (1978), 'Qué es la delincuencia para José Antonio de la Loma', *Los marginados*, February.

Colomer, M. (1977), 'La lucha urbana en el barrio de La Mina', *RTS: Revista de treball social*, no. 68, 11–20.

Comas, À. (2003), *Ignacio F. Iquino, hombre de cine*, Barcelona: Laertes.

Comas, J. (1981), '*"Deprisa, deprisa"* causó cierta decepción en Berlín', *Diario 16*, 20 February, n.p.

Connell, J. & C. Gibson (2003), *Sound Tracks: Popular Music, Identity and Place*, London: Routledge.

Corachán J. & B. Gasulla (1991), 'El SIDA pudo con "el Torete"', *El Periódico*, 3 March, 33.

Crespo, P. (1981), '"Los últimos golpes de El Torete" de J. A. de la Loma', *ABC*, 21 January.

Creswell, T. (2006), *On the Move: Mobility in the Western World*, New York and London: Routledge.

Cuesta, A. (2009), 'Quinquis del barrio' in (ed.) A. Cuesta, *Quinquis del 80. Cinema, Premsa I Carrer*. Barcelona: Centre de Cultura Contemporània de Barcelona, 185–195.

Cuesta, M. (2009), 'Trenzar el mito: Volteretas estéticas, cine de urgencia y prensa sensacionalista' in (ed.) A. Cuesta, *Quinquis del 80. Cinema, Premsa I Carrer*, Barcelona: Centre de Cultura Contemporània de Barcelona, 64–103.

D'Lugo, M. (1991), *The Films of Carlos Saura: The Practice of Seeing*, Princeton, NJ; Oxford: Princeton University Press.

Dasca, S. (1984), 'El Vaquilla: "Me he fugado porque me maltrataban"', *Diario 16*, 16 December, 32–33.

Davies, A. (2016), *Contemporary Spanish Gothic*, Edinburgh: Edinburgh University Press.

de Certeau, M. (1984), *The Practice of Everyday Life*, Berkeley: University of California Press.

de la Loma, J. A. (1984), 'Perros callejeros', *ABC*, 21 November.

de las Heras, J. & J. Villarín (1974), *La España de los quinquis*, Madrid: Editorial Planeta.

Díaz, E. (1999), 'Ideologies of the Making of the Spanish Transition' in (ed.) P. Heywood. *Politics and Policy in Democratic Spain: No Longer Different*, London: Frank Cass, 26–39.

Dolar, M. (2006), *A Voice and Nothing More*, Cambridge, MA: MIT Press.

Donnelly, K. J. (2002), *Pop Music in British Cinema: A Chronicle*, London: BFI Publishing.

Donnelly, K. J. (2013), 'Extending Film Aesthetics: Audio Beyond Visuals' in (eds.) J. Richardson, C. Gorbman & C. Vernallis, *The Oxford Handbook of New Audiovisual Aesthetics*, Oxford; New York: Oxford University Press, 357–371.

Donnelly, K. J. (2016), 'Emotional Sound Effects and Metal Machine Music: Soundworlds in Silent Hill Games and Films' in L. Greene and D. Kulezic-Wilson, *The Palgrave Handbook of Sound Design and Music in Screen Media: Integrated Soundtrack*, London: Palgrave Macmillan, 73–88.

Doyle, Peter (2005), *Echo & Reverb: Fabricating Space in Popular Music Recording 1900–1960*, Middletown, CT: Wesleyan University Press.

Draper Miralles, R. (1984), *De las prisiones de Franco, a las cárceles de la democracia*, Barcelona: Argos Vergara.

Dyer, R. (2000), 'Action', in J. Arroyo (ed.) *Action/Spectacle Cinema: A Sight and Sound Reader*, London: British Film Institute, 17–21.

EFE (1985), '"Yo, el Vaquilla" tendrá 40 copias para su estreno', *Noticiero Universal*, 17 August.

Esteban, J. C. (1981), '"Deprisa, deprisa". Una historia de amor', *Diario de Barelona*, 10 April, 15.

Farley, P. & M. Symmons Roberts (2011), *Edgelands: Journeys into England's True Wilderness*, London: Jonathan Cape.

Farrall, S., J. Jackson & E. Gray (2009), *Social Order and the Fear of Crime in Contemporary Times*, Oxford: Oxford University Press.

Faulkner, S. (2013), *A History of Spanish Film: Cinema and Society 1910–1920*, New York, London: Bloomsbury.

Felman, S. & D. Laub (1992), *Testimony: Crises of Witnessing in Literature, Psychoanalysis and History*, New York; London: Routledge.

Fernández Molina, E. & C. Rechea Alberola (2003), 'Juvenile Justice in Spain: Past and Present', *Journal of Contemporary Criminal Justice*, 19 (4), 384–412.

Fernández Santos, J. A. (1992), 'Muere de sobredosis en el hospital penitenciario de Carabanchel', *El País*, 4 December.

Fernández Torres, A. (1980), 'Miedo a salir de noche', *Contracampo*, no. 10–11, 80.

Fernando, C. (1983), 'Con *El pico*, llegó el escándalo', *Diario 16*, 21 July, 20–21.

F.F. (1985), 'De la Loma presenta "Yo, el Vaquilla", una biografía fílmica del conocido delincuente', *La Vanguardia*, 10 November.

Florido Berrocal, J., L. Martín-Cabrera, E. Matos Martín & R. Robles Valencia (2015), 'Introducción', *Fuera de la ley: Asedios al fenómeno quinqui en la transición española*, Granada: Comares.

Fresneda, C. (1986), 'El Pozo Tío Raimundo dice adiós a las chabolas', *El País*, 29 May.

Fuembuena, E. (2017) *Lejos de aquí*, Albacete: Que Vayan Ellos.

Funes, J. (1984), *La nueva delincuencia infantil y juvenil*, Paidós Ibérica: Barcelona.

Galán, D. (1977), 'Una insólita película de José Antonio de la Loma. *Perros callejeros*', *Triunfo*, 22 October, 33–34.

Galán, D. (1979), 'Eloy de la Iglesia: la ambición de un cine popular', *Triunfo*, 24 April.

Galán, D. (1981), 'El lento y complicado rodaje de Deprisa, deprisa', *El País*, 28 March.

Galván García, V. (2007), 'Sobre la abolición de las cárceles en la Transición Española', *Historia Actual Online*, October, no. 14, 127–131.

Gamella, J. F. (1990), *La Historia de Julián. Memorias de heroína y delincuencia*, Madrid: Editorial Popular.

García, A. (1985), '"El Vaquilla" mantuvo secuestrados durante ocho horas a seis funcionarios en la prisión de Ciudad Real', *Diario 16*, 20 November, 37.

García, F. (1981), 'Durante el rodaje de "La patria del Rata" el equipo fue detenido', *Diario 16*, 17 October, 37–38.

García, J. (1981), 'José Antonio Valdelomar verá otra vez su película en la cárcel', *El País*, 9 August, n.p.

García Santa Cecilia, C. (1988), '"El Pirri" aparece muerto por sobredosis en Vicálvaro', *El País*, 10 May.

García-Egocheaga, J. (2003), *Minorías malditas. La historia desconocida de otros pueblos de España*, Madrid: Susaeta.

Garland, D. (2001), *The Culture of Control: Crime and Social Order in Late Modernity*, Oxford: Clarendon.

Gayo, A. (2004),'¡Ni más, ni menos!: Los Chichos y Estopa se juntan en Vallecas en su parculiar jornada de reflexión. ¡Que vivan los rumberos!', *Interviú*, 29 March, 46–50.

Gilbert, J. (2004), 'Signifying Nothing: "Culture", "Discourse" and the Sociality of Affect', *Culture Machine vol. 6*.

Goicoechea, G. (1978), 'Reformatorios. Un pasado que perdura', *Triunfo*, no. 805, 1 July, 35–37.

Gómez Gufi, J. M. (2014), Sleeve notes for *Gipsy Rhumba: The Original Rhythm of Gipsy Rhumba in Spain 1965–1974*, Soul Jazz Records.

Gómez, J. M. (1985), 'Los Chichos cantan al "Vaquilla" "porque es de los nuestros"', *Tiempo*, 24 November, n.p.

Gómez Méndez, C. A. (2015), *Eloy de la Iglesia: Discursos del disenso del franquismo a la post-Transición*, unpublished PhD thesis, Universidad Carlos III de Madrid.

Gorbman, C. (1987), *Unheard Melodies: Narrative Film Music*, Bloomington and Indianapolis: Indiana University Press.

Gracia, F. (1979), 'El Terror está manipulado', *Diario 16*, 23 September, 13.
Gracia, F. (1980a), 'Según su director, Eloy de la Iglesia "Miedo a salir de noche es una película optimista"', *Diario 16*, 5 March.
Gracia, F. (1980b), 'Eloy de la Iglesia estrena película sobre el niño delincuente. "He realizado un homenaje a 'El Jaro'"', *Diario 16*, 4 October.
Gracia, V. (1978), '"El Torete", protagonista de "Perros callejeros", salió de prisión: "¿Qué queréis, buscarme la ruina?"', *Interviú*, 16 March, 90–91.
Green, S. & L. Meyer (2018), *The Granny and the Heist (La estanquera de Vallecas)*, Liverpool: Liverpool University Press.
Gubern, R. & K. Vernon (2013), 'Soundtrack' in (eds.) J. Labanyi & T. Pavlović, *A Companion to Spanish Cinema*, Malden, MA: Wiley-Blackwell, 370–388.
Gurruchaga, C. (1983), 'José Luis Manzano: "Vivimos en una sociedad drogada"', *Diario 16*, 19 September.
Halliday, M. A. K. (1976), 'Anti-Languages', *American Anthropologist*, 78 (3), September 1976, 570–584.
Harries, D. (2002), 'Film Parody and the Resuscitation of Genre' in (ed.) S. Neale, *Genre and Contemporary Hollywood*, London: BFI Publishing, 281–293.
Hart, P. (2007), 'Sound Ideas or Unsound Practices?: Listening for "Spanishness" in Peninsular Film' in (ed.) C. S. Conejero, *Spanishness in the Spanish Novel and Cinema of the 20th–21st Century*, Newcastle: Cambridge Scholars Press, 133–146.
Hayward K. J. & J. Young (2004), 'Cultural Criminology: Some Notes on the Script', *Theoretical Criminology*, 8 (3), 259–273.
Hebdige, D. (1979), *Subculture: The Meaning of Style*, London: Methuan.
Helmreich, S. (2007), 'An Anthropologist Underwater: Immersive Soundscapes, Submarine Cyborgs, and Transductive Ethnography', *American Ethnologist*, 34 (4), 621–641.
Hemsworth, K. (2015), 'Carceral Acoustemologies: Historical Geographies of Sound in a Canadian Prison' in (eds) Karen M. Moran and Dominique Moran, *Historical Geographies of Prisons: Unlocking the Usable Carceral Past*, London: Routledge, 17–33.
Herman, R. (1979), 'Ads Removed for a Gang Movie after Sporadic Violence at Theaters', *The New York Times*, February 23, 18.
Hernández Les, J. (1986), *El cine de Elías Querejeta: Un productor singular*, Bilbao: Mensajero.
Hernando Sanz, F. J. (2001), *Espacio y Delincuencia*, Madrid: Consejo Económico y Social.
Hewitt, C. (1993), *Consequences of Political Violence*. Aldershot: Dartmouth.
Hidalgo, M (1983), 'Arrojarse a los pies del "caballo"', *Diario 16*, 18 September, 38.
Highmore, B. (2005), *Cityscapes: Cultural Readings in the Material and Symbolic City*, Basingstoke: Palgrave Macmillan.

Holmes, J. (2001), *Terrorism and Democratic Stability*, Manchester: Manchester University Press.

Hooper, J. (1995), *The New Spaniards* (Fourth Edition), London: Penguin.

Hopewell, John (1995), *Out of the Past: Spanish Cinema after Franco*, London: British Film Institute.

Huertas, J., Joan J. Caballero & Remei de Pascual (1978), *Los hijos de la calle*, Barcelona: Bruguera.

Hurtado Martínez, M. (1999), *La inseguridad ciudadana de la transición a una sociedad democrática: España (1977–1989)* (no. 89). Univ. de Castilla-La Mancha.

Iñiguez, F. (2001), 'La rumba vallecana cumple un cuarto de siglo', *El País*, 14 January.

Jazeel, T. (2005), 'The World Is Sound? Geography, Musicology and British-Asian Soundscapes', *Area* 37, 233–241.

Jímenez, J. (1978), 'Trato de hacer un cine honesto y objetivo', *Baleares* (Palma), 4 April.

Jordan, B. & R. Morgan-Tamosunas (1998), *Contemporary Spanish Cinema*, Manchester: Manchester University Press.

Katz, J. (1988), *Seductions of Crime: Moral and Sensual Attractions in Doing Evil*, New York: Basic Books.

Klein, A. A. (2011), *American Film Cycles: Reframing Genres, Screening Social Problems, and Defining Subcultures*, Austin, TX: University of Texas Press, 2011.

Kowalsky, D. (2004), 'Rated "S": Softcore Pornography and the Transition to Democracy, 1977–1982' in (eds.) A. Lázaro-Reboll & Andrew Willis, *Spanish Popular Cinema*, Manchester: Manchester University Press, 188–208.

Labrador Méndez, G. (2017), *Culpables por la literatura: Imaginación y contracultura en la transición española (1968–1988)*, Madrid: Ediciones Akal.

LaBelle, B. (2010), *Acoustic Territories: Sound Culture and Everyday Life*, New York: Continuum.

LaBelle, B. (2012), 'Acoustic Spatiality', *Književnost i kultura*, Broj 4.

LaBelle, B. (2018), *Sonic Agency: Sound and Emergent Forms of Resistance*, London: Goldsmiths Press.

Laborde, E. (1981), 'De cómo censurar sin censurar y otras contradicciones', *ABC*, 7 April, n.p.

Labrador Méndez, G. (2009), *Letras arrebatadas: Poesía y química en la transicíon española*, Madrid: Devenir.

Lahera, E. (1980), 'Reducción de la edad penal. Mocosos a la cárcel', *Interviú*, 28 February, 60–62.

Lardín, R. (2006), 'Menos que nada: Una aproximación al último cine negro español (1980–2005) in (ed.) J. Palacias, *Euronoir: Serie negra con sabor europeo*, Madrid: T&B, 389–401.

Lawlor, T. & M. Rigby (1998), *Contemporary Spain: Essays and Texts on Politics, Economics, Education and Employment and Society*, London: Longman.
Lázaro Carreter, F. (1979), 'Una jerga juvenil: El cheli', *ABC*, 16 October, 6–7.
Lázaro Carreter, F. (1980), *Estudios de Linguística*, Barcelona: Editorial Crítica.
Lefebvre, H. & C. Regulier (2003), 'The Rhythmanalytical Project' in (eds.) S. Elden, E. Lebas & E. Kofman, *Henri Lefebvre: Key Writings*, New York; London: Continuum, 190–199.
Lefebvre, Henri (2004), translated by S. Elden and G. Moore, *Rhythmanalysis: Space, Time and Everyday Life*, London and New York: Continuum.
Lenore, V. (2014), 'Los macarras que salvaron al hip hop cañí', *El Confidencial*, 6 April, https://www.elconfidencial.com/cultura/2014-04-06/los-macarras-que-salvaron-al-hip-hop-cani_112278/.
Llano, S. (2019), *Discordant Notes: Marginality and Social Control in Madrid, 1850–1930*, New York: Oxford University Press.
Llano, S. & T. Whittaker (eds) (2019), 'Spanish Sound Studies', *Journal of Spanish Cultural Studies*, 20 (3).
Llinás, F. & J. L. Téllez (1981), 'El primer plano y el aceite de colza', *Contracampo*, December, no. 25–26, 27–36.
Llopis, S. (1981), 'La loca carrera de El Mini', *Cambio 16*, 23 March, no. 486, 100–102.
López, G. (1981), 'Confesiones de Genoveva López. "Creo que mi marido cometió el atraco influido por la película de Saura"', *Semana*, no. 897, 6–7.
López Pintor, R. (1985), 'Francoist Reformers in Democratic Spain; The Popular Alliance and the Democratic Coalition' in (eds.) H. R Penniman & E. M. Mujal-León, *Spain at the Polls, 1977, 1979, 1982: A Study of the National Elections*, Durham, NC: Duke University Press.
Lozano, S. (1984), 'El Pico 2', *Indiscreta*, 17 December.
Marchena, D. (2014), 'Los motes de los delincuentes', *La Vanguardia*, 5 December, https://www.lavanguardia.com/sucesos/20141215/54421429484/motes-de-los-delincuentes.html.
Marías, J. (1981), 'Señoritismo', *Gaceta ilustrada*, no. 837.
Marinero, M. (1980), 'Navajeros', *Diario* 16, 9 October.
Mariño, Henrique (2016), 'El Coleta, rima o revienta', *Público*, 6 July 2016, https://www.publico.es/sociedad/coleta-rima-o-revienta.html.
Marks, L. (1998), 'Video Haptics and Erotics', *Screen*, 39 (4): 331–348.
Marks, L. (2000), *The Skin of the Film: Intercultural Cinema, Embodiment and the Senses*, Durham NC: Duke University Press.
Marsh, S. (2003), 'Luis García Berlanga', http://sensesofcinema.com/2003/great-directors/berlanga/.
Marsh, S. (2013), 'Neville, Berlanga, and de la Iglesia: A Strategically Disruptive Auteurism' in (eds.) J. Labanyi and T. Pavlović, *A Companion to Spanish National Cinema*, Chichester: Wiley-Blackwell, 153–167.

Martín-Cabrera, L. (2015), 'Los quinquis nunca fueron blancos: Infrarrealismo, interseccionalidad y postsoberanía en el cine de José Antonio de la Loma' in (eds.) J. Florido Berrocal, L. Martín-Cabrera, E. Matos Martín & R. Robles Valencia, *Fuera de la ley: Asedios al fenómeno quinqui en la transición española*, Granada: Comares, 109–130.

Martínez Álvarez, J. (2018), 'El "Decreto Miró" y su repercusión en la producción de películas relaccionadas con la violencia de ETA (1983–1989)', *Comunicación y Sociedad*, 31 (3), 261–279.

Martínez, G., (ed.) (2012), *CT o La Cultura de la Transición: Crítica a 35 años de cultura*, Madrid: Debolsillo.

Martínez, R. (1980), 'De la Iglesia: "Hay delincuencia juvenil por el paro existente"', *Noticiero Universal*, 14 October.

Martínez Reguera, E. (1982), *La calle es de todos, ¿De quién es la violencia?*, Madrid: Editorial Popular.

Martínez Tomás, A. (1977), 'Perros callejeros', *La Vanguardia*, 16 November.

Masó, A. (1979), 'De nuevo, una crónica negra sobre la juventud', *La Vanguardia*, 30 October.

Massey, D. (2005), *For Space*, London: Sage.

Massumi, B. (2002), *Parables for the Virtual: Movement, Affect, Sensation*, Durham, NC: Duke University Press.

Mauri, F. (1998), *Agujero negro: Conversaciones con Eloy de la Iglesia*, La Coruña: Ediciones Montaner.

Melero, A. (2010), *Placeres ocultos: Gays y lesbianas en el cine español de la transición*, Madrid: Notorious Ediciones.

Melero, A. (2013), *La noche inmensa: La palabra de Gonzalo Goicochea*, Volumen 3 de Cuadernos Tecmerin, Madrid: Universidad Carlos III.

M.I.J.A.C. (Movimiento Infantil y Juventil de Acción Católica) (1977), 'Crítica a "Perros Callejeros". El M.I.J.A.C. manifiesta su desacuerdo con el planteamiento de esta película', *Mundo Diario*, 24 December.

Miralles, M. (1983), 'Policias compran información con heroína en el País Vasco', *Diario 16*, 27–28, 1 August.

Miralles, M. (1984), 'Dos vidas entre la realidad y la ficción', *Diario 16*, 24 December, 29.

Molina Roy, E. (1984), *Los otros madrileños: El Pozo del Tío Raimundo*, Madrid: Avapiés.

Monferrer I Celades, J. M. (2013), *El Campo de la Bota: Un espacio y una historia*, Barcelona: Octaedro.

Montaout, A. (1985), 'Un hermanastro de "El Vaquilla" muere al estrellarse cuando huía de la policía', *El País,* 7 February, 1.

Montgomery, M. (2008), *An Introduction to Language and Society*, London: Routledge.

Mora, Francisco (1979), 'José A. de la Loma. La delincuencia juvenil al cine', *Diario de Barcelona*, 14 August.

Moreiras Menor, C. (2002), *Literatura y cine en la España democrática*, Madrid: Ediciones Libertarias.

Moreno Cuenca, J. J. (1984), 'Exclusiva, tras su spectacular captura: "Así me convertí en delincuente"', *Interviú*, 19, December 1984, 6–13.

Moreno Cuenca, J. J. (1985), *Yo, El Vaquilla*, Barcelona: Seix Barral.

Moreno Cuenca, J. J. (2001), *Hasta la libertad*, Barcelona: Ediciones B.

Moreno-Caballud, L. (2015), *Cultures of Anyone: Studies on Cultural Democratization in the Spanish Neoliberal Crisis*, Liverpool: Liverpool University Press.

M.R.E. (1981), 'Esta vez sí: "Real como la vida misma". Estreno "Deprisa, deprisa", Carlos Saura', *Diario 16*, 2 April.

Naremore, J. (1988), *Acting in the Cinema*, Berkeley; London: University of California Press.

Ofer, I. (2017), *Claiming the City and Contesting the State: Squatting, Community Formation and Democratization in Spain (1955–1986)*, London: Routledge.

Ollero, D. (2016), 'Lo quinqui vuelve a estar de moda', *El Mundo*, 2 March.

O'Malley, P. (1995), 'Turning Point: The 1970 Education Act' in (eds.) O. Boyd-Barrett & P. O'Malley, *Education Reform in Democratic Spain*, London & New York: Routledge, 25–31.

Otero, L. (1988), 'El Vaquilla: Borrón y cuenta nueva', *Interviú*, 11 October 1988, 115–121.

Palacio, M. (2011), 'Introducción' in (ed.) M. Palacio, *El cine y la transición política en España (1975–1982)*, Madrid: Biblioteca Nueva, 7–18.

Parrado, D. (2017), 'El drama del joven de "La estanquera de Vallecas" que murió de sobredosis', *El Español*, 11 June, https://www.elespanol.com/corazon/famosos/20170610/222727939_0.html.

Pavlović, T. (2011), *The Mobile Nation: España cambia de pie*, Bristol: Intellect.

Pavlović, T., I. Álvarez, R. Blanco-Cano, A. Grisales, A Osorio, & A Sánchez (2009), *100 Years of Spanish Cinema*, Chichester: Wiley-Blackwell.

P.E. (1983), 'Eloy de la Iglesia, el director de la película más polémica del año, "El pico": "nos asesoró un ex-etarra herionómano"', *Interviú*, 12 October, n.p.

Peiró, J. (1983), 'De la Loma prepara su segundo asalto a la "vía americana"', *El Periódico*, 12 November.

Peña, R. & J. Valderrama (2004), *Nosotros los Chichos*, Barcelona: Ediciones B.

Penfold-Mounce, R. (2009), *Celebrity Culture and Crime: The Joy of Transgression*, Basingstoke: Palgrave Macmillan.

Pereda, E. (1984), '"El Torete" y "El Vaquilla", vidas paralelas', *El País*, 16 December.

Poc, S. (1984), 'Eloy de la Iglesia: "La droga más dura que existe hoy es la familia"', *El Correo Catalán*, 10 November.

Preston, P. (1995), *The Politics of Revenge: Fascism and the Military in Twentieth-Century Spain*, London: Unwin Hyman.

Queipo, A. (2015), 'MOvida Madrileña: El Coleta reescribe la cultura quinqui más cañí en su nuevo disco M.O.vida Madrileña', *Notodo.com*, 11 June 2015, http://www.notodo.com/musica/flamenco/8465_sonido_cao_roto_el_motown_espaol.html.

Queipo, A. (2016), 'Sonido Caño Roto. ¿El Motown español?', *Notodo.com*, 2 March 2016, http://www.notodo.com/musica/flamenco/8465_sonido_cao_roto_el_motown_espaol.html.

Quinlivan, D. (2012), *Place of Breath in Cinema*, Edinburgh: Edinburgh University Press.

Radcliff, P. (2011), *Making Democratic Citizens in Spain: Civil Society and the Popular Origins of the Transition, 1960–78*, Basingstoke: Palgrave Macmillan.

Radcliff, P. (2017), *Modern Spain: 1808 to the Present*. Huboken, NJ: Wiley Blackwell.

Reynolds, S. (2011), *Retromania: Pop Culture's Addiction to its Own Past*, London: Faber.

Ríos Carratalá, J. A. (2014) *Quinquis, maderos y picoletos*, Seville: Renacimiento.

Rodríguez Cárcela, R. (2012), '*El Caso*. Aproximación histórico-periodística del semanario español de sucesos'. *Correspondencias & Análisis*, 2. 219–236.

Rodríguez Ortega, V. R. (2014), 'The Thriller' in (eds.) J. Labanyi and T. Pavlović, *A Companion to Spanish National Cinema*, Chichester: Wiley-Blackwell, 265–275.

Román, M. (2014), 'Cuando los chunguitos cantaban en la calle', *Libertad Digital*, 16 November, https://www.libertaddigital.com/cultura/musica/2014-11-16/cuando-los-chunguitos-cantaban-en-la-calle-1276533465/.

Rosenthal, C. & D. Vanderbeke (2015), 'Introduction' in (eds.) Rosenthal and Vanderbeke, *Probing the Skin: Cultural Representations of Our Contact Zone*, Newcastle: Cambridge Scholars Publishing, 1–11.

Ruiz, J. (1980), '"Los últimos golpes de El Torete". A la tercera va la vencida', *El Correo Catalán*, 4 October.

Sainz Cantero, J. A. (1983), 'Realidad Social y Política Criminal en la España de la Transición', *Cuadernos de Política Criminal*, no. 21, 745–756.

Sánchez, A. (1979), 'Así hablan los marginados', *Interviú*, 4 January, 61–63.

Sánchez Costa, J. J. (1984), 'Eloy de la Iglesia insiste en su reflexión sobre la Guardia Civil', *El Periódico*, 11 November.

Sánchez Costa, J. J. (1985a), 'Rodaje de la primera película sobre la vida de "El Vaquilla"', *El Periódico*, 23 June.

Sánchez Costa, J. J. (1985b), 'Los Chichos presenta su disco "Yo, El Vaquilla" entre presos', *El Periódico*, 3 November, 51.

Sánchez, M. A. (1983), 'Dos actores de "Deprisa, deprisa", detenidos por sendos atracos', *Pueblo*, 6 September.

Sánchez Vidal, A. (1988), *El cine de Carlos Saura*, Zaragoza: Caja de Ahorros de la Inmaculada de Aragón.

Sánchez-Gijón, A. (1987), 'The Spanish Press in the Transition Period' in (eds.) Robert Clark and Michael Haltzel, *Spain in the 1980s: The Democratic Transition and a New International Role*, Cambridge, MA: Ballinger, 123–139.

Saura, C. (1981), 'Notas sobre *Deprisa, deprisa*', *Accompanying press notes to the film*.

Sconce, J. (1995), '"Trashing" the Academy: Taste, Excess, and an Emerging Politics of Cinematic Style', *Screen*, 36: 4, Winter, 371–394.

Seferi (1976), 'El automóvil, imprescindible en atracos y asesinatos. La incidencia en delitos graves del "hurto de uso"', *El Caso*, no. 1260, 26 June, 21–22.

Serres, M. and L. R. Schehr (1983), 'Noise', *SubStance*, vol. 12, no 3, issue 48–60.

Shaviro, S. (1993), *The Cinematic Body*, Minneapolis; London: University of Minnesota Press.

Shaw, L. and R. Stone (2012), *Screening Songs in Hispanic and Lusophone Cinema*, Manchester: Manchester University Press.

Sheller, M. (2004), 'Automotive Emotions: Feeling the Car', *Theory, Culture and Society*, 21 (4–5), 221–242.

Sherry, J. J. (1992), 'Arruinado, Enfermo y Solo', *Interviú*, 16 March, 55–57.

Sibley, D. (1995), *Geographies of Exclusion: Society and Difference in the West*, London: Routledge.

Silva, L. (2011), 'Carne de Presidio', *El mundo del siglo veintiuno*, 12 November 2011, 26–3.

Smith, J. (2008), *Vocal Tracks: Performance and Sound Media*, Berkeley, CA; London: University of California Press.

Smith, Jacob (2012), 'Sound and Performance in *Night Dreams* and *Café Flesh*' in (ed.) X. Mendik, *Peep Shows: Cult Films and the Cine-Erotic*, London: Wallflower Press, 41–56.

Smith, P. J. (1992), *Laws of Desire: Questions of Homosexuality in Spanish Writing and Film 1960-1990*, Oxford: Clarendon Press.

Smith, P. J. (1998), 'Homosexuality, Regionalism, and Mass Culture: Eloy de la Iglesia's Cinema of Transition' in (eds.) J. Talens and S. Zunzunegui, *Modes of Representation in Spanish Cinema*, Minneapolis, MN: University of Minnesota Press, 216–252.

Song, R. (2016), *Lost in Transition: Constructing Memory in Contemporary Spain*, Liverpool: Liverpool University Press.

Stangeland, P. (1995), *The Crime Puzzle: Crime Patterns and Crime Displacement in Southern Spain*, Málaga: Miguel Gómez.

Tasker, Y. (2004), 'Introduction: Action and Adventure Cinema' in (ed.) Y. Tasker, *Action and Adventure Cinema*, London: Routledge, 1–144.

Thompson, M. (2017), *Beyond Unwanted Sound: Noise, Affect and Aesthetic Moralism*, New York: Bloomsbury Academic.

Tomlinson, J. (2007), *The Culture of Speed: The Coming of Immediacy*, London: Sage.

Torre Iglesias, M. (1980), 'Hablan los especialistas', *Interviú*, 28 February, 63–64.

Torres, A. M. (1996), *Diccionario Espasa. Cine español*, Madrid: Espasa Calpe.

Torres, M. (1979), 'Ángel Fernández: "El Torete": "Me arrepiento cantidá"', *Fotogramas*, 21 October, no. 1617, 3–7, 33.

Trenzado Romero, M. (1999), *Cultura de masas y cambio politico: El cine español de la transición*, Madrid: Centro de Investigaciones Sociológicas.

Triana-Toribio, N. (2003), *Spanish National Cinema*, London: Routledge.

Trueba, F. (1977), 'Las buenas intenciones', *El País*, 4 November.

Turner, B. (2003), 'Social Fluids: Metaphors and Meanings in Society', *Body and Society*, March, vol. 9, 1–10.

Umbral, F. (1983), *Diccionario cheli*, Barcelona: Grijalbo.

Unión de Centro Democrático (1979), 'Vota UCD', *El País*, 25 February, 27.

Urrutia Valenzuela, A. (2007), 'La música en el barrio como elemento de afirmación identitaria (el ejemplo de Vallecas)', *Revista de Antropología*, 62 (1), 85–110.

Vázquez, C. (2018), 'Los Chichos: Hasta que el cuerpo aguante', *Efe Eme. com. Diario de Actualidad Musical*, 15 January, https://www.efeeme.com/los-chicos-hasta-que-el-cuerpo-aguante/.

Vernallis, C. (2004), *Experiencing Music Video: Aesthetics and Cultural Context*, New York: Columbia University Press.

Vernon, K. (2009), 'Queer Sound: Musical Otherness in Three Films by Pedro Almodóvar' in (ed.) B. Epps, *All About Almodóvar: A Passion for Cinema*, Minneapolis, MN: University of Minnesota Press, 51–70.

Vernon, K. (2016), 'El sonido cinematográfico', *Hispanófila* 177 (1) 11–26.

Vernon, K. (forthcoming), *Listening to Spanish Cinema*, Liverpool: Liverpool University Press.

Viana, I. (2018), '"Los Chichos": Los 40 principales nos vetaba por denunciar en las rumbas lo que correspondía a los políticos', *El Salto*, 19 January, https://www.elsaltodiario.com/musica/entrevista-los-chichos-concierto-despedida-veto-cuarenta-principales-rumba.

Vilarós, T. (1998), *El mono del desencanto: una crítica cultural de la transición española*, México D.F.: Siglo Veintiuno.

Viola, H. (1984a), 'Sobre "El Pirri" y otras películas', *Noticiero Universal*, 10 November 1984.

Viola, H. (1984b), 'El pico 2, de Eloy de la Iglesia llega con olor a escándolo', *Noticierio Universal*, 10 November 1984.

Wheeler, D. (2019), (ed.) *Spanish Songs of the Transition*, Liverpool: Liverpool University Press.

Wheeler, D. (2020), *Following Franco: Spanish Culture and Politics in Transition*, Manchester: Manchester University Press.

Whittaker, T. (2008), 'No Man's Land: Transitional Space and Time in Carlos Saura's *Deprisa, deprisa*', *Bulletin of Hispanic Studies*, 45, 5.

Whittaker, T. (2012), 'Locating la *voz*: The Space and Sound of Spanish Dubbing', *Journal of Spanish Cultural Studies*, 13 (3), 292–305.

Whittaker, T. (2013), 'Mobile Soundscapes in the *Quinqui* Film' in (eds.) Lisa Shaw and Rob Stone, *Screening Songs in Hispanic and Lusophone Cinema*, Manchester: Manchester University Press, 98–113.

Whittaker, T. (2014), 'Ghostly Resonance: Sound, Memory and Matter in *Las olas* and *Dies d'agost*', *Journal of Spanish Cultural Studies*, 15 (1), 323–336.

Whittaker, T. (2016), 'Sonorous Flesh: The Visual and Aural Erotics of Skin in Eloy de la Iglesia's *Quinqui* Films' in (ed.) Santiago Fouz-Hernández, *Spanish Erotic Cinema*, Edinburgh: Edinburgh University Press.

Willem, L. M. (2003), 'Introduction' in (ed.) L. M. Willem, *Carlos Saura: Interviews*, Jackson: University Press of Mississippi, vii–xv.

Willis, A. (2003), 'Spanish Horror and the Flight from 'Art' Cinema, 1967–73' in (eds.) M. Jancovich, A. Lázaro Reboll, J. Stringer & A. Willis, *Defining Cult Movies: The Cultural Politics of Oppositional Taste*, Manchester: Manchester University Press, 71–83.

Wojcik, P. (2006), 'The Sound of Film Acting', *Journal of Film and Video*, 58 (1/2), 71–83.

Wollen, P. (2002), 'Introduction: Cars and Culture' in (eds) P. Wollen and J. Kerr, *Autopia Cars and Culture*, London: Reaktion, 10–19.

Woods Peiró, E. (2015), 'Surveillant Filmmaking, the Carceral and the Transnational: Image and Viewers in Celda 211', *Journal of Spanish Cultural Studies*, 16 (1), 61–75.

Wright, S. (2013), *The Child in Spanish Cinema*, Manchester: Manchester University Press.

Index

Milton Keynes UK
Ingram Content Group UK Ltd.
UKHW021337080823
426527UK00042B/609